INFERNAL TRIAD

*The Flesh, the World, and the Devil
in Spenser and Milton*

INFERNAL TRIAD

*The Flesh, the World, and the Devil
in Spenser and Milton*

Patrick Cullen

PRINCETON UNIVERSITY PRESS

Copyright © 1974
BY PRINCETON UNIVERSITY PRESS
Published by Princeton University Press,
Princeton and London
ALL RIGHTS RESERVED
LCC: 73-16753
ISBN: 0-691-06267-6
Library of Congress Cataloging in Publication Data will
be found on the last printed page of this book.
Publication of this book has been aided by a grant from
The Andrew W. Mellon Foundation
This book has been composed in Linotype Times Roman
Printed in the United States of America by
Princeton University Press,
Princeton, New Jersey

For

E. MASON COOLEY, *friend and teacher*

Quam enim testimonia mendacia esse non
debent, tam non debent favere mendacio.
Sed hoc intelligentiae relinquo tuae.

—AUGUSTINE, *Ep.* XXVIII

Contents

Preface

Infernal Triad explores one aspect of the imaginative continuity between Spenser and Milton—the role of the medieval *schema* of the Flesh, the World, and the Devil in Books I and II of the *Faerie Queene* and in the major poems of Milton. The perils of such an approach, especially to the works of Milton, are self-evident: one may always risk making a Renaissance writer read like Gower or Lydgate. Obviously, by the time of Milton, Dryden, and Bunyan allegorical writing had undergone considerable change, often to the point that "allegorical" seems too strong a word, and one might prefer another word, more tactful if less elegant, like "quasi-allegorical" or "semi-allegorical." Caution would seem all the more necessary since, in the last few years, we have all been schooled by such Spenserians as Tuve, Alpers, Roche, Sale, and others on the dangers of speaking of allegorical equivalences and of imposing *schemata* on Spenser's verse. To speak, as I will, of an even later poet's characters as representing the Flesh, the World, or the Devil may seem at the very least a critical anachronism, a perverse introduction into a new area of a mode of allegorical analysis that one might have thought to have been put to rest in another. Let me say, then, at the beginning, that I have not meant to imply that, for example, Dalila "equals" the World, or Moloch the Devil; nor have I meant to imply that any allegorical *significatio* I point to is the exclusive significance of a character or episode. That would be too doctrinaire, and it would flatten the poetry under the weight of abstractions. And yet, unfortunately, that is easily the impression one may give when one attempts to unravel an allegorical lineage and when, for the purposes of criticism, one brings to the foreground what may be, within the poetry itself, in the background.

ix

Preface

I should also like to emphasize at the beginning that I am not proposing that Milton can or should be read, consistently, as an allegorist: allegory is only one of Milton's modes, and only rarely is he as consistently and systematically allegorical as earlier writers. What I am proposing, simply, is that in Milton allegorical schematizing is much more prominent than we are accustomed to expect, and that Milton's indebtedness to the allegorical tradition through Spenser and the neo-Spenserians is a matter of considerably greater importance than most criticism since Greenlaw has been willing to grant. The problems of reading the allegory of the seventeenth century, especially the allegory of Spenser's imitators, is largely unexplored terrain, and these problems will not be resolved by a study of this sort. Were this book a full-fledged study of the variety of allegorical modes in the seventeenth century and their historical lineage, I would, of course, have dwelt on these problems more than I have; but that is the subject of a future study, to which this one is a small preliminary. For the time being, if this study brings its two major Renaissance writers into a closer relationship than we have seen them in before, it will have served the purpose for which it was intended.

The debts I owe to a happily large number of friends and fellow scholars are as congenial to acknowledge as they are profound. No acknowledgment can measure up to my indebtedness to two former teachers of mine at Brown University, Leicester Bradner and Barbara Lewalski; many of the ideas for this book began many years ago in my studies under them. I owe Mrs. Lewalski special thanks for her helpfulness with the chapter on *Paradise Regained*, a work she has made so much her own that I scarcely dared venture into it. I have also benefited from the conversation of fellow Renaissance scholars in New York: J. Max Patrick, whose erudition served constantly to remind me that my timidity in writing on Milton was not altogether unjustified; John T. Shawcross, who has been so generous to me with his ideas, consistently adventurous and far-reaching, that my occasional disagreements with him in this work must seem ungrateful cavilling; David Kalstone, who responded to my monologues on Spenser always with intelligence and *mansuetudo*. Appreciation of another, but not less important, order is due my friend Edward Silverman; it is an acknowledgment that requires no elaboration.

Nothing I can say would be adequate to the memory of Marius Bewley. He outstripped all praise due him.

I should also like to thank the following people who have helped me in ways too various to do justice to them here: Isadore From, for guiding me to essential things, of which this book is not necessarily one; Richard Sáez, for the benefit of our constant disagreement over Spenser and Milton; Mitchell Leaska, for his vigorous and penetrating criticism of my earlier work; Richard Curtis, for challenges he was gracious enough not to expect me to meet; Henry Turin, for his assistance in helping me reach the right destination; Eric Applegate, for unwavering loyalty and kindness even at most difficult times; and my parents, whose weaknesses rival most people's strengths.

My association with Princeton University Press has been a rewarding one. Mrs. Martyn Hitchcock, warned by me that *Infernal Triad* might antagonize members of certain critical camps, was astute enough to discover readers severe but also sympathetic; and like all good editors, she did not flinch when informed that the book might be controversial. To her I am especially grateful, as I am also to Benjamin F. Houston for his guiding the manuscript through press, with a solid efficiency graced by good nature.

Grants from the American Council of Learned Societies and the City University of New York made possible some of the research for this study. I am grateful for the assistance of the library staffs of the British Museum, the Union Theological Seminary, Columbia University, and the Berg Collection of the New York Public Library. The editors of *ELH* kindly allowed me to include some of the material from my article, "Guyon *Microchristus*: The Cave of Mammon Reexamined" (*ELH*, 37 [1970], 153-174). Except for the account of the schematic structure of the Cave and the relationship of Books I and II, this essay has been almost totally recast from its original form.

My chief debt is acknowledged—it cannot be repaid—in the dedication. Mason Cooley deserves a better book, but he alone could be its author. Gifted with an intelligence as compassionate as it is capacious and elegant, he has taught me much, forgiven me much. For many lessons and much forgiveness, I offer him this small token of immense gratitude.

P.C.

New York City
November 1973

Prologue

Few of the schemata of medieval Catholicism survived the light of the Reformation. One of those that did was the infernal triad of the Flesh, the World, and the Devil—the three all-inclusive temptations of intemperance (or despair), avarice, and vainglory, which Adam experienced in the garden, Christ in the wilderness, and which all Christians vow at their baptism to renounce. The central contention of this book is that the infernal triad is the major structural motif for Spenser's Legend of Holiness and Cave of Mammon as well as Milton's *Paradise Regained* and *Samson Agonistes*, and that it also enters into the portrayal of Pandaemonium and the Fall in *Paradise Lost*. A book on Spenser and Milton, however, always runs the risk of being only half read. Unfortunately, the importance of each essay cannot be fully grasped outside the context of the whole argument of the book, and the reader's conviction for any single essay can be won only with the knowledge of the conclusions that have preceded and will follow that essay. A preliminary overview of the argument may therefore compensate in usefulness for what it lacks in elegance.

The Legend of Holiness (Chapter 1) belongs to a subgenre of romance, the literature of Christian pilgrimage. The sixteenth-century reader, I believe, would have immediately recognized this and would therefore have brought to Spenser's work expectation of discovering the conventions of such exemplary pilgrimage works as Deguileville's *Pilgrimage of the Life of Man*, Hawes's *Example of Virtue* and *Pastime of Pleasure*, and Cartigny's *The Wandering Knight*. Chief among these conventions was the very conception of the pilgrimage itself as a war against the Flesh, the World, and the Devil— a conception also found in the reader's own baptismal vow, which inaugurated him into a lifelong combat between the

xiii

old Adam, or unregenerate self, and the new Adam, or regenerate self. After the opening two episodes, which comprise a parody of the two main *vitae* open to the Renaissance pilgrim and hero, the active life (the defeat of Errour) and the contemplative life (Archimago), Red Crosse is separated from his true guide and encounters the Flesh (Duessa), the World (Lucifera), and the Devil (Orgoglio), so that an imitation of Christ's triumph in the wilderness is replaced by an imitation of Adam's fall in the garden. Upon his reunion with his true guide, Red Crosse once again encounters or is educated in terms of the Flesh (Despaire), the World (the House of Holiness), and the Devil (the dragon), thereby fulfilling the *imitatio Christi* of his baptismal vow. In both sequences, the World is a composite episode: the house of the World comprises "all sin" in that it subsumes the Flesh, the World, and the Devil in the form of the seven deadly sins; the House of Holiness comprises all virtue. If I may adopt a useful, if somewhat old-fashioned, device, the structure of Red Crosse's pilgrimage (eliminating, for the sake of convenience, the two prefatory episodes and the banquet) can be diagrammed as follows:

FLESH	WORLD	DEVIL
(Duessa)	(Lucifera)	(Orgoglio)
	Flesh	
	(sloth, gluttony, lust)	
	World	
	(avarice)	
	Devil	
	(envy, wrath, pride)	

FLESH	WORLD	DEVIL
(Despaire)	(House of Holiness)	(dragon)

A comparable parallel triadic structure emerges in the Cave of Mammon (Chapter 2). Events outside the Cave almost exactly duplicate the triadic structure of events within the Cave. The offer of gold corresponds to the first chamber of the Cave; the offer of glory corresponds to the second Chamber. In the third episode outside the Cave, Guyon mentions intemperance but Mammon does not offer it as a temptation. That temptation is made in the third episode within the Cave, the Garden of Proserpina; also, the Garden answers Guyon's question, introduced in the third episode, about the source of Mammon's wealth. The point of having two sequences is to provide a means for demonstrating the limits of human virtue. There is no question that had a temptation of the Flesh been offered outside the Cave Guyon could have resisted it as he had the others and would therefore have successfully imitated Christ in the wilderness. In entering the Cave, however, another performance, in addition to the Temptation in the Wilderness, is required of him, the Harrowing of Hell; and that more-than-mortal performance requires more than human virtue, it requires the assistance of Christian grace. Accordingly, although within the Cave Guyon succeeds, as far as the limits of his fallen nature permit, in imitating Christ's resistance in the wilderness, he fails in imitating Christ in Hell. A combined imitative triumph is permitted him only with the return of the Palmer, when on his voyage to the Bower of Bliss he resists the Flesh, the World, and the Devil in the form of the seven deadly sins, and on the third day, in imitation of Christ's Harrowing of Hell, he defeats Acrasia. The Cave of Mammon and the Bower of Bliss are thus contrasting parallel episodes conceived against the backdrop of the wilderness and Hell, as are also the comparable episodes in Book I at Orgoglio's castle and in the garden of Una's parents. From this perspective, the two books emerge as complementary parts of a unit developed in terms of Book I's opening figure for original sin, Errour, the Woman and the Serpent.

In *Paradise Lost* (Chapter 3), the infernal triad appears twice. The first appearance is in Pandaemonium, a house of the World indebted for its portrayal to the allegorical houses of Spenser and the neo-Spenserians. There Moloch, Belial, and Mammon are identified with the Devil, the Flesh, and the World, respectively. Although Satan, in a comic parody

of Christ's Temptation in the Wilderness, ostensibly rejects
their proposals, the same three sins appear again in Eden in
the first stage of Satan's temptation of Eve, and they appear
in precisely the same order that they appeared in Pandaemonium, namely vainglory (the Devil), intemperance (the
Flesh), and avarice (the World); the introduction of the
orthodox version of the three sins is followed in the second
stage of the temptation, which occurs before the tree itself,
by a lengthy appeal to the Flesh as the Protestants understood
that temptation, a temptation to disbelief. A schematic comparison of Satan's account of his ostensible experience with
the tree with Eve's meditation and response suggests that although "all sin" is involved in both, the primary sin is different, with vainglory dominating Satan's account, disbelief
and gluttony Eve's meditation and eating. What Milton seems
to be doing is using the triadic scheme as a means of clarifying the contrast between the nature and degree of Satan's sin
and Eve's, a contrast he reinforces by schematic parallels between Adam's speeches and Eve's. The intention behind this
contrast is to justify God's Augustinian account of why man
receives grace and the devil none. If these schematic contrasts and parallels do in fact function to show why man
receives both mercy and justice, one reaches the inevitable
conclusion, which without knowledge of the schematic evidence might seem an evasion of the episode's difficulties:
ambivalence is the theologically proper response to the Fall.

Paradise Regained (Chapter 4) has generated more controversy over its structure than any other work of either Spenser or Milton. Although Elizabeth Pope has made a pioneering attempt to elucidate the poem's structure in terms of the
infernal triad, the clearest explanation, Barbara Lewalski's,
focuses on the association of each day with a temptation to
one of Christ's three mediatorial roles and subordinates the
Flesh-World-Devil triad to the first three temptations of the
second day. Although I will attempt to bolster Lewalski's
connections (controverted, I think, mistakenly), I will argue
that the association of each day with one of Christ's mediatorial roles is Milton's addition to, not replacement of, the

structural pattern he inherited from Spenser and Fletcher (in "Christ's Victory on Earth"). What we have, then, is a linear triadic sequence combining *both* the three mediatorial roles and the infernal triad; and in the World-temptation, we have, as in Deguileville, Spenser, and Fletcher, a complex episode comprising "all sin." Milton has, in fact, not one but two repetitions of the Flesh-World-Devil triad in the World-temptation of the second day. The following two diagrams, the first of Fletcher's "Christ's Victory," the second of *Paradise Regained*, should make clear the Spenserian ancestry of Milton's structure:

FLESH	DEVIL	WORLD
(stones; despair)	(temple; presumption)	(kingdoms; vainglory)
		Flesh
		(luxury)
		World
		(avarice)
		Devil
		(ambition)

Book	
	Preface: perspectives on baptism and the word
I	FLESH; PROPHET (stones-temptation)
II	Link: meditations; infernal council
	WORLD; KING (kingdoms-temptation)
	Flesh (banquet)
	World (gold)
III	*Devil* (glory)
	Transition: Israel
	Devil (Parthia; glory)
IV	*Flesh* (Rome; intemperance) [king?]
	World (Athens; avarice) [prophet?]
	Link: storm
	DEVIL; PRIEST (pinnacle-temptation)

These diagrams cannot, of course, illuminate numerous more subtle similarities between the two works—the pastoral-mountain progression in the World-temptation, or the Circean attributes of the worldly temptor, e.g.; nor do they demonstrate more than the general thrust of each particular episode, whose total complexity obviously cannot be found in any single structural *significatio*. But skeletal though these diagrams are, they reveal *Paradise Regained* as a tour-de-force transformation of an inherited structure. Moreover, once the triadic structure comes into focus, so does the tetradic. Book I deals with the issue which was, for the Protestant, the very substance of Christ's Temptation in the Wilderness, the truth of God's word and promise. Book II, appropriately introduced by meditations, deals with the inner kingdom, Christ's first step in realizing the divine word and promise. Book III, framed by Devil-glory temptations, deals with the relationship of private virtues to public kingdoms. And Book IV provides a grand recapitulation of the work, presenting the infernal triad in the same order that it appears in the three-day sequence; it may also recapitulate the mediatorial triad.

Like the structure of *Paradise Regained*, which I believe it imitates, the structure of the "middle" of *Samson Agonistes* (Chapter 5) emerges from the double-triadic scheme of Spenser's Legend of Holiness and Fletcher's "Christ's Victory." The order of temptation is identical to that in the Legend of Holiness and *Paradise Regained*: the Flesh (Manoa), the World (Dalila), and the Devil (Harapha). Once again the World-temptation is complex, with Dalila tempting Samson in her second speech (as Samson himself explicates it) to accept her avarice as feminine weakness and her lust as love, and in her third speech asking him to accept her vainglory as true glory. The diagram should by now be familiar:

FLESH	WORLD	DEVIL
(Manoa)	(Dalila)	(Harapha)
	World (avarice)	
	[lines 772-789]	
	Flesh (lust)	
	[lines 790-818]	
	Devil (glory)	
	[lines 843-870]	

xviii

By overcoming the infernal triad, Samson imitates Christ's triumph in the wilderness. This triumph becomes the focus for Milton's Christian redefinition of tragedy.

That, in brief, is the process of imitation and metamorphosis with which this work is concerned. For many readers, I realize, I have brought to the foreground procedures and conclusions they may find anachronistic or even offensive. Nonetheless, a real line of literary development is here, which opens up questions of critical as well as historical interest; for, if my reading is accurate, we find two of the greatest English Protestant poets, one of them writing at the very end of the Renaissance, using an allegorical formula inherited from medieval Catholicism. I have absolutely no pretensions to any ability to answer with much certainty the questions emerging from this study, but perhaps it will be useful at least to raise one or two of them. The crucial question, and it is a large one, is the nature and extent of Milton's relationship to English literary traditions and to medieval and Renaissance allegory. Obviously of neither the school of Donne nor the school of Jonson, Milton seems to have the historical anomalousness we tend to attach to the great. So wide-ranging in his learned syncretism, Milton is for few of us an English poet among English poets. We have emphasized the Latinate quality of his style, now the Italianate, perhaps too quickly forgetting the grand line of the Elizabethans. We have emphasized the classical and continental writers, and wisely; but less wisely, we have de-emphasized, or simply ignored, the role of the native, English tradition. Milton emerges from this study as a much more English Milton than present scholarship is inclined to present him. For Milton's indebtedness to Spenser and the neo-Spenserians extends beyond structure even to matters of argument: his stones-temptation seems partly indebted for its argument to Spenser's Despaíre episode and Fletcher's stones-temptation, and the gold- and glory-temptations have (as has long been recognized) similarities in argument to the Cave of Mammon. His indebtedness extends even more to the conception of individual episodes and the artistic machinery he uses in them: for example, the grove-mountain progression in *Paradise Regained*, though it goes back ultimately to Ariosto and Tasso, is principally indebted to Spenser's Fradubio-Lucifera progression and, especially, Fletcher's garden-mountain progression; the portrayal of Dalila goes back, as far as non-biblical sources are concerned, to the worldly Circes of "all sin" in Spenser, Fletcher, and Quarles; the conception of Harapha as a giant Devil-figure goes back to Spenser's Orgoglio.

Conclusions such as these suggest that we must redefine Milton's relationship not only to Spenser and the neo-Spenserians but also to the larger area of Renaissance allegory and romance. Milton—and one might add Cowley, Bunyan, Dryden, and others—dwells in the twilight of Renaissance allegory. It is true, of course, that the surface of Milton's poetry does not obviously invite an allegorical reading, as do the *Faerie Queene*, *Apollyonists*, and *Psyche*, for example. Allegorical personifications, which have the effect of calling immediate attention to the allegorical texture of a work, are few in Milton. When we encounter Sin, Death, and Chaos, we are inclined to view them somewhat as a Miltonic anomaly or freak event; or for some they simply suggest that the late poetry is in reality early poetry. These allegorical personifications are not freak events, however, nor are they necessarily a safe basis for dating the verse; for they are, I am inclined to believe, merely the most obvious manifestation of the very nature of Milton's poetry, which, in its use of allegorical schemata or formulae, is characterized much more than we are accustomed to assume by an allegorical habit of thinking. Milton is not, to be sure, so elaborately and systematically allegorical as allegorists preceding him. Allegory in Milton tends to be part of an overarching general outline; it is neither intrusive nor obtrusive; it seems almost to hover at a distance, refraining from controlling every detail of the literal level of the verse but supplying details with a context of meaning. Needless to say, the degree of distance and control varies within all allegory. Britomart, for example, seems to me a much less allegorically controlled character than either Errour or Acrasia. But even so, the distance in Milton is more variable, subtle, and complex. That Adam and Eve represent respectively *mens* and *sensus*—an argument which has been made more than once and which has at least some plausibility—is infinitely more difficult to prove than a comparable argument in terms of the Bower of Bliss, where Guyon clearly represents restored Adamic *mens* and Acrasia unrestored Evian *sensus*. All events in the Bower of Bliss are allegorically accountable; this is not true of all events of Eden. Although there may be an allegorical dimension to their portrayal, Adam and Eve are not primarily allegorical figures operating in an allegorical fiction. Milton simply does not sufficiently restrict the *significatio* of his characters or events for this to be so. That is to say that Milton's works seem largely to lack the symbolic specificity of much Spenserian allegory. In His first two days of temptation in *Paradise Regained*, Christ demonstrates the powers of right reason at its finest, but to say that He represents Reason or Temperance is much less an adequate or complete account of Him than it is of Guyon. And yet at the same time, the glories-sequence is, in terms of merely what is offered, as allegorical as the Cave of Mammon episode. Mammon and the devil both make allegorical offers of gold, but only in Spenser do we get an allegorical description, pictorial and emblematic, of what is meant by avarice. Milton also informs us of the nature of avarice, but argument has replaced allegorical paraphernalia. Similarly, Manoa, Dalila, and Harapha represent the Flesh, the World, and the Devil every bit as much as Spenser's Lucessa, Lucifera, and Orgoglio. The allegorical idea and structuring are identical; it is the unfolding or portrayal of the abstraction that is different. Lucifera and Dalila are both World-figures; the *significatio* is the same, the *illustratio* is not. Spenser's episode is replete with the symbolic description of traditional allegory, but Milton offers only a few lines of that in the Chorus's opening account of Dalila's arrival.

Similarly, for both Spenser and Milton the World-figure is associated with the triad of vices comprising "all sin": in Spenser these sins are represented through an emblematic pageant of sins; in Milton they emerge from the structuring of Dalila's argument. Once again, the same allegorical formula; once again, a vast difference in the artistic execution of the formula. It is as though in Milton we have allegory's conceptual structuring without allegory's detailed elaboration of symbolic images, or at least only the residue of that technique.

In Milton the symbolic pictures that are traditional allegory's *illustratio* are usually less important than argument, speeches, debate. We learn of the allegorical significance of Milton's characters largely through what is said not what is done. In Milton we learn through Mammon what it is to be an avaricious man not, as in Spenser, through piles of gold, a ladder of ambition, and lists of emblematic personifications, but through (primarily) his argument; we learn through Belial what it is to be an intemperate man not, as in Spenser, through lovely clothes camouflaging an animal lower part, but through his lovely words camouflaging sloth. In Milton, then, we learn what avarice or intemperance is by witnessing the avaricious or intemperate mind in action. Now Spenser can do this, too, though on a much smaller scale; but much more than Milton he will portray the mind through systematic correspondences between it and the external world. Detailed symbolic imagery of landscape and gesture is Spenser's main method of revealing the abstract and the interior. Milton, of course, is also fond of establishing defining correspondences between the landscape and the psyche, like those between Satan's mind and Hell, Adam's and Eve's minds and Eden; but these correspondences are general, not systematically symbolic in all particulars. Spenser's systematic working out of abstractions through symbolic images, the specificity and particularity of his allegory, are rare in Milton. Nonetheless Milton inherits from Spenser, and from the allegorical and romance tradition in general, a tendency to place characters and events within an abstract conceptual framework, a penchant to structure his work according to schematic formulae. Milton was not in the beginning of his career or in the end an allegorist of such sustained specificity and completeness as his predecessor. He is never the complete allegorist, for the full repertory of allegorical techniques never entirely suffuses and permeates his art and thinking. Allegorical episodes in the old manner are few, as are allegorical landscapes and personifications. Even so, something of the old tradition remains, sometimes intact as in the portrayal of Sin, but more commonly transformed. Milton, as we will see in the coming chapters, could use the old allegorical formula of the Flesh, the World, and the Devil as much as his master; but the formula tends primarily to provide only a general context of meaning, preserving a discrete distance between itself and the letter. Allegory's correspondences are still being made, but they are being made less systematically, less specifically, less pictorially.

The distinctions I have drawn are not intended to be anything more than explorations; they may well be inaccurate, they are certainly imperfect and incomplete. Nonetheless, some kind of relationship is there, and when we finally discover it, we may have to revise our notions of the literary moment in which Milton operated. I present my speculations on these matters here at the beginning, not at the end; for they are not meant to seem conclusions. Speculations they remain; and if they serve to encourage the reader to his own speculations on the larger implications of this study, they have served well enough until another time and a different argument.

Introduction

Doest thou forsake the deuil and all his workes, the
vaine pompe and glorye of the world, with al couetous
desires of the same, and the carnal desires of the flesh,
so that thou wilt not folow, nor be led by them?

Aunswere. *I forsake them al.*

("The Ministracion of Baptisme")[1]

Renaissance man, no less than medieval man, inherited the
belief that as a son of Adam, he was heir to the temptations
Adam experienced; and that as man born again in Christ, he
was, like Christ, to overcome the sins the first Adam had
succumbed to—an infernal triad of sins, comprising all the
sins of the world and all the lures of the devil: lust, avarice,
pride; *concupiscentia carnis, concupiscentia oculorum, super-*
bia vitae; the Flesh, the World, and the Devil.[2] The ultimate
origins of this concept of an inclusive triad of sins are
uncertain;[3] but within Christianity the idea seems to have

[1] *The Prayer-Book of Queen Elizabeth* (London: Thynne, 1912),
p. 114.

[2] The pioneering and, for the purposes of Renaissance literature,
still most useful study of the three inclusive vices is that of Elizabeth
Marie Pope, *"Paradise Regained": The Tradition and the Poem* (Baltimore, Md.: The Johns Hopkins Press, 1947), pp. 51-69, 80-92.
More detailed treatment of the medieval background can be found in
Donald R. Howard, *The Three Temptations* (Princeton, N.J.: Prince-
ton Univ. Press, 1966), pp. 41-75. Also useful in that it studies ap-
pearances of the triad not only in literature but also in art is Samuel C.
Chew, *The Pilgrimage of Life* (New Haven, Conn.: Yale Univ. Press,
1962), pp. 70-78. There are also scattered references in Morton W.
Bloomfield, *The Seven Deadly Sins* (East Lansing, Mich.: Michigan
State Univ. Press, 1952).

[3] Howard, *The Three Temptations*, pp. 46-47, speculates that the
notion of three chief vices was formulated in the early Christian era

developed from an attempt to bring the temptations of the first Adam in Eden in tandem with the temptations of the second Adam in the wilderness.[4] Since Christ, acting as the new Adam, resisted three temptations in the wilderness, so must the old Adam have succumbed to three temptations. The classic analogy is Gregorian:

> Antiquus hostis contra primum hominem parentem nostrum in tribus se tentationibus erexit, quia hunc videlicet gula, vana gloria et avaritia tentavit; sed tentando superavit, quia sibi eum per consensum subdidit. Ex gula quippe tentavit cum cibum ligni vetitum ostendit, atque ad comedendum suasit. Ex vana autem gloria tentavit cum diceret: *Eritis sicut dii* (*Genes.* III, 6). Et ex provectu avaritiae tentavit cum diceret: *Scientes bonum et malum.* Avaritia enim non solum pecuniae est, sed etiam altitudinis. Recte enim avaritia dicitur cum supra modum sublimitas ambitur. . . .
>
> Sed quibus modis primum hominem stravit, eisdem modis secundo homini tentato succubuit. Per gulam quippe tentat cum dicit: *Dic ut lapides isti panes fiant.* Per vanam gloriam tentat cum dicit: *Si Filius Dei es, mitte te deorsum.* Per sublimitatis avaritiam tentat cum regna omnia mundi ostendit, dicens: *Haec omnia tibi dabo, si procidens adoraveris me.* Sed eisdem modis a secundo homine vincitur, quibus primum hominem se vicisse gloriabatur. . . .[5]

---

under the influence of oriental mystery religions and Hellenistic philosophy. The germinal conception of the idea probably goes back as far as Plato's conception of the tripartite soul in Book IV of *The Republic* and the discussion of the chief objects of sin—wealth, honors, indulgence of appetites—of a declining people in Book VIII.

[4] The biblical accounts of the temptations of Adam and Christ are contained in the Appendix.

[5] *XL homiliarum in evangelia*, in *Patrologiae cursus completus, Series latinae* (Paris: Garnier, 1844-1903) [hereafter cited as *P.L.*], 76:1136. *Trans.*: The ancient foe set himself up against the first man, our parent, in three temptations, since clearly he tempted him by

This is the formulation followed throughout the Middle Ages.[6] Just how common and influential it was, is testified to by the fact that it appears in at least three of the miracle

---

gluttony, vainglory, and avarice; and indeed in tempting him he overcame him, since he placed him under by his own consent. To gluttony he tempted him when he showed him the forbidden fruit of the tree and persuaded him to eat. To vainglory when he said, "Ye shall be as gods." And to avarice he tempted him when he said, "knowing good and evil." For there is avarice not only for money but also for loftiness and high estate. For it is rightly called avarice when loftiness is sought immoderately. . . . But by the same means whereby he led the first man astray, he himself succumbed in tempting the second man. To gluttony he tempted Him when he said, "Command that these stones be made bread." To vainglory he tempted Him when he said, "If thou be the Son of God, cast thyself down." To avarice for loftiness, he tempted Him when he showed all the kingdoms of the world, saying, "All these things I will give thee, if thou wilt fall down and worship me." But by the same means whereby he boasted that he had conquered the first man, he was himself conquered by the second man. . . .

[6] Both before and after Gregory; see, *inter alia*, St. Hilary, *In evangelium Matthaei commentarius*, *P.L.* 9:929-931; Ambrose, *Expositio evangelii secundum Lucam*, *P.L.* 15:1701-1709; Augustine, *In epistolam Joannis ad Parthos*, *P.L.* 35:1996-1997; Venerable Bede, *In Lucae evangelium expositio*, *P.L.* 92:369-370, and *Expositio in primam epistolam S. Joannis*, *P.L.* 93:92-93; Rabanus Maurus, *Commentariorum in Matthaeum*, *P.L.* 107:784-785; Haymo of Auxerre (possibly Haymo of Halberstadt), *Homiliae de tempore*, *P.L.* 118:200-201; Walafridus Strabus, *Glossa ordinaria*, *P.L.* 114:254, and *Expositio in quatuor evangelia*, *P.L.* 114:869-870; Angelom of Luxeuil, *Commentarius in Genesin*, *P.L.* 115:137; Werner, Abt. of St. Blase, *Deflorationes SS. Patrum*, *P.L.* 157:866; Radulphus Ardens, *In epistolas et evangelis dominicalia homiliae*, *P.L.* 155:1794; Hugh of St. Victor, *Miscellanea*, *P.L.* 177:790-792, and *Hugh of Saint Victor on the Sacraments of the Christian Faith (De Sacramentis)*, trans. Roy J. Deferrari (Cambridge, Mass.: Medieval Academy of America, 1951), pp. 122-124; Peter Lombard, *Sententiae*, *P.L.* 192:1048-1049; Pope Innocent III, *Sermones de tempore*, *P.L.* 217:371-376; Aquinas, *Summa theologica*, III, q. 41, art. 4; *Twelfth Century Homilies*, ed. A. O. Belfour, Early English Text Society [hereafter cited as EETS], o.s. 137 (London: Kegan Paul, Trench, and Trübner, 1909), pp. 96-107; *A Stanzaic Life of Christ*, ed. Francis A. Foster,

plays of the late Middle Ages.[7] Indeed, the explication of Christ's temptation by the Expositor in the Chester Plays (161-168) is little more than a versification of Gregory:

> Loe! lordinges, Gods righteousnes,
> as St. Gregorie makes mynde expresse,
> since our forefather ouercomen was
> by three thinges to doe evill:
>
> Gluttony, vayne glorye there be twooe,
> Covetousnes of highnes alsoe,
> by these three thinges, without moe,
> Christ hath overcome the Devill.

The Expositor goes on to complete the commonplace connections: Adam was tempted to gluttony "when of the frute falsly / the Deuill made hym to eate" (171-172), to vainglory "when he height hym great mastery, / to haue godhead, unworthely" (174-175), and to avarice "when he het hym to be wise" (178); so Christ was tempted to gluttony "When he entyced hym . . . / to turne Stones into bread" (189-190), to vainglory "when he excited hym downe to goe / the pynacle of the temple froe" (194-195), and to covetousness "when he shewed hym such riches / and het hym landes" (198-199).

This, then, was the basic pattern; but inevitably, of course, such a pattern was subject to revision and expansion. The most important expansion involved the yoking together of

---

EETS, o.s. 166 (London: Oxford Univ. Press, 1926), pp. 176-179. There are, of course, variations—*iactantia* for *vana gloria*, *curiositas* for *avaritia*, e.g.—and not all of the above equate the temptations of Adam and Christ, and those who do make the equation do not always agree on what specifically is being equated; but for the most part their differences with Gregory's formulation of the three vices are not substantial.

[7] *The Chester Plays, Part I*, ed. Hermann Deimling, EETS, e.s. 62 (London, 1892), pp. 217-225; *Ludus Coventriae*, ed. K. S. Block, EETS, e.s. 129 (London, 1922), pp. 193-200; *York Plays*, ed. Lucy Toulmin Smith (1885; rpt. New York: Russell and Russell, 1963), pp. 178-184.

the three temptations of either Christ or Adam, often both, with the description in I John 2:15-16 of the three sins of the world: "Love not the world, neither the things that are in the world. If any man love the world, the love of the Father is not in him. For all that is in the world, the lust of the flesh, and the lust of the eyes, and the pride of life, is not of the Father, but is of the world." The first term of this triad posed no problem: everyone agreed on the meaning of *concupiscentia carnis*, and almost everyone associated it with Satan's showing Adam the fruit and his asking Christ to make bread from the stones. There was, however, considerable confusion over the last two terms. It was partly a problem of definition: both terms could refer to a love of glory, honor, and great estate. This problem was complicated by the fact that Matthew and Luke do not present the last two temptations in the same order: for Matthew, of course, the order is stones-tower-kingdoms; for Luke, stones-kingdoms-tower. Consequently, if the Matthew sequence was being used, the equation would generally be: stones = *concupiscentia carnis*; tower = *concupiscentia oculorum*; kingdoms = *superbia vitae*; whereas if the Luke sequence was being used, the equation would generally be: stones = *concupiscentia carnis*; kingdoms = *concupiscentia oculorum*; tower = *superbia vitae*. Let me give a miniature example of the kind of confusion that could occur. Augustine, Haymo of Auxerre (or Haymo of Halberstadt), Radulphus Ardens, Hugh of St. Victor, and Martin of Leon[8] all agree that the kingdoms-temptation is a temptation to avarice and/or worldly honor and ambition; but whereas Radulphus and Hugh relate the temptation to *concupiscentia oculorum*, Augustine, Haymo, and Martin relate it to *superbia vitae*. Similarly, Augustine and Martin both interpret *concupiscentia oculorum* as curiosity (a version of avarice, also a lust of the eyes) and relate it to the tower; but Radulphus and Hugh interpret *concupiscentia oculorum* as avarice (i.e., *avaritia sublimitatis*) and relate it

[8] *P.L.* 35:1996-1997; *P.L.* 118:200-201; *P.L.* 155:1794; *P.L.* 177:791; *P.L.* 209:262-263, respectively.

to the kingdoms, while Haymo, interpreting it as vainglory, relates it to the tower. So many correspondences were being made, and with so many different terms, that one can hardly expect all aspects of any one theologian's equation to agree with another's. For the sake of clarity, however, it will be useful for us to adopt the table made by Professor Howard summarizing the mainstream of the triads:[9]

	I John 2:16	Genesis 3	Matt. 4	Luke 4
gluttony	lust of the flesh	fruit	stones	stones
avarice	lust of the eyes	knowledge	tower	mount
vainglory	pride of life	be like gods	mount	tower

The Reformation perpetuated the medieval formulae but with modifications. The most important of these concerned the first temptation, which most Protestant theologians from Calvin on preferred to see as a temptation to doubt, distrust, or despair rather than a temptation to gluttony. Calvin, refuting Romans who would have "magnifié outre mesure l'abstinence" by interpreting the first temptation of Christ as a temptation to "friandise, ou que c'estoit d'intemperance," argues that there is no intemperance in eating when one is hungry. To understand Christ's temptations, he says, we must first understand Adam's, which Calvin interprets as doubt, ambition-pride, and rebellion:

> Or il est certain que le diable a assailli Adam et l'a tenté d'incredulite, de rebellion, et d'orgueil. Et on le peut veoir par les propos dont il use, quand il dit, Vous estes pareils à Dieu. . . . Il ne dit pas, Vous gousterez au bout de la langue un fruict qui vous sera delectable: mais il dit, Vous serez pareils à Dieu. Voyla donc l'orgueil dont il vient assaillir Adam et Eve. Et puis il y a l'incredulite. Car quand on luy replique qu'l y a menace de mort, Ho, il n'en sera pas ainsi. Et finalement il y a la rebellion, laquelle l'Escriture note si expressement, quand l'homme

[9] *The Three Temptations*, p. 53.

ose bien attenter contre le commandement de Dieu. . . .
Or l'ambition et l'orgueil, pour vouloir monter plus haut
qu'il ne nous est licite: apres, l'incredulité pour aneantir
la parole de Dieu: et puis, la rebellion pour nous vouloir
opposer à Dieu manifestement, et pour lui faire la
guerre: voyla les coups mortels que le diable nous
donne.[10]

The devil's purpose in the stones-temptation was to get Christ
to doubt the word of God. This reading worked in well with
Christ's reply that "Man shall not live by bread alone, but
by every word that proceedeth out of the mouth of God"
(Matt. 4:4), and it worked in well with Calvin's, and Protestantism's, insistence on a return to that word. The devil's
purpose in the tower-temptation was to induce "desfiance"
and presumption: "il [le diable] a voulu induire Iesus Christ
à une folle presomption, d'attenter plus qu'il ne luy estoit
licite."[11] And his purpose in the kingdoms-temptation was to
get Christ to sin through "ambition ou avarice."[12] Distrust,
rebellious presumption, avarice-ambition—this, in essence, is
Calvin's formulation; and it was this formulation which provided the main precedent for Protestant theologians after

---

[10] Sermon XLIX, in *Sermons sur l'harmonie évangélique*, in *Corpus
Reformatorum*, 46 (Brunvigae: Schwetschke, 1891), col. 610. *Trans.*:
Now it is certain that the devil assaulted Adam and tempted him to
unbelief, rebellion, and pride. And one can see this in the issues he
makes use of, when he says, "You are like God. . . ." He does not
say, "You will taste at the tip of your tongue a fruit you will find
delicious"; but he says, "You will be like God." There is, therefore,
the pride whereby the devil comes to attack Adam and Eve. And
then there is the unbelief, because when they reply to him that there
is the threat of death, "O, that will not be the case." And finally
there is the rebellion, noted expressly by the Scripture, when man
dares actually to make an attempt against the commandment of
God. . . . First, then, ambition and pride, for desiring to climb higher
than we are permitted; after that, unbelief in denying the word of
God; and, finally, rebellion in wishing manifestly to oppose God and
in making war against Him: these are the mortal blows the devil
gives us.

[11] Sermon L, col. 621.   [12] Sermon LI, col. 630.

Calvin.[13] If I may oversimplify, we have by the time of the Reformation two different yet related forms of the triple temptation: both the Catholic and the Protestant, despite different connections and orders, largely agree that avarice or ambition, pride or vainglory, were the determining lures for the second and third temptations; it was on the first temptation that the two parted company, with the Catholic into the seventeenth century interpreting it as a temptation to an excess of fleshly desire, the Protestant interpreting it as a temptation to disbelief in the word of God.

Gluttony, avarice, vainglory; the lust of the flesh, the lust of the eyes, the pride of life: these were the "capita draconis,"[14] all his temptations, and all the sins of the world. Although it was really another way of saying the same thing, the related triad of the Flesh, the World, and the Devil does not, as far as I can determine, figure prominently in theological discussions of the three temptations. Of course, since pride was commonly seen as the Devil's own sin ("hoc est proprium diaboli"),[15] gluttony as the lust of the Flesh, and avarice as the sin of the World, the connection is at least implicit; but it was explicitly made only by a few theologians, among them Radulphus Ardens:

> His tribus [i.e., "concupiscentia carnis, aut oculorum, aut superbia vitae"] victus homo fuit subjectus omni malitiae, carnis, mundi et diaboli. Jejunare igitur et tentari voluit Christus, ut nobis triumpharet de diaboli, carne simul et mundo. Diabolus quidem, in iisdem tribus tentaverat et vicerat Adam, tentavit et Christum, sed ab eo devictus est. De gula quippe tentavit eum cum dixit: *Si Filius Dei es, dic ut lapides isti panes fiant.* . . . De cupiditate tentavit Christum, cum ei dixit: *Haec omnia tibi dabo, si cadens adoraveris me.* . . . De vana gloria

---

[13] See Pope, *"Paradise Regained,"* pp. 55-63, 80-92.
[14] Isaac of Stella, *Sermones, P.L.* 194:1795.
[15] Hugh of St. Victor, *P.L.* 177:791.

sive de superbia tentavit eum, cum dixit ei: *Si Flius* [sic]
Dei es, mitte te deorsum.[16]

Radulphus does not specifically make a connection, but rather
through quotation implies a connection, between the Flesh,
the World, and the Devil and I John 2:16, with *concupiscentia carnis* obviously being gluttony and the Flesh; *concupiscentia oculorum*, cupidity (avarice) and the World; *superbia
vitae*, vainglory and the Devil. Hugh of St. Victor[17] implies
but does not specifically make the same equation as Radulphus, and Ludolphus of Saxony[18] makes the equation but
attributes avarice to the Devil and vainglory to the World.

While the Flesh-World-Devil triad does not figure prominently in exegeses of the temptations of Adam and Christ, it
was of course part of the monastic vows, the litany, the baptismal rites, and the catechism; and apparently it was a fairly
popular subject among the sermon writers.[19] A brief glance at

[16] *P.L.* 155:1794. *Trans.*: By these three things [i.e., the lust of the
flesh, the lust of the eyes, and the pride of life] was man conquered,
subject to all sin—the Flesh, the World, and the Devil. Christ wished,
therefore, to fast and be tempted that He might triumph for us over
the Devil, the Flesh, and the World. For certain the devil, in the
same three things he tempted and overcame Adam, also tempted
Christ, but was vanquished by Him. To gluttony he tempted him for
certain when he said to Him, "If thou be the Son of God, command
that these stones be made bread. . . ." To cupidity he tempted Christ
when he said, "All these things will I give thee, if thou wilt fall down
and worship me. . . ." To vainglory or pride he tempted Him when
he said to Him, "If thou be the Son of God, cast thyself down."

[17] *P.L.* 177:791.

[18] *Vie de Jesus-Christ*, ed. A. LeCoy de La Marche (Paris, 1870),
p. 79.

[19] Literary uses of the Flesh, the World, and the Devil are extremely commonplace. The triad enters literature written in England at
least as early as Robert Grosseteste's *Templum Domini* (pp. 105-106
in the fifteenth-century "translation" reprinted by Roberta D. Corne-
lius, *The Figurative Castle*, diss. Bryn Mawr 1930) and *Château
d'amour* (p. 43 in the English translation, *Castel Off Loue*, ed. Richard Francis Weymouth [London: Asher, 1864]), and the *Ancrene*

Introduction

W. Ross's collection of Middle English sermons[20] reveals
much about the popularity and versatility of uses this pattern
had for the medieval sermon writer. Sermon 7 informs us
that the first deed of gratitude to God is to be "clene shryven
and full repentante and do penaunce of þe vij dedely synnes,"
that is, pride, wrath and envy, "þe wiche þe dewell temptes
þe in day by daye"; covetousness, "where-in þe worlde
temptes þe in at all tyme"; and sloth, gluttony, and lechery
"in þe wiche þi flessh temptes þe euermore." Sermon 19 exhorts all men to rise from their sleep and clothe themselves
(with, one assumes, the armor of St. Paul); "for the iij
stronge enmyes þat haue throwe þe down in synne, nyght and
day þei strenght þem to brynge þe euerlenger þe lowere vn-to
þe pitt of hell—þat is þe flesshe, þe world, and þe feend. Me
vexant triplici certamine tres inimici: hostis antiquus, caro
lubrica, mundus iniquus." In Sermon 37, the writer equates
" 'Euery synne þat is donne in þis werlde' "—he is obviously
paraphrasing I John 2:16—with pride, covetousness, and
lust; which are, though the connection is not specifically

Riwle (p. 147 in The Nun's Rule, modernized by James Morton [Lon-
don: Chatto and Windus, 1924]); and will be found, among many
other places, in the Cursor Mundi, ed. Richard Morris, EETS, o.s.
57, 59, 62, 66, 68, 99, 101 (London: Kegan Paul, Trench, and Trübner, 1877-92), lines 10095-10122; John Gower, Mirour de l'omme in
The Complete Works, ed. G. C. Macaulay (Oxford: The Clarendon
Press, 1899-1902), lines 241ff.; Piers Plowman (B, xvi.1ff.); "Jesus,
Mercy for My Misdeeds" and "Our Three Foes," in Religious Lyrics
of the Fifteenth Century, ed. Carleton Brown (Oxford: The Clarendon Press, 1939); "The Mirror of the Periods of Man's Life," in
Hymns to the Virgin and Christ, "The Parliament of Devils" and
Other Religious Poems, ed. F. J. Furnivall, EETS, o.s. 24 (London:
Trübner, 1867), lines 641-642; and Chaucer's "Tale of Melibee,"
1420-1426; and it plays an important role in the moralities and interludes, most notably of course The Castle of Perseverance. For our
purposes, the most important literary use of the Flesh-World-Devil
triad is in the pilgrimage literature, and discussion of that will await
the chapter on Book I of the Faerie Queene.
[20] Middle English Sermons, ed. Woodburn O. Ross, EETS, o.s. 209
(London: Oxford Univ. Press, 1940).

made, the sins associated with the Devil, the World, and the Flesh respectively. Sermon 40 is more explicit. There are, it argues, three great spiritual drinks: the first is the drink of pride, offered by the devil, along with the drinks of envy and vengeance (i.e., wrath); the second principal spiritual drink is lechery (which is the wine of the taverner flesh; gluttony is implied, sloth apparently omitted); the third is worldly covetousness. Sermon 42 also uses the Flesh-World-Devil triad to organize the seven deadly sins, but the context here is an exegesis of three things Solomon, in Proverbs 30:18-19, found hard to understand (the way of an eagle, a serpent, and a ship) and a fourth thing he found impossible to understand, the way of a young man. The bird is interpreted as the prideful man, the serpent as the covetous man, and the young man naturally as the lustful man (the ship is interpreted in terms of the worldliness of the serpent, apparently; the sea is the world, the ship great men who sustain the poor people, and the officers of the ship the oppressors of the poor). The prideful man is the victim of lust, envy, and wrath; the covetous man the victim of covetousness alone; the lustful man the victim of sloth and gluttony. The seven deadly sins are thus reduced to three categories, corresponding, as the concluding exhortation suggests, to "þe devell [pride], þe world [covetousness], and þe flessh [lust]."

The Royal MS Sermons point to what was undoubtedly one of the most popular uses of the Flesh-World-Devil triad, namely to organize the seven deadly sins.[21] The most common formulation, at least from the late fourteenth century on,

[21] See references in note 19 to Grosseteste's *Templum Domini* and *Château d'amour*, the *Ancrene Riwle*, the *Cursor Mundi*, Gower's *Mi[r]our de l'omme*, *Piers Plowman*, and "Jesus, Mercy for My Misdeeds." Also, John Wyclif, "De virtutibus peccatisque et de salvatore," in *Trialogus*, ed. G. Lechler (Oxford, 1869); John Gregory, "Per propriam sanguinem," in Homer G. Pfander, *The Popular Sermon of the Medieval Friar*, diss. New York University (New York, 1937). Other examples will be found in the discussion of pilgrimage literature in my chapter on Book I of the *Faerie Queene*. See also Chew, *Pilgrimage of Life*, pp. 70-87.

is that found in these sermons.[22] But the formulation was highly variable (Bishop Grosseteste, for example, even disagrees with himself, in the *Templum Domini* attaching anger to the World, in the *Château d'amour* attaching it to the Devil). Sloth might be attached to the Devil (and in fact frequently was before the end of the fourteenth century), and envy and wrath might be attached to the World. Nonetheless, despite variations, certain constants remain: the Flesh is almost always linked with gluttony and lust, the World with avarice, and the Devil with pride—so that in its essence the Flesh-World-Devil triad reduces itself basically to the same three principal sins of Gregory's pattern.

What I have outlined is, for our critical and literary purpose, as much theological apparatus as we will need: a knowledge that there was an infernal triad of sins, the inclusive lures of the devil and the world, which were variously formulated—gluttony, avarice, vainglory; lust, riches, glory; lust, glory, power; despair, ambition, presumptuous rebellion; the Flesh, the World, the Devil—to which lures the old Adam succumbed, and over which the new Adam triumphed to set an example so that "nú maeʒ ealc mon deofel ofercumen."[23] That, in brief, is the pattern the following chapters will deal with. We must be wary, however, not to expect too precise a correlation between this theological pattern and the literature; that is the vice undermining more than one study of this type. The theology itself is not very precise but extremely protean, and much more so the literature. Almost invariably, moreover, we will find Spenser and Milton, as we might well expect, more indebted to literary antecedents than theological sources for their structural schemata; and invariably, the works themselves will define their own terms.

[22] According to Bloomfield, *Seven Deadly Sins*, p. 141.
[23] *Twelfth Century Homilies*, p. 99.

I. SPENSER

1. Red Crosse and the Pilgrimage of Christian Life
2. Guyon *Microchristus*

1. Red Crosse
and the Pilgrimage of Christian Life

*Dearly beloved, I beseech you as strangers and pilgrims,
abstain from fleshly lusts, which war against the soul.*

(I Pet. 2:11)

*Put on the whole armour of God that ye may be able to
stand against the wiles of the devil. For we wrestle not
against flesh and blood, but against powers, against the
rulers of the darkness of this world, against spiritual
wickedness in high places.*

(Eph. 6:11-12)

These and related texts, elaborated on by the Christian
fathers, gave birth to one of the grand conceptions of
Christian life: man's life is a pilgrimage to God, a war against
the forces of evil. "First, þan, [fight] manly aȝens þe devell,
þe world, and þe flessh, and ouercome hem—ȝe, þe vij devels
þat beþ chefe vppon þe vij dedely synnes, as Lucifere, Mam-
mona, Asmodeus, and oþur. / Slee also þe world and þe
flesshe. And when þou hast slayn þise felons, þan þou shalst
be þe Kynges of heven champion while þou lyvest here, euer to
reigne with hym after þe dethe in þe kyngedam of heven,"
exhorts the preacher.[1] These words might well serve as a
gloss to Book I of the *Faerie Queene*; for it is this conception of the Christian soldier in pilgrimage to the celestial city
of his salvation, attaining sainthood by overcoming the Flesh,
the World, and the Devil, that chiefly informs the structure
of the work. My argument, briefly, is this: upon his separation from Una, Red Crosse encounters but is, like the first

[1] *Middle English Sermons*, ed. Woodburn O. Ross, EETS, o.s. 209
(London: Oxford Univ. Press, 1940), p. 270.

3

Adam, ultimately defeated by the Flesh (Duessa), the World (Lucifera), and the Devil (Orgoglio); and upon his rescue by Arthur and reunion with Una, Red Crosse successfully resists or is educated in terms of the Flesh (Despaire), the World (the House of Holiness), and the Devil (the dragon), whereupon he becomes Red Crosse *microchristus*.[2]

This pattern is, in many respects, unique with Spenser. Nonetheless, the sixteenth-century reader would not, I think, have been surprised to discover the Flesh-World-Devil triad as the dominant structural scheme underlying Red Crosse's pilgrimage. The scheme abounds in the dramatic literature of England up to Spenser's time.[3] More important, it also abounds in the genre Spenser's readers, as much as Bunyan's readers later, would have recognized immediately as part of the first book's tradition, a genre in this book at least as important as the Italianate epic—the literature of Christian pilgrimage. To survey the whole scope of this literature would be as tedious as unnecessary. Instead, I will focus on pilgrimage works of four writers: Guillaume de Deguileville, *The Pilgrimage of the Life of Man*, in Lydgate's translation; John Lydgate, *The Assembly of Gods*; Stephen Hawes, *The Example of Virtue* and *The Pastime of Pleasure*; and Jean Cartigny, *The Wandering Knight*, in William Goodyear's translation. These works have special interest in that all of

2 Jean MacIntyre, "*The Faerie Queene*: Book I: Toward Making It More Teachable," *College English*, 31 (1970), 473-482, also relates Red Crosse Knight's adventures to the infernal triad. MacIntyre divides Red Crosse's career into four stages: Error (Errour, Archimago, Duessa), Sin (Luifera, Orgoglio, Despaire; or the World, the Flesh, and the Devil), Regeneration (the House of Holiness), and Victory (the slaying of the dragon, the betrothal to Una).

3 The pilgrimage against "all sin" can be found in such moralities and early interludes as the Digby *Mary Magdalene*, *The Castle of Perseverance*, *Mankind*, *The Interlude of Youth*, *Mundus et Infans*, to mention only a few. Later moral interludes of the second half of the sixteenth century, like *The Tide Tarrieth No Man*, *Enough Is as Good as a Feast*, *All for Money*, *The Conflict of Conscience*, continue the tradition, though the sins are not generally portrayed as schematically as before.

them have at one time or another been suggested as analogues to, or even sources for, the Legend of Holiness;[4] and yet, curiously, Spenserians have never examined them systematically and collectively as a body of literature with conventions and recurring motifs. Certain features decidedly do recur, however; and chief among them is the infernal triad.

Deguileville's *Pilgrimage*[5] embodies the central impulse of pilgrimage literature and the allegorical romance: the hero must, by overcoming obstacles, purge himself of vice in order to attain the object of his quest. The object of Deguileville's Pilgrim's quest, however, is not the rose of his desire but the New Jerusalem of his salvation. Pilgrim, excited by a vision he has had of the New Jerusalem, undertakes a journey there with the assistance primarily of Grace Dieu. At the beginning of his journey, Pilgrim reaches a crossroads; one way is "large & pleyn, esy to pace; / The tother, streight, & hard to trace" (11167-11168). Here he receives conflicting advice from true and false guides: Youth and Idleness urge Pilgrim to take the broad path; Labour, Moral Virtue, Mortification

[4] See Appendix IV, "The Sources of Book I," in *The Works of Edmund Spenser: A Variorum Edition*, I, *The Faerie Queene: Book One*, ed. Frederick Morgan Padelford (Baltimore, Md.: The Johns Hopkins Press, 1932), esp. 404-418. Of particular interest are the articles of F. M. Padelford, "Spenser and *The Pilgrimage of the Life of Man*," *Studies in Philology*, 28 (1931), 211-218; and Dorothy F. Atkinson [Evans], "*The Wandering Knight*, the Red Cross Knight and 'Miles Dei,'" *Huntington Library Quarterly*, 7 (1944), 109-134. Many additional correspondences between Spenser and Cartigny are pointed out by Mrs. Evans in the Notes to her edition of *The Wandering Knight* (Seattle, Wash.: Univ. of Washington Press, 1951), pp. 133-161. Of course C. S. Lewis, *The Allegory of Love* (London: Oxford Univ. Press, 1936), esp. ch. 6, should always be consulted. Stephen Batman's *The Travayled Pylgrime* is not discussed here since the work is not as promising as its title might suggest; even for Book II, the correspondences pointed to by Kathrine Koller, "*The Travayled Pylgrime* by Stephen Batman and Book Two of *The Faerie Queene*," *Modern Language Quarterly*, 3 (1942), 535-541, seem to me rather slight.

[5] The edition used is F. J. Furnivall's, EETS, e.s. 77, 83, 92 (London: Kegan Paul, Trench, and Trübner, 1899-1904).

of the Body, and Grace Dieu urge Pilgrim to overcome the lust of the flesh and take the narrow path. But as in other pilgrimages, the pilgrim succumbs to the weakness of the flesh and makes a false choice of the broad path. Youth drops Pilgrim onto "a weye large and brood" (12744), where he encounters the seven deadly sins and their various subspecies: gluttony, lust (Venus), and sloth; pride, envy, and wrath; and avarice; or the Flesh, the Devil, and the World, respectively. Escaping the infernal triad, Pilgrim then encounters in a dark forest Necromancy, Heresy, and Satan himself. Pilgrim flees into the Sea of Worldliness and reaches the Tower of Worldly Gladness in which Satan (the Devil) and a siren (the Flesh) dwell. Grace Dieu rescues Pilgrim and brings him to the Ship of Religion, where he is educated in truth and purged of vice. The *Pilgrimage* concludes with the arrival of Old Age and Sickness. Mercy comforts the dying Pilgrim. Death swings his scythe and the author awakens.

Despite the rambling organization of Deguileville's narrative, most of the major motifs of pilgrimage literature can be found in it: the baptism and arming of the knight; the crossroads situation; the contention between true guides and false; the false choice; the encounter with the Flesh, the World, and the Devil; the *selva oscura* of error, false truth, and worldliness; a house of the World containing the infernal triad; the rescue by grace; the re-education of the hero. Deguileville's *Pilgrimage*, then, would seem to provide the prototypical language of Spenser's work.

John Lydgate's *The Assembly of Gods: or the Accord of Reason and Sensuality in the Fear of Death*[6] does not portray a pilgrimage as such, but since it is concerned with the pilgrimage of life and the conflict of virtue with the Flesh, the World, and the Devil, it merits our attention. In this poem a dreamer witnesses a Prudentius-like battle between the vices and the virtues on the Field of Microcosm. Vice has as his captains the seven deadly sins. As in Spenser's pageant, the

[6] The edition used is Oscar Lovell Triggs's, EETS, e.s. 69 (London: Kegan Paul, Trench, and Trübner, 1896).

seven deadly sins all ride animals and are organized around the infernal triad: pride, envy, and wrath (the Devil); covetousness (the World); gluttony, lechery, and sloth (the Flesh). Virtue has as his knights the four cardinal virtues, Righteousness, Prudence, Strength, and Temperance; and also Humility, Charity, Patience, Liberality, Abstinence, Chastity, and Good Business, seven virtues to counter seven vices. Conscience judges the contest. Vice is defeated with the predictable consequences of repentance, a curbing of sensuality, reason becoming the deputy of free will, and so forth. Death enters Microcosm, and the field dries up, whereupon Virtue is exalted above the firmament, taking with him "the swete Frute of Macrocosme" (st. 210). After the dreamer hears a rather non-descript exegesis of the vision at the School of Doctrine, the *Assembly of Gods* concludes with the dreamer's reflection on the meaning of his experience:

> But alway beware, be ye yong or olde,
> That your frewyll ay to Vertu moore
> Apply than to Vyce, the eysyer may be boore
> The Burdyn of the fylde, that ye dayly fyght
> Agayn your iii enemyes, for all her gret myght.
>
> That ys to sey, the Deuyll & the Flesshe
> And also the Worlde. . . .
> . . . .
> And then shall ye haue the triumphall guerdoun
> That God reserueth to euery creature
> Aboue in hys celestiall mansioun. . . .
> (sts. 297-299)

The *Assembly of Gods* presents us with fundamentally the same conception of the pilgrimage of life we encountered in Deguileville and will encounter in Spenser: the Christian pilgrim is engaged in a vices-and-virtues combat in which sainthood stipulates victory over the triple threat of the Flesh, the World, and the Devil.

Stephen Hawes may not be, as some of the older critics

7

contended, the Spenser before Spenser, but his two major works, *The Example of Virtue* and *The Pastime of Pleasure*, viewed side by side, reveal a rather remarkable resemblance to Spenser's Legend of Holiness; for both of his works are allegorical chivalric romances structured around the infernal triad. In the *Example of Virtue*,[7] Youth agrees to be led by Dame Discretion, sister of Wisdom, to overcome "this brytell Worlde" (I;13). The novice pilgrim boards a ship with Dame Discretion and crosses the Sea of Vainglory to reach an island where he undergoes an education at the hands of Dame Prudence. There, Dame Sapience decides that the pilgrim should have a wife, Cleanness, daughter of the King of Love. Youth and Discretion leave and pass through the "great derkenesse" of "a ryght great wyldernesse" (VIII;158). In this *selva oscura* are found serpents and wild beasts, "the lyon / Wolfe / and beere" (VIII;160), the first two of which would seem to signify, as in the *Inferno*, pride (the Devil) and covetousness (the World), with the third probably signifying lust (the Flesh). These three wild beasts, or the triple pleasures of the World, anticipate Youth's next series of encounters: first, a lady on a goat "Prayenge me to her for to assent / As to fulfyll the flesshly pleasure" (VIII;161), whose name is Dame Sensuality; second, a lady riding an elephant while sitting in a castle holding a cup of gold, who identifies herself as "the lady of ryches / The quene of Welthe and Worldly glory," and who is identified by Discretion as "pryde endued with couetyse" (IX;163-168). Youth's resistance of these two women comprises a rejection of the infernal triad, though the scheme is manifested in only two figures, the avarice of the World and the pride of the Devil being conflated in a single figure. But having resisted the infernal triad, the pilgrim proceeds to get lost in a worldly labyrinth, "the busy-

---

[7] Citations are to *The Example of Vertu* (London, 1510). Roman numerals following quotations refer to the chapter number of the 1510 edition; arabic numerals indicate the stanza number in the inadequate but only accessible edition of Edward Arber in *English Songs*, I, *The Dunbar Anthology* (London, 1901), pp. 217-295.

ness of worldly operacyon" (IX;169), from which he is rescued by Sapience, who guides both the pilgrim and his guide
to the castle of the King of Love. In order to enter the castle,
"the kyngdome of the great grace" (IX;180), and to reach
Cleanness, Youth must cross a bridge over perilous waters,
which probably signifies baptism.[8] To marry Cleanness,
Youth must overcome one more obstacle. Although in the
selva oscura of the World he resisted the Flesh, the World,
and the Devil, now he must defeat them in the form of a
three-headed dragon: "a serpent of great subtylte / Whiche
well bytokeneth as we do fynde / The worlde the flesshe and
the deuyll by kynde" (XI;192). Youth cuts off the heads of
the Flesh and the World and, after some difficulty, drives the
head of the Devil back to Hell. The triad defeated, Youth is
renamed Virtue. Saint Jerome marries him to Cleanness, and
the marriage is celebrated by a great feast, the Eucharist. We
next meet the couple sixty years later; having been granted
a vision of the Hell they avoided, they are both taken to the
celestial garden "That longeth to us by inherytaunce" (XII;
236). The *Example of Virtue* is, therefore, replete with characters, episodes, and settings at once referring it back to
Deguileville's work and anticipating Spenser's: the true guide,
the education and preparation of the hero, the fusion of romantic and religious quests, the *selva oscura*, Dame Sensuality (Duessa in Spenser), the labyrinth of worldly error, the
defeat of a dragon, the marriage feast with apocalyptic overtones, and of course, in several guises, the Flesh, the World,
and the Devil.

A similar generic vocabulary presents itself in Hawes's
Pastime of Pleasure.[9] The pilgrim in this work, however, fol-
lows a different route from his counterpart in the *Example of
Virtue*: whereas Virtue vanquishes the triad in pursuit of a

---

[8] A similar scene occurs in Deguileville's *Pilgrimage*, lines 872ff.,
in which Pilgrim must be baptized in the river before the house of
Grace Dieu.

[9] The edition used is William Edward Mead's, EETS, o.s. 173 (London: Oxford Univ. Press, 1928).

true love assisted by true guides, Grande Amoure succumbs
to it in pursuit of a false love, La Bel Pucell, assisted by false
guides, and must therefore undergo a re-education in purgatory. The work opens with the conventional crossroads situation; Grande Amoure confronts two paths, *vita contemplativa*
and *vita activa*:

> This is the streyght waye / of contemplacyon
> Vnto the Ioyfull toure pedurable
> Who that wyll walke / vnto that mancyon
> He must forsake / all thynges varyable
> With the vayneglory / somoche deceyuable
> And though the waye / be harde and daungerous
> The laste ende therof / shall be ryght precyous
> And in the other hande / ryght fayre wryten was
> This is the waye / of worldly dygnyte
> Of the actyfe lyfe / who wyll in it passe
> Vnto the toure / of fayre dame beaute
> Fame shall tell hym / of the waye in certaynte
> Vnto labell pucell / the fayre lady excellent
> Aboue all other / in clere beaute splendent

(85-98)

Choosing the fame and beauty of the "more playne" (101)
path of the active life, Grande Amoure makes a "false
choice": he has chosen the World.

That, at any rate, is the message with which the poem
opens. The events of the first part of the poem, however, do
not clearly support that message. Grande Amoure's training
in doctrine, logic, rhetoric, chivalry, courtesy, and astronomy,
which occupies the first and highly discursive half of the
work, does not seem to bear out the initial moralism, nor
does his defeat of the two multi-headed giants and the dragon
with the head and face of a maiden. Though there are a few
obvious indications of the fallacy behind Grande Amoure's
quest for La Bel Pucell, especially in the speech of Fortune
at Mars's Tower of Chivalry and in the blatant naturalism
of Venus' letter to La Bel Pucell in Grande Amoure's behalf,

not until the end of the work does it become entirely clear that this *Romance of the Rose* quest is in actuality a quest for the three lures of the World—glory, lust, and (in Grande Amoure's old age) gold. Not inconceivably Hawes is making the same point that Spenser makes in Red Crosse Knight's degeneration sequence, that it is part of the craftiness of evil to persuade us of our virtuousness in the very process of our corruption. Or perhaps Hawes is attempting in the first half of his work to create a worldly parody of Pilgrim's elaborate education and preparation in Deguileville; or perhaps he is creating a worldly analogy to the pilgrimage in his own earlier *Example of Virtue*. Be that as it may, we do eventually return to the question of Grande Amoure's choice at the crossroads when the hero, having been married to La Bel Pucell for "full ryght many a yere" (5333), confronts the arrival of Age. Age moralizes that "my dedes of youthe were of grete foly" (5359): "the youthe is open to all fraylte / Redy to fall in to grete iniquyte / Full well is he that is brydled fast / With dame reason tyll his youth be past" (5365-5368). But ironically Grande Amoure simply replaces the vices of his youth with the vice of age, avarice. When death does come, Grande Amoure is buried by Dame Mercy and Dame Charity and sent to purgatory, where, to earn salvation, he is instructed in the seven deadly sins. From this instruction Grande Amoure finally learns that to attain salvation and "Ioye perdurable" the pilgrim must triumph over "the bryttle worlde," "the vyle flesshe," and "the deuyll":

> And my selfe called la graunde amoure
> Sekynge aduenture in the worldly glory
> For to attayne the ryches and honoure
> Dyde thynke full lytell that I sholde here ly
> Tyll dethe dyde marke me full ryght pryuely
> Lo what I am and where to you must
> Lyke as I am / so shall you be all dust
>
> Than in your mynde inwardely dyspyse.
> The bryttle worlde so full of doubleness

11

With the vyle flesshe / and ryght soone aryse
Out of your slepe / of mortall heuynes
Subdue the deuyll with grace and mekeness
That after your lyfe / frayle and transytory
You may than lyue in Ioye perdurable.

(5481-5495)

Now, if one looks back on Grande Amoure's life, one can see how he succumbed to the three temptations. As the first stanza of the preceding quotation shows, he succumbed to lust (he is called "la graunde amoure"), vainglory ("worldly glory"), and gold ("ryches"). The pilgrim's youth is governed by lust and glory. This is demonstrated by the fact that his quest is for the love of La Bel Pucell and that his false guide is Fame; also by the fact that Mars, "prynce of honoure and of worthy fame" (3046), and Venus, "of loue the goddess" (3764), are the patron gods assisting him. In addition, Fame, in her futile attempt to grant Grande Amoure an eternal name, bases her justification on the love and glory Grande Amoure attained in his youth:

Dyde not graunde amoure with his ryall dedes
Wynne la belle pucell the moost fayre lady
And of hyghe honoure attayned the medes
In the demeanynge hym so worthely
Sleynge the grete terryble gyauntes vgly
And also the fyry monster vyolente
And of the seuen metalles made by enchauntement

(5509-5515)

To the world's eyes, a great lover and a great hero; but *sub specie aeternitatis*, a victim of the temptations to lust and glory. And finally, of course, in his old age Grande Amoure completes the triad by falling victim to avarice.

The *Pastime of Pleasure* is, then, despite its discursiveness, a pilgrimage conceived in terms of man's war against the Flesh, the World, and the Devil. Accordingly, the work ends,

as Lydgate's *Assembly of Gods* did, with the author's petition
to Mary to aid him in his battle against the infernal triad:

> Pray to thy swete sone / which,is infynall
> To gyue me grace to wynne the vyctory
> Of the deuyll / the world and of my body [the Flesh]
> And that I may my selfe well apply
> Thy sone and the to laude and magnyfy.
>
> (5791-5795)

In the overall pattern of its pilgrimage, with the hero led by
a false love and assisted by false guides to make a false choice
and then put through a period of purgation in which he ultimately triumphs over the Flesh, the World, and the Devil
to which he had earlier succumbed, the *Pastime of Pleasure*
certainly anticipates Spenser's pilgrimage. Indeed, if we were
to combine the *Example of Virtue*'s triumph over the infernal
triad through a true love with the *Pastime of Pleasure*'s succumbing to the infernal triad through a false love, we would
be very close to the general outline of Book I of the *Faerie
Queene*.

Jean Cartigny's *The Wandering Knight*,[10] like Deguileville's *Pilgrimage*, Hawes's *Pastime of Pleasure*, and Spenser's
Legend of Holiness, portrays the moral degradation of the
pilgrim in terms of the Flesh, the World, and the Devil. Like
Hawes, but unlike Deguileville and Spenser, Cartigny does
not begin with his knight allied to his true mistress and guide.
Instead, the Wandering Knight, having spent his first twenty-
one years in "all folly and lasciviousness," determines to
make a voyage "in this world [to] find true felicity and happiness." Dame Folly provides the knight with a worldly counterpart to the Christian's armor, and the two set out on a worldly
parody of the Christian pilgrimage to find "riches, worldly

---

[10] The edition used is Dorothy Atkinson Evans' (Seattle, Wash.:
Univ. of Washington Press, 1951) of the William Goodyear translation (1581). On the popularity of this work, see pp. xi-xii, xxi-xxvi,
of Mrs. Evans' Introduction.

pleasure, strength, honor, and delights of the flesh." Folly and the Wandering Knight come to a crossroads where two ladies, Virtue and the fraudulent Voluptuousness, who pretends to the name of Felicity, try to persuade the knight to accept them as his guide in the world. Folly, claiming that Virtue is unfaithful, persuades the knight to follow Voluptuousness, who takes him to her Palace of Worldly Felicity. Leaving the palace for a temporary respite from pleasure, the knight sees it sink suddenly into the earth. A whirlwind, an earthquake, brimstone, and other signs of the last judgment occur. The knight finds himself in "a beastly bog sticking fast," whereupon God's Grace rescues him and takes him to the School of Repentance, where he is purged, makes confession, takes Communion, and is awarded the hermit Understanding as his new governor. God's Grace then takes the knight to the Palace of Virtue, where he is instructed in the seven cardinal virtues and granted a vision of the City of God. This vision causes the knight to desire never to return to earth, at which point God's Grace has him instructed by Perseverance.

The structure of the Wandering Knight's pilgrimage bears a genuinely striking resemblance to Red Crosse's. Folly separates the knight from Virtue by causing him to doubt her; Hypocrisy separates Red Crosse from Truth. Spenser, in portraying the Adamic degeneration of his knight upon separation from Truth, employs three episodes, one for each member of the infernal triad, while Cartigny has really only one episode, the Palace of Worldly Felicity—or two, if one counts the initial encounter with Voluptuousness. In both narratives, however, subservience to the Flesh leads to subservience to the World and the Devil (as it did also in Deguileville and Hawes): Voluptuousness leads the Wandering Knight to the Palace of Worldly Felicity, Duessa leads Red Crosse to the House of Pride. Both writers, moreover, portray the palace of the World as the home of all the sins of the World: both palaces contain the seven deadly sins organized according to the Flesh, the World, and the Devil. In Spenser the pageant of sins is organized as the Flesh (idleness, gluttony, lechery), the World (avarice), and the Devil (envy, wrath, pride). In Cartigny the seven towers of the palace are organized around the Devil (pride, envy, wrath), the World (covetousness), and the Flesh (gluttony, lechery, sloth). The infernal triad manifests itself further in Cartigny's palace in that, as the palace of the World, it is ruled by Lucifer (the Devil) and Voluptuousness (the Flesh); and a similar conjunction is made by Spenser at the House of Pride in the simultaneous presence of Duessa (the Flesh), Lucifera (the World), and Satan (the Devil). Cartigny in fact specifically explicates the concept of "worldly felicity" in terms of I John 2:16 in the fourteenth chapter of Part One. He quotes John and remarks that "The eye, the flesh, and the pomp of life is the worldling's felicity; that is their heaven"; and he devotes the remainder of the chapter to an explanation of the meaning of these three vices. What the Flesh involves is obvious enough. The concupiscence of the eyes involves "covetousness and desire of riches," or the World, and the concupiscence of pride "honor, authority, might, estimation, and dignity in the world," all of which are "of the devil." Accordingly the palace itself is architecturally structured around the three vices. In the ninth chapter the knight is taken by Voluptuousness, as Red Crosse will later be taken by Duessa, to see the prince of the castle of the World, the richly arrayed Lucifer. In a gesture which is obviously linked with Satan's request of Christ in the temptation of the kingdoms and which will be repeated by Red Crosse Knight in the House of Pride, the Wandering Knight reverences Lucifer. He is then guided to the different sections of the palace: the treasury house (the lust of the eye, or the World); the gallery of Pomp ("the pomp of life," or the Devil); and the apothecary shop of Lasciviousness, the wine-cellar of Drunkenness, the kitchen of Lickerousness, a room apparently designed for homosexuals, and the temple of Venus (the lust of the Flesh). The Palace of the World thus contains the three kingdoms of the infernal triad. The degradation sequences of Cartigny and Spenser are, therefore,

15

remarkably alike: in both the knight ignores a true guide and follows a false guide, the Flesh (Voluptuousness, Duessa), who pretends to be a true guide and adopts a false name (Felicity, Fidessa); and in both the Flesh leads the knight to a house ruled by pride and signifying the World which contains the infernal triad. The principal difference is that Spenser's worldly palace is not ruled by Lucifer but by Lucifera, and his hero reaches his moral nadir not in the palace of the World but in a separate episode in which he succumbs to the pride of the Devil. The result of this additional episode is that Red Crosse in his degeneration experiences the temptations of the Flesh, the World, and the Devil not once but twice.

Cartigny's regeneration sequence also resembles Spenser's, though it is not structured, as Spenser's is, around the infernal triad. Both the Wandering Knight and Red Crosse must be rescued by God's grace out of a situation from which they cannot physically or morally escape. Both fall into despair; both undergo purgation and illumination and are granted a vision of the celestial city; and both are restrained from the desire to retreat from the world and are returned to the world to complete their pilgrimage. I think one is forced to conclude, therefore, that the number and consistency of the analogues between Cartigny and Spenser justify claiming the *Wandering Knight* as not merely an analogue but a major source for the Legend of Holiness. At the very least one must conclude that Cartigny's work best exemplifies the literary tradition of the Christian pilgrimage that Spenser inherited and within which he worked.[11]

[11] One might expect the legend of St. George to incorporate the Flesh-World-Devil scheme, but supportive evidence is slender. Associated with the Crusades, patron and protector of English soldiers since the Crusades, and patron saint of the Order of the Garter, he was obviously eligible for the title "Christi miles nobilis" (see Dreves, *Analectica Hymnica Medei Aevi*, vol. 21, no. 101, p. 60, edition of 1895); and the most influential treatment of his life, Jacobus de Voragine's in the *Legenda Aurea*, translated by Caxton, portrays George not only as a tiller of the earth ("that is his flesshe") but also as a holy *agonistes* and pilgrim: "Or George may be sayd gera: that is holy /

and of gyon that is a wrasteler. For he wrasteled with the dragon. or it is sayd of george that is a pylgrym. . . . He was a pylgryme in the syght of the worlde . . ." (from the Caxton translation, reprinted in the Appendix to Alexander Barclay, *The Life of St. George*, ed. William Nelson, EETS, o.s. 230 [London: Oxford Univ. Press, 1955], p. 112). But the *Legenda Aurea* makes no mention of the infernal triad, nor do Mantuan and Barclay—though Barclay does dwell on George's ability to subdue "carnall lust / and worldly vanyte" (366), and he celebrates his "manly resystence / Agaynst all pleasures / of worldly vanyte" (396-398), both of which suggest the concept "all sin"; but it is only a suggestion. Artistic representations in England of St. George yield no more fruit. E. C. Williams, "Mural Paintings of St. George in England," *Journal of the British Archeological Association*, 3rd Series, 12 (1949), 19-36, mentions a fifteenth-century St. George at the parish church of Broughton, Bucks, in which the dragon's tail has three heads; but that, she says, is "an original touch, not found elsewhere" (p. 25). The only specific connection I know of between St. George and the infernal triad is Lydgate's, in his tapestry poem on "The Legend of St. George" (in *The Minor Poems of John Lydgate, Part I*, ed. Henry Noble MacCracken, EETS, e.s. 107 [London: Kegan Paul, Trench, and Trübner, 1911], p. 145; some useful comments on this tapestry poem and another edition of it can be found in E. P. Hammon, "Two Tapestry Poems by Lydgate," *Englische Studien*, 43 [1910-11], 10-26):

> þis name George by Interpretacioun
> Is sayde of tweyne, þe first of hoolynesse,
> And þe secound of knighthood and renoun,
> As þat myn Auctour lyke þe for to expresse,
> þe feond venqwysshing of manhoode and prowesse,
> þe worlde, þe fleeshe, as Crystes owen knight,
> Wher-euer he roode in steel armed bright.

The similarities between this poem and Spenser's are rather striking, but one would be hard pressed to prove that Spenser actually knew the poem. One can say, however, that in the traditional legend itself, in the defeat of the dragon and the rescue and conversion of the city of the unconverted and damned, lay an imitation of Christ's role as rescuer of man and victor over Satan. St. George's great act of sainthood was rich with implications of the pilgrim's *imitatio Christi*. The marriage of the legend with the pilgrimage genre's combat against the Flesh, the World, and the Devil, therefore, was for Spenser a natural one, whether or not he knew the Lydgate poem or any other (to me unknown) work.

On Spenser's use of the St. George legend, see Appendix IV, pp.

Among the recurring features of pilgrimage literature the dominant feature, as we have seen, is the very conception of the pilgrimage itself as a combat against the Flesh, the World, and the Devil. The reason for this common denominator is simple: the conception of the pilgrimage found in the literature is precisely that found in the baptismal rites. The infernal triad figures three times in the baptismal ceremony. The first vow the godparents make for the child is to "forsake the deuil and all his workes, the vaine pompe and glorye of the world, with al couetous desires of the same, and the carnal desires of the flesh." The triad also forms part of the minister's prayer on behalf of the child, and it is part of the minister's words upon receiving the child into the church as he makes the sign of the cross on the child's forehead:

> We receiue this Childe into the congregacion of Christes flocke, and do sygne him with the signe of the crosse, in token that hereafter he shal not be ashamed to confesse the faith of Christ crucified, and manfully to fight under his banner against sinne [the Flesh], the world, and the deuyll, and to continue Christes faithful souldiour and servaunt vnto his liues ende.[12]

370-390, of the Variorum Edition. Of especial value in that it provides English texts of the *Legenda Aurea* account and of Mantuan's *Georgius* is F. M. Padelford and Matthew O'Connor, "Spenser's Use of the St. George Legend," *Studies in Philology*, 23 (1926), 142-156, reprinted in the Variorum Edition. On Spenser's use of the conception of St. George as a knight of holiness, see Grace Warren Landrum, "St. George *Redivivus*," *Philological Quarterly*, 29 (1950), 381-388. Of general interest are J. E. Matzke, "Contributions to the History of the Legend of St. George," *Publications of the Modern Language Association* (hereafter cited as *PMLA*), 17 (1902), 464-535; E. K. Chambers, *The Medieval Stage* (Oxford: The Clarendon Press, 1903), I, 205-227, and *The English Folk-Play* (Oxford: The Clarendon Press, 1933), pp. 170-185; James George Frazer, *The Golden Bough*, 3rd ed. (1911; rpt. London: Macmillan, 1966), I, ii, 163ff., 330ff.

[12] *The Prayer-Book of Queen Elizabeth* (London: Thynne, 1912), p. 111.

From the beginning of his life in Christ, the child is, like Red Crosse Knight, a Christian soldier bearing on his person the sign of the cross; he has become engaged in a pilgrimage that stipulates an unceasing combat against the Flesh, the World, and the Devil.

Baptism at once embodies and begins a recapitulation of Christ's life. "Know ye not," says Paul,

> that so many of us as were baptized into Jesus Christ were baptized into his death? Therefore we are buried with him by baptism into death: that like as Christ was raised up from the dead by the glory of the Father, even so we also should walk in newness of life. . . . Knowing this, that our old man is crucified with him, that the body of sin might be destroyed, that henceforth we should not serve sin (Romans 6:3-6).

If Christ on the cross crucified the old man, or Adam, correspondingly for the individual Christian baptism signals his entry into a life of continuous mortification of the old Adam and restoration in the image of the new. For neither the Calvinist nor the Anglican does baptism mean the total removal of the Adamic taint. According to Calvin, "we are baptized into the mortification of our flesh, which begins with our baptism, and which we pursue day by day and which will, moreover, be accomplished when we pass from this life to the Lord";[13] and according to the minister's exhortation concluding the Anglican baptism, "Baptisme doeth represent vnto vs our profession, which is to folow the example of our sauiour Christ, and to be made like vnto hym, that as he died and rose again for us: so should we (which are Baptised) dye from sinne, and ryse again vnto righteousness, continually mortifying al our euyll and corrupt affections, and dailye procedynge in all vertue and godlynes of liuing."[14] But if

[13] *Institutes of the Christian Religion*, ed. John T. McNeill and trans. Ford Lewis Battles, The Library of Christian Classics, XXI (Philadelphia: The Westminster Press, 1960), II, 1312 (IV.xv.11).

[14] *The Prayer-Book*, pp. 111-112. Dean Nowell, whose catechism

19

baptism signifies a recapitulation of the Crucifixion, it also signifies a recapitulation of the first event following Christ's own baptism, the Temptation in the Wilderness. The new Adam's resistance in the wilderness of the three sins to which the old Adam succumbed in the garden provides the pattern for Christian victory in this world; what is typology in the wilderness is a psychomachia for the Christian soldier.

These are the conceptions underlying Spenser's portrayal of Red Crosse's pilgrimage. They also underlie Spenser's account of his knight's experiences in the court of Gloriana.[15]

Elizabeth declared the official catechism of the Church of England, expresses the same ideas; see Alexander Nowell, *A Catechism*, ed. G. E. Corrie, Parker Society, 53 (Cambridge, Eng.: Cambridge Univ. Press, 1853), pp. 208-209.

[15] For a different analysis of the events described in Spenser's letter to Raleigh, see Donald Cheney's chapter, "Plowman and Knight: The Hero's Dual Identity," in *Spenser's Image of Nature: Wild Man and Shepherd in "The Faerie Queene"* (New Haven, Conn.: Yale Univ. Press, 1966); according to Cheney, Red Crosse, like the narrator, is portrayed as "abandoning the pastoral mode" (p. 19). See also Virgil K. Whitaker, *The Religious Basis of Spenser's Thought* (Stanford, Cal.: Stanford Univ. Press, 1950), pp. 47-49, who argues that because the organization of Book I is theological not biographical, Red Crosse experiences his "first baptism" not until he falls into the Well of Life in canto xi. It seems to me, however, that confusing Red Crosse's falling into the Well of Life with the actual rites of baptism or his slipping into the balm of the Tree of Life with his partaking of the Lord's Supper demeans the sacraments. The two events should be seen in terms of Arthur's falling to the ground and accidentally ("by chaunce" [viii.19]) loosening the veil of his shield. The act of falling characterizes all three episodes in which Arthur and Red Crosse, though acting as instruments of grace, themselves receive the benefits of grace, which are continuous. Man does not slip into baptism, but he does, as Spenser reminds us, "daily fall" unless "heauenly grace doth him vphold" (viii.1). Fallen man is therefore in constant need of the grace afforded through the sacraments. In the Christian pilgrimage, as Paul writes in II Corinthians 4:16, "the inward man is renewed day by day." Calvin therefore writes of baptism that "we obtain in Christ continual and unceasing forgiveness of sins," "assurance of that sole and perpetual cleansing which we have in Christ's blood" (*Institutes*, II, 1307 [IV.xv.3-4]);

The "clownishe younge man" who enters Gloriana's court is man unbaptized and unregenerate. George's "clownish" or rustic connection with the earth implies his connection through the flesh with Adam: "The first man is of the earth, earthly" (I Corinthians 15:47); and of course George's name means "of the earth, earthly." His rustic unworthiness, which makes him "vnfitte . . . for a better place," identifies him as man *sub lege*, not *sub gratia*. George's assuming the armor of Ephesians and his transformation into "the goodliest man in al that company," which makes him "well liked of the Lady [i.e., the church]," indicates his baptism and reception "into the congregacion of Christes flocke." He has put on, as the mid-century Protestant divine, Thomas Becon, had said, the "most beautiful and goodly virtues"[16] of the new Adam. Spenser's portrayal of Red Crosse's baptism in his letter to Raleigh thus prepares us for a work of pilgrimage, in which the knight will set out, in accordance with all that his baptism means, to defeat the Flesh, the World, and the Devil to which the old Adam succumbed, to triumph over the vestiges of the old man within, to continue the regeneration of the inner, spiritual man; he sets out in *imitatio Christi*. That is the intent, it is not the result; for Red Crosse, like Deguileville's Pilgrim and Cartigny's Wandering Knight, ends the first stage of his pilgrimage in *imitatio Adamis*, at which point he must be rescued by grace to begin again to fulfill the *imitatio Christi* of his baptismal vow.

I

Spenser, as much as Milton, was not one to leave a genre as he found it. From the beginning of his career, imitation

---

and of the Lord's Supper that "it reminds us that he [Christ] was made of the bread of life, which we continually eat . . . ; [and assures us] that this quickening is eternal, we being ceaselessly nourished, sustained, and preserved throughout life by it" (*Institutes*, II, 1364 [IV.xvii.5]).

16 *The Catechism of Thomas Becon . . . with Other Pieces*, ed. John Ayre, Parker Society, 13 (Cambridge, Eng.: Cambridge Univ. Press, 1844), p. 208.

stipulated transformation, so that when, in the *Shepheardes Calender*, he turned to the pastoral, he did so that he might explore the range and limits of its perspectives.[17] So now, turning to the greater things of the heroic, he adopts the terminology of the pilgrimage genre that he may question and revise its, and our own, conventional and simplistic understanding of the heroic pilgrimage of Christian life. From the opening two stanzas it becomes clear that Spenser will not permit us to embrace a steady, simple, and easy perspective on the pilgrim of Holiness any more than he will permit us to embrace the inherited simplicities of the genre within which he is working. Underlying these stanzas is the orthodox, and expected, conception of the pilgrimage as a fulfillment of the baptismal vow to imitate Christ's victory over Adam in the wilderness; but the strategy behind the stanzas is to tempt us for a moment to perceive the novice knight as comfortably and simplistically as he perceives himself, in clear *imitatio-Christi* terms, only to trip us over our simplicities. For, in the concluding lines of both stanzas, Spenser introduces a scheme that will recur like a *leitmotif* throughout the book, the dual scheme, summarizing man's inheritance from Adam, of pride and intemperance. (Here as elsewhere Spenser schematizes his materials that he may clarify and unfold their fundamental complexity.) Accordingly, the portrayal of Red Crosse in the opening lines of the first stanza contains no surprise. What we see is largely what we would expect to see: in a legend of Holiness appears a knight of Holiness:

> A gentle Knight was pricking on the plaine,
> Y cladd in mightie armes and siluer shielde,
> Wherein old dints of deepe wounds did remaine,
> The cruell markes of many' a bloudy fielde . . .[18]

But from the deceptive simplicity of this portrait of Red Crosse Knight as Christ the stanza shifts to a portrait of him as Adam:

[17] See Patrick Cullen, *Spenser, Marvell, and Renaissance Pastoral* (Cambridge, Mass.: Harvard Univ. Press, 1970), pp. 29-119.
[18] Citations from Spenser are to the Variorum Edition.

His angry steede did chide his foming bitt,
As much disdayning to the curbe to yield . . .

The angry and unruly horse disdaining the bit of reason signifies the intemperance of the irascible appetite inherited through Adam. Red Crosse embodies the lawless intemperance of Sansloy, whose steed, like his, "the sharpe yron did for anger eat" (iii.33).

The second stanza also begins with a portrait of Red Crosse in terms of his vowed *imitatio Christi*:

But on his brest a bloudie Crosse he bore,
The deare remembrance of his dying Lord,
For whose sweete sake that glorious badge he wore,
And dead as liuing euer him ador'd:
Vpon his shield the like was also scor'd:
For soueraine hope, which in his helpe he had:
Right faithfull true he was in deede and word . . .

And once again a qualifier:

But of his cheere did seeme too solemne sad . . .

Red Cross is "too solemne sad" for the same reason that the House of Pride is said to be "that sad house of Pride" (v.53), and for the same reason that Sansjoy gravitates there; for while Red Crosse bears the shield of faith and has "soueraine hope" in Christ, he also embodies Adam's pride. As with the House of Pride, so with Red Crosse Knight: the prideful man's *fiducia carnalis*, his imperfect faith in God, and his prideful faith in the limited resources of the fallen self, render him ultimately helpless and therefore joyless or "sad."

The opening stanzas thus intimate the form Red Crosse's pilgrimage will take, a conflict between the new man of the spirit, *sanctus*, and the old man of the earth, *georgos*. Though baptized, the pilgrim nonetheless has something of that old Eden and old Adam he is to restore. Some of the original concupiscence of our corrupted nature remains: "And this infection of nature doth remain, yea in them that are regenerated; whereby the lust of the flesh . . . which some do expound the wisdom, some sensuality, some the affection, some the desire, of the flesh, is not subject to the Law of God" (Article IX). These corrupt affections of the old Adam are for Spenser, as we will see time and again, dual; they are the same two tendencies to error and sin which were implied in the opening two stanzas and which are now to take on their full monstrous realization in the figure of Errour: intemperance and pride.

The opening two episodes operate against the background of the convention of the false choice in pilgrimage literature. In entering the Woods of Errour, Red Crosse makes a false choice. Led by delight, he succumbs to *vita voluptuosa* and proceeds to a combat with Errour which parodies *vita activa* and the true form it will ultimately take in a battle with another monster in canto xi. Moreover, in an ironic reversal of pilgrimage convention, the progress in vice from fleshly pleasure to error is done with the companionship of the pilgrim's true guide, and parallels his future progress in vice with the false guide, Duessa. Our simplified expectations are reversed again in the next episode. The conventions of the pilgrimage would lead one to expect that once the pilgrim has made a false choice of the worldly labyrinth he would, with the assistance of his true guide, correct that choice for a true and otherworldly one, *vita contemplativa*. In fact what happens is that the Adamic intemperance which led the pilgrim to embrace a worldly parody of the active life also leads him to embrace a worldy parody of the contemplative life. The simplistic expectations of the pilgrimage genre do not hold for the world Spenser portrays. Spenser reworks the conventions of the genre in order to expose the genre's naive perspectives on the relationship of good and evil in the real world; and in so doing, he also exposes the hero's—and our own—perilous simplicities. The re-examination of the genre involves, therefore, a re-examination of its subject. Spenser's upsetting of our conventional expectations becomes one of the means whereby he engages us in the complexities of his pilgrim's world, making us, as the metaphor of the voyage in the final canto reveals, fellow voyagers, fellow pilgrims.

Wandering Wood is the *selva oscura* of pilgrimage literature, the dark labyrinthine forest of the World in which Dante found himself at the beginning of the *Inferno* and Youth in the *Example of Virtue*, and in which Dequileville's Pilgrim encountered Necromancy and Heresy.[19] It is also a figure for the garden in which the first Adam was tempted and the wilderness in which the second Adam overcame the error to which the first Adam had succumbed. Accordingly, Wandering Wood presents the primal source of error, the taint of the flesh we have inherited through Adam's fall. The hybrid monster, part woman, part serpent, is the "child" of Eve and the devil.[20] The monster in the dark forest is the monster in

[19] On the significance of the *selva oscura* as the world, see John Steadman, "Spenser's *Errour* and the Renaissance Allegorical Tradition," *Neuphilologische Mitteilungen*, 67 (1961), 32-39. Steadman, pp. 37-38, finds the woods "a symbol of worldly wisdom" or more narrowly "a symbol of secular erudition," the episode as a whole representing "the vain effort to find true happiness in the world through secular wisdom." William Nelson, *The Poetry of Edmund Spenser* (New York: Columbia Univ. Press, 1963), pp. 158-160, discusses the Virgilian forest (*Aeneid*, I.314) as it was interpreted by commentators from Servius on as signifying worldliness, sinfulness, the domination of passion over reason; and he argues that the episode exemplifies the "folly" of "the knowledge of this world" (p. 164). A stimulating and detailed analysis of the episode is contained in Donald Cheney, *Spenser's Imagery of Nature*, pp. 22-28.

[20] Virgil K. Whitaker, "The Theological Structure of the *Faerie Queene*, Book I," in *That Soueraine Light*, ed. William R. Mueller and Don Cameron Allen (Baltimore, Md.: The Johns Hopkins Press, 1952), pp. 75-77, provides a solid theological basis for viewing Errour as "Red Crosse's liability to error as a son of Adam." Whitaker does not discuss the significance of the monster's dual nature as part-woman, part-serpent, as I do; but his interpretation of the vomit full of books as "false doctrines that must be overcome by faith" and the "spawne of serpents small" as "the lusts of the flesh" is not inconsistent with the monster's dual nature. D. Douglas Waters, "Errour's Den and Archimago's Hermitage: Symbolic Lust and Symbolic Witchcraft," *ELH, A Journal of English Literary History* (hereafter cited as *ELH*), 33 (1966), 283-386 (rpt. *Duessa as Theological Satire*

the darkness of our own nature. She embodies the two fundamental sins which occasioned the Fall and were passed on to all men, and which were suggested in the structure of the opening two stanzas—the pride of the Serpent and the intemperance of the Woman. She is the monster that makes of our inner garden a wilderness. Indeed, in this figure for original sin, Spenser provides the image which informs the quests of both Red Crosse Knight and Guyon, and thereby unites the opening two books of the *Faerie Queene*: Red Crosse through holiness and faith will destroy the pride of the Serpent, Guyon through temperance will contain the intemperance of the Woman, in order to restore the garden that is at the end of both their quests.

Like pilgrims before them, Red Crosse and Una make a false choice; but in contrast to the clear-cut moral alternatives offered earlier pilgrims, the right alternative seems wrong, the wrong alternative right. Taking cover from the rain seems, on the human level, a perfectly natural act, and

---

[Columbia, Mo.: Univ. of Missouri Press, 1970], pp. 22-25) follows Whitaker in seeing the serpent-brood as fleshly lusts and the books as false doctrines resulting from "high lusts" or "symbolic lusts." Waters finds the latter most important in Errour's appeal to Red Crosse since the episode is primarily a temptation to Red Crosse's "pride of intellect." The pride of the intellect signified by the books and the fleshly intemperance signified by the spawn of serpents, which Waters detects, are a natural extension of the dual sins which Errour embodies and which are repeatedly linked throughout the episode. The best support for my reading, however, comes from one of Spenser's seventeenth-century imitators. In Phineas Fletcher's *Apollyonists*, Sin, whose characterization is to a large extent based on Errour, is said to be "Of the first woman, and th'old serpent bred" (i.11); and in *The Purple Island*, Hamartia, or Sin, whose characterization is also based on Errour, is said to be begotten by "the Dragon" "Of that first woman" (xii.29). (Citations are to *The Poetical Works of Giles Fletcher and Phineas Fletcher*, ed. Frederick S. Boas, 2 vols., Cambridge, Eng.: Cambridge Univ. Press, 1908-1909). For additional information on the ancestry of Errour, see Roland H. Botting, "Spenser's Errour," *Philological Quarterly*, 16 (1937), 73-78; and John Steadman, "Spenser's *Errour*," pp. 32-39, and "Sin, Echidna, and the Viper's Brood," *Modern Language Review*, 57 (1961), 62-66.

wise, the only sensible choice; on the moral level, it is still a
perfectly natural act, but unwise. It is natural to err; man
daily falls. Not only is this true of Red Crosse and Una, but
also of ourselves as well: their responses are our responses
as readers. For us as for them, nothing seems wrong, no error
committed, in wandering in the woods, enjoying the comfort-
ing shelter of "loftie trees yclad with sommers pride" (i.7).
How pleasant and harmless this seems! Not until later do we
realize that these "loftie trees yclad with sommers *pride*" are
in awful conjunction with the fecund pride of Errour, who
will spew forth her vomit "As when old Father *Nilus* gins
to swell / With timely *pride* aboue the *Aegyptian* vale"
(i.21; my additional italics). What seems at first merely the
natural "pride" of summer flourishing is in fact the flourishing of another pride. Not until later do we discover that the
seemingly protective darkness of the forest "that heauens
light did hide" (i.7) is the "desert darknesse" (i.16) of the
monster; that the "pathes and alleies wide, / With footing
worne" (i.7) which lead to shelter are the same paths "that
beaten seemed most bare" (i.11) which lead us to Errour.
This is the psychology of error and the error in our psychology. The monster is within us, the landscape an image of our
own minds:

> And foorth they passe, with pleasure forward led,
> Ioying to heare the birdes sweete harmony,
> Which therein shrouded from the tempest dred,
> Seemd in their song to scorne the cruell sky.
> Much can they prayse the trees so straight and hy,
> The sayling Pine, the Cedar proud and tall,
> The vine-prop Elme, the Poplar neuer dry,
> The builder Oake, sole king of forrests all,
> The Aspine good for staues, the Cypresse funerall.
>
> (i.8)

With obvious delight, Red Crosse and Una identify each tree,
how the world uses and perceives it. Once again, everything
seems innocent, but it is they themselves who are innocent—

27

of their own nature. The pair recognizes the familiar without realizing the reason for their recognition: the landscape is a mirror; it is they themselves that they confront. Their misperceived familiarity deceives them, leads them to demonstrate in their wandering, or erring, the Errour in themselves they prefer not to see. Their accurate science is an ignorance of self, and their blocking out of the darkness of their corrupted nature serves only to increase its sway over them. Their very efforts to avoid the confrontation with their own evil make the inevitable confrontation all the more difficult. Denying their own fallen nature, they fall; denying their affinity with Errour, they err, lose their way, come spatially and spiritually closer to the monster. Theirs is a false identity of innocence in a world where innocence is not possible. They have entered the wilderness of the world as though it were Eden and they the unfallen parents. And now they do not know where they are or who they are:

> Led with delight, they thus beguile the way,
> Vntil the blustring storme is ouerblowne;
> When weening to returne, whence they did stray,
> They cannot finde that path, which first was showne,
> But wander too and fro in wayes vnknowne,
> Furthest from end then, when they neerest weene,
> That makes them doubt, their wits be not their owne:
> So many pathes, so many turnings seene,
> That which of them to take, in diuerse doubt they been.
>
> (i.10)

The placing of "led with delight" at the beginning of the stanza echoes the opening line of stanza 8, "And Foorth they passe, with pleasure forward led," and works to stress that concupiscence they share with the monster: "that slimy snake, the first betrayer and the father of restlessness, never ceases to watch and lie in wait beneath the heel of woman, whom he once poisoned. By 'woman' we mean of course the carnal or sensual part of man. For this is our Eve, through whom the crafty serpent entices and lures our minds to deadly pleasures."[21] "Led with delight," the pair has succumbed to the error of the Woman in Eden; *sensus* has overcome *mens*, as the two are impelled by the monster within them. Once again the Adamic dualism appears, for Eve's intemperance has in fact led them to manifest that other aspect of the monster, the Serpent's pride, in their praising of the trees in stanzas 8 and 9. Should we wonder why the catalogue of trees is so long, the answer is found not in Spenser's obligation to imitate a literary convention found in Ovid and Chaucer; rather it is found in the line prefacing the catalogue, "Much can they prayse the trees so straight and hy." We as readers tend, like the characters, to look at the trees and forget that real subject is not the trees but the praising of the trees— trees, "loftie . . . with sommers pride," that image the pride of the Serpent and of Errour. The praising and naming of the trees finds its counterpart not, as it may have seemed at first, in Adam's naming of the animals in prelapsarian Eden but in Eve's postlapsarian idolatry in her worship of the tree. Behind Red Crosse's and Una's wandering, Spenser has once again suggested, in an almost subliminal use of his interpretive *schema*, the two sins of pride and intemperance which lost us Eden and which, as the opening two stanzas of the canto indicated, constitute the Errour of the knight's, and our own, fallen nature. In a moral progression to be repeated in Red Crosse's Adamic degeneration with Duessa, intemperance ("delight," "pleasure") has led to subservience to pride. The episode thus anticipates Red Crosse's captive

---

[21] Erasmus, *Handbook of the Militant Christian (Enchiridion Militis Christiani)*, trans. John P. Dolan (Notre Dame, Ind: Fides, 1962), p. 62. This work, indebted to the pilgrimage tradition, has a number of remarkable similarities to Spenser's, not the least of which is its sending the pilgrim out to combat the Flesh (lust), the World (avarice), and the Devil (ambition, pride, anger). Undoubtedly one of the most widely read books in the sixteenth century, it was translated into every major European language, and in England alone there were no fewer than eight editions of the Tyndall translation between 1533 and 1576. Consequently, Spenser may well have been familiar with it.

helplessness before his own nature when, in the last stage of
the Adamic sequence, he is captive to the intemperance of the
Woman (Duessa) and the pride of the Devil (Orgoglio).

The problem of the pilgrim's progress against evil is not
simply that the corruption of his nature allies him to his combatants but that, simplifying his complex identity as *sanctus*
and *georgos*, he refuses to recognize that corruption and
community. Even after Una has recognized their error, warning the knight to "Be well aware . . . / Least suddaine mis-
chief ye too rash prouoke" (i.12), Red Crosse persists in his
rash claim to innocence. He appeals to the strength of his
own virtue, but in that very appeal he manifests once again
the dual nature of his opponent's vice. Red Crosse ignores
the warnings of both Una and the dwarf, willfully disregard-
ing the two aids granted him for his pilgrimage, and "full of
fire and greedy hardiment" (i.14) enters the cave. In ignoring the dwarf, who represents reason, prudence, or common-
sense, he acts irrationally, intemperately; like his horse, he
does not wish to be curbed by the bit of reason. He also acts,
again completing the familiar dualism that links him to the
monster, through pride in his own virtue:

> Ah Ladie (said he) shame were to reuoke
> The forward footing for an hidden shade.
> Vertue giues her selfe light, through darkenesse
>   for to wade.
>
>   (i.12)

Errour's pride underlies the Christian aphorism Red Crosse
tosses off so lightly, for his "vertue" is not only that of the
faithful Christian but also that of the pagan, that is, *virtus*,
manliness. Red Crosse's pride in his male prowess, his brute
force, is what is at stake. His rashly claimed virtue masks
Orgoglio's pride. In the very act of denying his error to Una
and the dwarf, then, Red Crosse manifests the pride and intemperance of Errour. Red Crosse would like to act as though
the Fall had not left its impress upon him. Until he reaches

his despairing sense of the depths of his corruption in Orgoglio's dungeon, Red Crosse will add sin unto sin as though he were an unfallen Adam in exile from his garden. He is a victim as much of innocence as evil.

The irony governing Red Crosse's combat with Errour is that she must be fought because the knight's own motivations for fighting her are rooted in error. Red Crosse's denial of his own error makes Errour all the stronger. The battle with Errour is so difficult because of Red Crosse's naive confidence in an uncontaminated virtue. Again and again, however, the imagery of battle, as Paul Alpers has effectively shown,[22] suggests the real community that exists between the two combatants. Intemperate fury links the two, as does pride. Even when Una exhorts the knight to substitute faith for prideful reliance on his own powers, Red Crosse's response is somewhat less than ideal: "That when he heard, in great perplexitie, / His gall did grate for griefe and high disdaine, / And knitting all his force got one hand free" (i.19). What this implies is less faith added to force than force redoubled through wounded pride. In his final and victorious attack on Errour, however, Red Crosse is only "Halfe furious" and is "Resolv'd in minde" (i.24). His fallen tendency to Mars's intemperate *ira* is at least partly restrained. Simultaneously, he seems to display at last something of the faith Una had demanded of him as he strikes the monster with "more than manly force" (i.24); but the phrase properly preserves the ambiguity that has governed the episode, and we are not permitted the confidence of an affirmation. We are, in fact, left with an ambivalent reaction to this victory, despite Una's enthusiastic celebration of the "great glory" of the victory over "a strong enimie" (i.27). It was, in a sense, a victory, and the enemy was certainly strong; but the battle was necessary only because the knight had erred, and the enemy was strong only because the knight was weak. Una

[22] *The Poetry of "The Faerie Queene"* (Princeton, N.J.: Princeton Univ. Press, 1967), pp. 336-339.

offers the touching but perilously naive optimism that "many such I pray, / And henceforth euer wish, that like succeed it may," but she will pay dearly for that naïveté. She must learn through a long wandering in the wilderness to distinguish, as she fails fully to do now, and as she will fail to do when confronted with Archimago masquerading as her knight, between what the knight seems and what he is. Una is scarcely much more prepared to guide Red Crosse Knight, instructing him in all that the Christian life entails, than Red Crosse is to be guided. Immediately following her careless celebration are the less enthusiastic lines of the narrator:

> Then mounted he vpon his Steede againe,
> And with the Lady backward sought to wend;
> That path he kept, which beaten was most plaine . . .
>
> (i.28)

The adventure has in a sense led them nowhere. They return the way they came.

Within the woods of Errour man pursues not only the life of this world but also a parody of the active life and its quest to defeat the dragon: all action is pointless there; to triumph over Errour is merely to triumph over the error of being in the woods in the first place. The only viable action is to leave. The conventions of pilgrimage literature would lead us to expect that once Red Crosse has made a false, worldly choice, he would turn away from the *vita activa* of the world and embrace *vita contemplativa*. Spenser of course does not accept this simple opposition of the two *vitae*. Nonetheless, he does have his pilgrim turn away from one way of the world only to have him encounter another, parodying the other-worldly life of contemplation. (As parodies of the two *vitae*, the Errour and Archimago episodes are linked, as a ring, to the Contemplation and dragon episodes.) In another respect, too, the second episode complements the first: the error of Red Crosse's claim to innocence leads inevitably to hypocrisy. Blinding himself to original sin in the first episode, he now denies his own corrupt impulses, as we would say, by "projecting" them onto Una. The false vision of himself in the first episode now leads to a false vision of Una. Red Crosse now hypocritically distorts Truth in order to preserve the myth of his own innocence.

Archimago is an obvious foil to the hermit Contemplation in canto x. The worldly hermit is in fact involved with the otherworld, but it is the otherworld of Satan, the underworld; his aid is the word, but the word of diabolic necromancy; his purpose is to convert man, but to doubt, this world, and his own infernal faith. The two visions Archimago sets before Red Crosse are, like their maker, a parody of the contemplative life. Accordingly, the false hermit of contemplation produces not, as the later hermit will, spiritual visions of truth but infernal illusions of truth in the two visions of the false Una. As in the Errour episode, Red Crosse Knight is vulnerable largely because of his illusions about his own nature, his inability to confront his own concupiscence. And yet the appeal to intemperance is even stronger here than in the previous episode. Indeed the two visions seem to be organized as a double-barrelled attack on the appetitive soul, the first directed primarily to the concupiscible, the second primarily to the irascible appetite. In the first of these visions, Red Crosse is tempted to err by succumbing to the fleshly pleasures and delights that the true contemplative life requires to be renounced:

> Then seemed him his Lady by him lay,
> And to him playned, how that false winged boy,
> Her chast hart had subdewd, to learne Dame Pleasures
> toy.

> And she her selfe of beautie soueraigne Queene,
> Fair *Venus* seemde vnto his bed to bring
> Her . . .

> (i.47-48)

For a moment the syntax equates truth and beauty in an infernal parody of the Platonic doctrine underlying the portrayal of the true Una. Red Crosse's response to this vision is purposefully ambiguous:

> In this great passion of vnwonted lust,
> Or feare of doing ought amis,
> He started vp . . .

(i.49)

Red Crosse's unfocused sense of a darker side of his own nature leads to a confusion over not only who Una is but also, as in Wandering Wood, who *he* is. His confusion over Una's identity is an extension of his own disoriented sense of identity. Ironically, he grieves "to thinke that gentle Dame so light" while at the same time he succumbs to desire for her, as he dreams of "bowres and beds, and Ladies deare delight" (i.55). Red Crosse's externalizing of evil, his denying of his Adamic self, which led him to err in his battle with Errour, now leads him to become hypocritical in his battle with Hypocrisy.

In the first vision, Red Crosse is tempted (to use the symbolic terminology of the induction to Book I) to the excess of Venus; in the second, to the excess of Mars, "bloudy rage." The lust of Venus has made him vulnerable, but it is the excessive *ira* of Mars that completely overcomes his reason as he, cast ironically in the role of Vulcan, watches his Venus with the squire:

> Which when he saw, he burnt with gealous fire,
> The eye of reason was with rage yblent,
> And would haue slaine them in his furious ire,
> But hardly was restreined of that aged sire.

(ii.5)

And "Pricked with wrath and fiery fierce disdaine" (ii.8), the pilgrim abandons his guide. In a parody of the Contemplation episode, Red Crosse draws himself away from the false vision of the hermit and goes out into the world. Naively and now hypocritically he has denied the reality of his own nature; his rage for innocence has led him to repudiate the divine word itself. But for Spenser the acknowledgment of one's corruption is the indispensable prerequisite for what goodness man can achieve in this world; man cannot deny the complexity of his own nature and cope with the complexities of the outer world. The first half of Spenser's pilgrimage of life shows us, through Red Crosse, the evils men commit in the name of goodness, through belief in their own innocence; it is an exemplum of the evils wrought by men blind to their limitations.[23] From this perspective, the movement of the Legend of Holiness is towards the pronouncing of the hero's name and its correcting of his attempt to evade the full complexity of the nature and identity embodied in that name. Denying the paradoxes of his fallen identity, Red Crosse will deny his name, George, man of earth, to avoid the difficult conflict with Adam, man of clay, that sainthood stipulates. He will act as though baptism had released his nature from sinning. He will act with the confidence of an antinomian in the powers of grace and the privileges of his being one of the elect, only to fall victim to the very vices the Protestant reformers attached to their Roman opposition. Obviously enough Spenser's portrayal of Red Crosse's degeneration at the hands of Catholic tempters—in which he experiences a gradual loss of faith at the same time that he continues to perform ostensible good works against evil—constitutes an attack on Catholicism's emphasis on the redemptive efficacy of works rather than faith; for Spenser's point throughout the degeneration sequence is that, without faith, good works are increasingly corrupted by the evil against which the saint contends. But if, in these episodes,

[23] Richard Hooker in "A Learned Discourse of Justification" (1586?), in *Of the Laws of Ecclesiastical Polity* (London: Dent, 1909), I, 23, provides a useful gloss to Spenser's portrayal of both Red Crosse and Guyon. Speaking of the "fruit of holiness," Hooker argues: "Our very virtues may be snares unto us. The enemy that waiteth for all occasions to work our ruin, hath ever found it harder to overthrow an humble sinner, than a proud saint. There is no man's case so dangerous as his, whom Satan hath persuaded that his own righteousness shall present him pure and blameless in the sight of God."

Spenser is making one of the standard Protestant criticisms of Roman Catholicism, simultaneously he may also be suggesting, in terms of Red Crosse and later Guyon, one of the potential vices behind radical Protestantism that can adulterate both faith and works, namely a false faith in one's being numbered among the elect, which is in reality not true faith at all but a prideful perversion of faith into a presumptuous confidence in one's spiritual superiority. The excesses of the Protestant meet the excesses of the Catholic in the coming together of an infernal circle. Spenser's satire, grounded as it is in the Anglican *via media*, is almost invariably double-pronged; and it would seem to direct itself against the radical excesses of Protestantism as well as, more obviously, those of Roman Catholicism. It is a satire that refuses us, and shows us the dangers of, any oversimplified view of our own nature. And so Red Crosse, denying the limitations Adam has imposed on his nature, is cursed to become him, as he now joins Duessa to repeat the Fall and to succumb to the same triad of sins to which Adam himself had succumbed—the Flesh, the World, and the Devil.

Duessa's significance is, of course, multiple. She exemplifies at various times false faith, false religion, the Church of Rome, Mary Queen of Scots, and possibly, as has recently been suggested, "Mistress Missa."[24] All of these significances, however, are subsumed within what is, from the perspective of the pilgrimage genre, her most important significance as a counterpart to Lady Voluptuousness or Folly, that is, the Flesh. Through intemperance and lust, Duessa lures the pilgrim—Red Crosse Knight or Fradubio—into disbelief of God's word. In Duessa, then, Spenser fuses the Calvinist and

[24] See Appendix V, "The Moral and Spiritual Allegory," pp. 422-448, and Appendix VI, "The Historical Allegory," pp. 449-495, of the Variorum Edition. On Duessa as a whore symbolizing the Roman mass, see D. Douglas Waters, " 'Mistress Missa,' Duessa, and the Anagogical Allegory of *The Faerie Queene*, Book I," *Papers on Language and Literature*, 4 (1968), 259-275 (ch. 1 of *Duessa as Theological Satire*).

in general Protestant interpretation of the temptation of the Flesh as doubt, unbelief, and despair, with the older, Catholic interpretation of the temptation of the Flesh as intemperance. Accordingly, it is appropriate that Duessa, representing false faith, is portrayed as the Whore of Babylon and that, correspondingly, Sansfoy, Faithlessness, is in lustful alliance with her.

Red Crosse's battle with Sansfoy operates against the literary background of the vices-and-virtues combat. However, here as in the previous two episodes, Spenser employs the genre to tempt the reader to false expectations of moral simplicity. The literary background would lead us to expect, in a combat between a pagan and a Christian knight, clear-cut moral polarities: Sansfoy will be defeated by Foy in a kind of moral mathematics. In fact, however, the defeat of an evil does not necessarily testify to the triumph of a good. In the worldly arena the worldly facsimiles of Christian virtues can at least temporarily triumph; and false faith—in the flesh, in the material—can provide an *ad hoc* solution to the problem of faithlessness. The Archimagoan semblances have an operative value in the world; they permit the knight to defeat evil, to have the semblance of Christian victory, and to preserve the illusion of innocence. Increasingly, Red Crosse survives on the secular surrogates for the Christian virtues which appearance leads him to believe are his own. Red Crosse Knight *is* Archimago. But that is not, I suspect, the way we view the battle at first. The terminology of the genre confuses us, as does the rhetoric, so that at first we embrace the simplicities to which Red Crosse has himself fallen victim. A principle of symbolic space seems to operate in this episode, as in others; for Sansfoy's rushing towards the knight images, as we are later to realize, a moral coming together of the two combatants:

> His foe was nigh at hand. He prickt with pride
> And hope to winne his Ladies heart that day,
> Forth spurred fast . . .
>
> (ii.14)

37

Red Crosse and Sansfoy are momentarily conflated by the ambiguous pronominal referent, and the conflation is prophetic; it is repeated in the simile describing their battle:

> As when two rams stirrd with ambitious pride,
> Fight for the rule of the rich fleeced flocke,
> Their horned fronts so fierce on either side
> Do meete, that with the terrour of the shocke
> Astonied both, stand sencelesse as a blocke,
> Forgetfull of the hanging victory:
> So stood these twaine, vnmoued as a rocke,
> Both staring fierce, and holding idely
> The broken reliques of their former cruelty.

(ii.16)

Both combatants are contained within the same image: their fierce *fiducia carnalis* transforms them into rams fighting for mastery of the flock. For both knights the motives of combat are rooted in the dual nature of Errour: "ambitious pride" provokes their fight for hegemony; the satisfaction of their fleshly lust for Duessa is the privilege of "the rule of the rich fleeced flock." Lust becomes the basis for false faith and faithlessness, as Red Crosse slays Sansfoy only to supplant him and to establish, like the mother of Errour, a sexual alliance with the forces of evil.[25]

The Fradubio episode firmly relates Red Crosse's experience with Duessa to Adam's succumbing to the Flesh in

[25] Harry Berger, Jr., "Spenser's *Faerie Queene*, Book I: Prelude to Interpretation," *Southern Review* (University of Adelaide), 2 (1966), 30-31, has some penetrating remarks on the psychological complexity of the Sansfoy episode: "In killing Sansfoy, Redcross not only conquers the enemy but also suppresses the symptom"; "the Saracen's proper allegorical title would seem to be, not merely *Faithlessness*, but *Consciousness of Faithlessness*: he threatens to disclose to the hero the extent to which Redcrosse himself has unwittingly become infidel to the very source of his life. Ignorance of anything but his romance conditions is at this point the hero's salvation."

Eden.[26] The episode contains the complex of meanings Spenser has attached to the temptation of the Flesh: Fradubio is placed "in doubt" (Protestant reading) through lust (Catholic reading) for the Circean sorceress. The parallels between Fradubio and Adam are not continuous and exact on a literal level: Duessa's transforming Fradubio into a tree is not, as narrative, equivalent to Adam's experience. Nonetheless, a general correspondence exists: the subservience in the garden of Adam's *mens* to Eve's *sensus* is imitated by Fradubio's intemperate subservience to Duessa, and the dimming of Adam's reason and faith through intemperance is imitated in Fradubio's relationship with Fraelissa. The transformation of Fraelissa into a tree culminates the corrupting transformation of Fradubio's reason through fleshly intemperance. Fradubio's progress from faith to doubt to false faith, his sinful allegiance to the Woman, the dimming of his reason, his being contained within a tree, and his need to bathe "in liuing well" (ii.43) to return to his true form: all these factors establish Fradubio, and simultaneously Red Crosse, as a moral counterpart to Adam. Neither Fradubio's experience with Duessa nor Red Crosse's is a one-to-one correspondence to Adam's fall; rather, it is morally analogous to, because it is rooted in, Adam's experience. The episode exemplifies the Fall as a continuing event in time, a recurring aspect of human experience from which no man is exempt. It is a mirror not only to Red Crosse's personal experience with Duessa but also to the condition of the race as a whole. But once again Red Crosse's naive belief in his innocence leads him not to perceive his image in the Adamic mirror of the landscape. The episode involves, to be sure, a cry of conscience, a dimly articulated sense of guilt, but one which Red Crosse externalizes and thereby alienates from himself. His insistence on an absolute disjunction between himself and Adam-

---

[26] The Edenic context of the Fradubio episode is handled in some detail by William Nelson, *The Poetry of Edmund Spenser*, pp. 162-163.

39

Fradubio manifests itself in his final act: he thrusts the bleeding branch into the ground "That from the blood he might be innocent, / And with fresh clay did close the wooden wound" (ii.44). This ostensible act of charity is in reality a salving of the conscience; and later, true Remorse will require that that wound bleed. Red Crosse's insistence on seeing himself innocent, untainted by Adam's blood, blinds him to his own falling and the corrupt festering of Adam's sin within him. The knight who would restore Eden through an *imitatio Christi* now, by denying the corruption of his own garden, imitates not the new Adam and His sainthood but the old Adam and his fall.

In succumbing to the Flesh, Red Crosse takes the broad path taken by pilgrims before him in Deguileville, Hawes, and Cartigny; and like them, he is now led by the Flesh to become, in the second stage of his *imitatio Adamis*, a child of the World in Lucifera's House of Pride. In his portrayal of the World, Spenser was to provide the pattern for the World-temptation in both Fletcher and Milton. In the first place, although Lucifera is not portrayed specifically as Circe, the description of her House of Pride is primarily indebted to Ariosto's description of the palace of Alcina, who is a Circe-figure. The connection between Circe and the World is implicit in Spenser, but it remains for Fletcher and Milton to make that connection explicit. Secondly, and even more importantly, Spenser sets a pattern, assisted probably by Cartigny, for both his seventeenth-century imitators in having the temptation of the World include a temptation to "all sin," so that there are actually two versions of the Flesh, the World, and the Devil in Red Crosse's Adamic sequence, the secondary version being incorporated in the World-temptation. Though Spenser does not here, as he will in the Cave of Mammon, and as Fletcher will in the temptation of Panglorie and Milton in the kingdoms-temptation in *Paradise Regained*, portray the World's infernal triad as allegorically compartmentalized kingdoms, the pageant of the seven deadly sins is in fact organized around the Flesh-World-Devil

40

scheme. In this pageant Lucifera's coach is drawn by "six vnequal beasts" (iv.18): the sins of the Flesh (idleness, gluttony, and lechery); the sin of the World (avarice); and, finally, the sins of the Devil (envy, wrath), with Satan, the driver, being the third sin of the Devil, pride.[27] The order of this triad—from the Flesh to the World to the Devil—is precisely that of the linear, i.e., Duessa-Lucifera-Orgoglio, sequence. The seven deadly sins in this palace of the World are, therefore, "all the kingdoms of the world, and the glory of them" (Matthew 4:4).

The connection between the House of Pride and Christ's kingdoms-temptation is seen clearly in the parallels between it and the Cave of Mammon, which is also a composite World-temptation. Lucifera and Mammon both have the desire, like Satan and Adam, to be "sicut dei," worshipped by men. "God of the world and worldlings I me call," boasts Mammon; "Great *Mammon*, greatest god below the skye, / That of my plenty poure out vnto all . . . , / Riches, renowme, and principality, / Honour, estate, and all this worldes good" (II.vii.8). Lucifera also dispenses "this worldes good," and "to the highest she did still aspyre, / Or if ought higher were then that, did it desyre" (iv.11). But as commentaries on the kingdoms-temptation often point out, the kingdoms the devil offers are really God's; his claim to kingship is fraudulent. Accordingly, Guyon says to Mammon, "Ne thine be kingdomes, ne the scepters thine" (II.vii.13), and the narrator remarks of Lucifera that "rightfull kingdome she had none at all, / Ne heritage of natiue souereigntie, / But did vsurpe with wrong and tyrannie / Vpon the scepter, which now she did hold" (iv.12). Another and even more important feature relates Mammon and Lucifera to the kingdoms-

[27] I am anticipated in this observation by Samuel C. Chew, *The Pilgrimage of Life* (New Haven, Conn.: Yale Univ. Press, 1962), pp. 71-72, and "Spenser's Pageant of the Seven Deadly Sins," in *Studies in Art and Literature for Belle da Costa Greene* (Princeton, N.J.: Princeton Univ. Press, 1954), p. 46. Chew's chapter, "The Spiritual Foes of Man," pp. 70-113, offers an excellent survey of Spenser's relationship to past portrayals of the seven deadly sins.

temptation. In tempting Christ, Satan says, "All these things [i.e., 'all the kingdoms of the world, and the glory of them'] will I give thee, if thou wilt fall down and worship me" (Matthew 4:9); to which Christ replies, "Thou shalt worship the Lord thy God, and him only shalt thou serve." Correspondingly, Mammon offers "all these mountaines" to Guyon "if me thou deigne to serue and sew" (II.vii.9); and at the House of Pride, Duessa and Red Crosse "on humble knee / [Make] obeysance" (iv.13)—which may at first seem merely a courteous gesture, but the later gesture certainly is not, when Red Crosse, having defeated Sansjoy,

> . . . goeth to that soueraine Queene,
> And falling her before on lowly knee,
> To her makes present of his seruice seene.
>
> (v.16)

We recall at once Satan's offer in the wilderness, as once again the knight imitates not Christ but Adam.

The sin to which Satan tempts Christ in the kingdoms-temptation is identical to the sin Lucifera manifests in the House of Pride: the vainglorious pride of the World; *concupiscentia oculorum* in both its aspects, *avaritia sublimitatis* and *avaritia pecuniae*. That this particular sin extends to virtually every particular of Spenser's palace of the World—from the name of its ruler to its golden square bricks—requires no demonstration, nor does the fact that the abundant imagery of light, fire, and gold makes this episode, more than any other episode in Book I, a temptation to the eyes, the like of which in Spenser is found only in that other temptation to the eyes, the Cave of Mammon. The House of Pride is like a magician's act, teasing the eyes to accept as truth its visual and moral fraudulence; it tempts the pilgrim to perceive it, the city of man, as the city of God, tempts him to perceive its vainglory as glory. The new landscape Red Crosse Knight inhabits holds the mirror up to him, for if the House of Pride presents itself as something other than what it is, it is equally true that Red Crosse in the House of Pride continues to perceive himself as something other than what he has become: like the House of Pride itself, the knight blinds himself to his limitations; he covers his corruption with the gilt of virtue. Pride's blindness to her limitations takes the form with Red Crosse not only of a pursuit of vainglory but also of a refusal to acknowledge his growing evil. As in the den of Errour, Red Crosse's pride in his virtue blinds him to the fact that he is losing it. If the House of Pride is the earthly city pretending to be the heavenly city, Red Crosse is Adam pretending to be Christ. He turns to pride to mask from himself the Adamic corruption of his subservience to Duessa. Red Crosse adds one vice to another, pride to intemperance, in order to conceal vice and to preserve the illusion of innocence. Consequently, the battle with Sansjoy is, I think, performed to the end of quieting Red Crosse's growing despair of his righteous identity. Sansjoy functions, it is true, as an opposite to Christian hope. But perhaps more important, he is also the worldly man's facsimile of Christian humility, for he embodies the World's awareness of the limitations of self. A counterpart to the Christian's awareness of his moral limitations and corruption, Sansjoy is the power that provides the impetus to pride. Red Crosse fights Sansjoy, then, less because he is fighting to preserve his virtue than because he wishes to preserve the illusion of virtue and his pride in that virtue. He fights Sansjoy for the same reason that all worldly men must fight him, to be blind to his own limitations that he may better serve Lucifera, his own pride.

As in the battle with Sansfoy, however, both Spenser's generic vocabulary and his rhetoric do not predispose us to see this complexity. We are tempted, and a large number of Spenser's critics have succumbed to this temptation, to a mistaken expectation of moral polarities. The genre's vices-and-virtues terminology tempts us to believe that Red Crosse is employing the remnants of his virtue against vice: Christian Hope combats atheistic Hopelessness, Joy combats Sansjoy. But the extent to which this conventional reading is true seems to me negligible: it is entirely inconsistent with the immediate motivation for the battle Spenser provides—a desire to preserve ownership of Duessa and Sansfoy's shield—and with the conclusion of the battle. As in his battle with Sansfoy, Red Crosse triumphs through the worldly facsimile of the Christian virtue, a hope not in eternal rewards but in earthly rewards; and this facsimile of virtue permits him to believe that in defeating a vice he has affirmed his own virtue. In actuality, of course, what happens here is what happened in Wandering Wood: denying his corruption, Red Crosse succumbs all the more readily to it. For in the Luciferan arena of the World, the worldly man copes with his despairing sense of his own limitations by becoming not less but more of the world; the same awareness that leads the Christian to humility leads him to pride. His behavior is almost classically compulsive: he attempts to cope with the hopelessness underlying his frantic pursuit of the things of this world by pursuing them all the more frantically; he attempts to block out Sansjoy by becoming more and more successful; he does not alter the unfulfilling behavior, but merely increases its intensity in order to reassert his self-image. The worldly man is constantly combatting Sansjoy and constantly keeping him alive, for Sansjoy both motivates and threatens his pride. Consequently, when the objects Red Crosse has fought for, Duessa and the shield, are in fact his again, Sansjoy is unseen but still alive. Sansjoy cannot be killed by pride, because his presence is inherent in the motivation for pride. A temporary blindness to Sansjoy is all that the prideful man can hope to accomplish. Ironically, as the blinding light of Lucifera's present suggests, pride's lust of the eyes stipulates blindness. The most that Red Crosse can do is repress Sansjoy, blind himself to him, send him away. Indeed, if we read the end of the battle as a psychomachia, the implication would appear to be that, for all of Red Crosse's hysterical attempts to see and kill his hopelessness, he is also, through Duessa, concealing him from himself and keeping him alive. For if Sansjoy were in fact slain, nothing that Red Crosse has won would mean anything at all. The whole scene would appear for precisely what it is, a vainglorious, hollow sham. Red Crosse would be required to confront himself for what he increasingly is, a hypocritical and Archimagoan fraud; and that, it becomes clear from his offering himself to Lucifera, is the last thing he wishes to do.[28]

To read Red Crosse's combat with Sansjoy as the last desperate efforts of a man to assert his own virtue is, then, to succumb to the naive simplicities of the hero's and the genre's moral vision. Red Crosse fights Sansjoy not because of his baptismal vow to renounce "the vaine pompe and glorye of the world, with al couetous desires of the same"; he fights him because he is of the World, struggling to reassert the prideful illusion of an uncontaminated virtue while laying claims to the rewards of his corruption. He is Archimago; and the simplistic moral terms of the genre are ironically the terms of the knight's Archimagoan hypocrisy. The genre, therefore, provides a temptation, which we must resist. So, too, I believe, does the rhetoric. The rhetoric of this episode has already been handled, often very ably, by Paul Alpers;[29] but the strategy of the rhetoric here does not, I think, follow the principles Alpers would like to make universal in Spenser's verse. Alpers' insistence that we are not encouraged to sit in judgment on the knight is at best a misleading truth. To be sure, we are not to judge the knight self-righteously or complacently; that would duplicate the knight's own errors

[28] For an admirable reading emphasizing, from a different perspective, Red Crosse's community with Sansjoy and the House of Pride, see Joan Heiges Blythe, "Spenser and the Seven Deadly Sins: Book I, Cantos IV and V," *ELH*, 39 (1972), 342-352.

[29] *The Poetry of "The Faerie Queene,"* pp. 340-343. Unavoidably my analysis must cover some of the passages Alpers' covers. Though he and I are often at opposite critical poles, it would be ungrateful of me not to acknowledge my admiration and debt. My own approach to Spenserian rhetoric has also been stimulated by Jerome S. Dees, "The Narrator of *The Faerie Queene*: Patterns of Response," *Tennessee Studies in Language and Literature*, 12 (1971), 537-568, and Lewis H. Miller, Jr., "The Ironic Mode in Books 1 and 2 of *The Faerie Queene*," *Papers on Language and Literature*, 7 (1971), 133-149.

of self-perception. But judge we must; otherwise we will also duplicate his errors. To be sure, the verse is an instrument of engagement and identification; this does not necessarily mean, however, a suspension of the need to disengage ourselves morally from the hero. For Red Crosse's subservience to Duessa and Lucifera manifests more than innate corruption; it manifests also a collapse of his will and reason—and this we must judge. We must of course recognize ourselves in Red Crosse, but that recognition consists of not only what we are through Adam but also what we may become and what—if there is to be any point in Spenser's teaching us by example—is in our power not to become. The technique of this battle is, then, the technique of earlier confrontations: we experience a *tentatio bona*, in which the ideal reader will experience the full attraction of Red Crosse's temptation, but the ideal man as well as reader will resist it. Spenser's verse in Book I, every bit as much as Milton's in *Paradise Lost*, tempts us to suspend our reason and judgment.[30] Alpers has come closer than anyone to understanding the importance of rhetoric in Spenser's verse; but perceiving the rhetoric, he misperceives its moral strategy, temporarily suspends his judgment, and therefore, in my opinion, succumbs.

More than any of the previous confrontations, the collapse of apparent moral opposition into equivalence is clear from the onset. We may be tricked in Wandering Wood up to the point of Una's awareness of the place, or in the battle with Sansjoy until the rams-simile or Red Crosse's offer of his services to Duessa. But as the margin of moral difference between the knight and his combatants diminishes, our awareness should simultaneously quicken and increase, make us all the more alert to the complexities to which the knight himself is blind. From the beginning of Red Crosse's encounter with Sansjoy, Spenser tempts us to embrace moral polari-

[30] See Stanley Fish, *Surprised by Sin: The Reader in "Paradise Lost"* (New York: St. Martin's Press, 1967). Frankly, I am inclined to feel that the rhetorical "good temptation" works more clearly in the Legend of Holiness than it does in *Paradise Lost*.

ties only to disabuse us of them. Listening to the vicious, spiteful recriminations of the pagan knight, Red Crosse may in his manly self-possession seem, for a moment, the true Christian hero opposed to the intemperate pagan:

> Him litle answerd th'angry Elfin knight;
> He neuer meant with words, but swords to plead
>   his right.

> But threw his gauntlet as a sacred pledge,
> His cause in combat the next day to try:
> So been they parted both, with harts on edge,
> To be aueng'd each on his enimy.
> That night they pas in ioy and iollity,
> Feasting and courting both in bowre and hall;
> For Steward was excessiue *Gluttonie*. . . .
>
> (iv.41-42)

I need quote no more. Unless we have wilfully chosen to ignore where Red Crosse is, who has brought him there, and why he is there, the narrator's tempting of us, his teasing shift from distinction to conflation, should be perfectly obvious. We experience Red Crosse's hypocrisy, and we quickly perceive the fraudulence behind his vision of himself. We recall the combat in the preceding canto between the false Red Crosse Knight (Archimago) and the irascibly intemperate Sansloy, who like Sansjoy is trying to avenge his brother; and we make the obvious connection the verse implies.

The strategy behind Spenser's portrayal of Red Crosse preparing for battle is also to seduce us into accepting the false Red Crosse Knight as the true:

> The noble hart, that harbours vertuous thought,
> And is with child of glorious great intent,
> Can neuer rest, vntill it forth haue brought
> Th'eternall brood of glorie excellent:
> Such restlesse passion did all night torment
> The flaming corage of the Faery knight,
> Deuizing, how that doughtie turnament

With greatest honour he atchieuen might;
Still did he wake, and still did watch for dawning light.

At last the golden Orientall gate
Of greatest heauen gan to open faire,
And *Phoebus* fresh, as bridegrome to his mate,
Came dauncing forth, shaking his deawie haire:
And hurld his glistring beames through gloomy aire.
Which when the wakeful Elfe perceiu'd, streight way
He started vp, and did him selfe prepaire,
In sun-bright armes, and battailous array:
For with that Pagan proud he combat will that day.

(v.1-2)

We are tempted to perceive Red Crosse as facilely as he perceives himself, as the *miles Christi* seeking eternal glory. But behind this pretense is the "restlesse passion" of his devising how "With greatest honour he atchieuen might," which is the vainglorious pride of the World: his is a quest for personal honor through self-reliance; it is *he* who will achieve the honor. Red Crosse will wear the image of the cross but keep the reward for himself; his hypocrisy permits him the claim of Christian innocence and the booty of his corruption.

In the second stanza, the surface of the verse continues to depict the surface of the knight. The image of Phoebus shining on Red Crosse "as bridegrome to his mate" seems to suggest Red Crosse as the *miles Christi*: the light shining on him seems the light of true glory, the light of Gloriana, the light of his own virtue, or even the light of the Christian's "armour of light" Paul speaks of in Romans 13:12. But in the House of Pride Lucifera is Aurora, coming "Out of the east [calling] the dawning day" (iv.16), and the false Phoebus (iv.8). The image thus embodies both the posture of innocence and the reality of corruption; it reveals what Red Crosse conceals. The verse, then, imitates not only the character but the character's perception of himself, as the Christian knight shining in the glory of God's son; and it exposes him for what by the end of the battle he will have become, the knight of the false sun.

The combat itself is immersed in the same moral ambiguity. As Alpers has nicely observed,[31] the combatants are contained within the same images of battle—light, fire—and heroic emotion—greed, wrath:

> Their shining shieldes about their wrestes they tye,
> And burning blades about their heads do blesse,
> The instruments of wrath and heauinesse:
> With greedy force each other doth assayle . . .
>
> (v.6)

The conventional terms of battle, of course, but also Luciferan: the light and fire are hers, and wrath and greed are wizards of her kingdom. The ambiguity is suggested, too, in the next stanza, whose movement is, typically, from distinction to conflation:

> The Sarazin was stout, and wondrous strong,
> And heaped blowes like yron hammers great:
> For after bloud and vengeance he did long.
> The knight was fiers, and full of youthly heat,
> And doubled strokes, like dreaded thunders threat:
> For all for prayse and honour he did fight.
>
> (v.7)

The cruel pagan seeks blood, the Christian honor; and if we ignore the fact that the praise Red Crosse is fighting for and will receive is that of the House of Pride, the combatants may seem morally distinct, and the genre's vices-and-virtues terminology accurate. But the remainder of the stanza undermines that simplicity, as the two combatants are physically and morally interlinked:

> Both stricken strike, and beaten both do beat,
> That from their shields forth flyeth firie light,
> And helmets hewen deepe, shew marks of eithers might.
>
> (v.7)

The narrative technique of this battle, like that of previous battles, involves a constant interplay of perspectives in which

[31] *The Poetry of "The Faerie Queene,"* p. 340.

49

our simplistic perspective on the knight is undermined by one asserting the genuine complexity of the event we are witnessing. So, too, the next stanza begins by asserting the genre's simplistic polarities, but concludes by undermining this simplicity:

> So th'one for wrong, the other striues for right:
> As when a Gryfon seized of his pray,
> A dragon fiers encountreth in his flight,
> Through widest ayre making his ydle way,
> That would his rightfull rauine rend away . . .
>
> (v.8)

Right versus wrong, Joy versus Sansjoy, like Christ (the griffin) versus Satan (the dragon). That is the Archimagoan pretense the knight embraces; but Spenser's similes, like Milton's do not always tell what they seem to tell. The combat of Christ and the dragon for the soul of man is reduced to a savage, animalistic contention for the booty of plunder. Red Crosse does indeed "plead his right" (iv.42) in the battle, but it is the "rightfull rauine" of Duessa and the shield of faithlessness. Ownership becomes the basis of Red Crosse's morality. That is what one would expect of the worldly man in the House of Pride: he defends not the right but his rights. Red Crosse's perspective on himself is as fraudulent as the objects for which he contends.

The rhetorical strategy co-operates, then, with the strategy behind Spenser's use of the pilgrimage genre; for again and again, the oppositions the narrator sets up are exposed as fraudulent. Both the genre and the rhetoric tempt us to an indulgent and sentimental sympathy for the knight, but sentimentality in Spenser is itself a spurious virtue. The temptation, in fact, is probably stronger for us than for the sixteenth-century reader, for our intimate relation to the knight through the rhetoric may easily court us to the tolerant suspension of judgment of our own century's liberalism. But judgment is precisely what is required: Spenser's reader, like the Christian knight, must be constantly on his watch. For we are involved with a rhetoric of deception that mirrors the nature of the House of Pride itself and thereby provides us with a counterpart to the temptation the character himself experiences. The rhetoric functions less to make a theological point—that we are all innately sinful and need grace—than to make a moral one: through the *tentatio bona*, we are forced to confront the very complexity the knight blinds himself to; tempted not only to what he sees but also to how he sees it, we are required to detach ourselves and exercise the rigorous scrutiny the knight evades. The *tentatio bona* forces us, then, to re-examine our own tendency to perceive ourselves as the knight perceives himself, loosely, simplistically. The lesson of the rhetoric and the genre is a lesson in the intellectual and emotional exigencies of the moral life.

It is not a lesson that Red Crosse has learned. No knowledge of himself motivates his flight from the House of Pride; he leaves not because of the guilt of self-recognition but because of fear. Seeing himself still, as the narrator tempts us to perceive him, as "The guiltlesse man" (vii.1), he enters the grove like Adam restored to the garden of his innocence. Red Crosse's pilgrimage has brought him full circle back to Wandering Wood. In both episodes, Red Crosse escapes from adversity (the storm; Lucifera's dungeon) to encounter in a deceptive landscape an image of his own self-deception—a *locus amoenus* of pleasant shade and singing birds within which the knight can act as though he had returned to Eden, safe from the outer world, secure in an uncorrupted nature. But once again he has made a false choice. In removing his armor and resting, the knight makes a perfectly natural gesture for a tired man in hot weather; like getting out of the rain in the Errour episode, it seems the only sensible thing to do. And no doubt we are meant to feel the full power of the grove's attraction. Nonetheless, this episode, like its earlier counterpart, is a temptation—to us as well as to the knight; a temptation to succumb not merely to the grove itself but also to the knight's unexamined vision of himself and the world. Red Crosse disarms himself not simply because the

51

grove is attractive but because it confirms the false-Edenic vision of himself that has plagued him from the onset of his quest. Thinking himself secure from temptation, his virtue safe in its restored self-sufficiency, he denies the need for the armor grace has given him. Eden has no need for soldiers. The illusion of Eden permits him his illusion about himself and his mission. But as in Wandering Wood, the knight demonstrates his corruption by denying it. His fall occurs in the denial of the Fall; and as before in Wandering Wood, Red Crosse, led by delight, confronts in the figures of Duessa (the Woman) and Orgoglio (the Devil) the Adamic corruption he has denied. The action in Wandering Wood, already repeated in the knight's subservience to Duessa and Lucifera, is repeated once again in the Orgoglio episode as Red Crosse completes his *imitatio Adamis* by succumbing to the intemperance and pride of his own Errour.[32]

In the House of Pride, Red Crosse succumbs to pride; in the Orgoglio episode, he also succumbs to pride. The question inevitably arises, and it has received countless answers: Can and should the two episodes be distinguished from each other, or are they redundant?[33] I would suggest that we are

[32] On the presumption involved in this episode, see Vern Torczon, "Spenser's Orgoglio and Despaire," *Texas Studies in Language and Literature*, 3 (1961), 126-127; on the lust, John Shroeder, "Spenser's Erotic Drama," *ELH*, 29 (1962), 144-148. See also A. C. Hamilton, *The Structure of Allegory in "The Faerie Queene"* (Oxford: The Clarendon Press, 1961), pp. 73-76; and S. K. Heninger, Jr., "The Orgoglio Episode in *The Faerie Queene*," *ELH*, 26 (1959), 174-175. A quite different reading from these readings or my own is Paul Alpers', *The Poetry of "The Faerie Queene,"* pp. 142-143: "It is perfectly natural to give oneself to this grove, and simply reading the verse makes it impossible for us to sit in judgment on the Red Cross Knight."

[33] Most critics at least attempt to make some sort of distinction. Ruskin suggests that "This Orgoglio is Orgueil, or Carnal Pride; not the pride of life [which Lucifera represents], spiritual and subtle, but the common and vulgar pride in the power of this world" (Var. Ed., p. 423). Whitney identifies Lucifera with "worldly or ostentatious pride" and Orgoglio with "braggard, carnal, or physical pride" (Var.

expected to view them as *both* complementary parts of a unit and separate episodes. The reason for this dual expectation is simple: the three episodes of Red Crosse's *imitatio Adamis* respond not to one governing allegorical *schema* but two. Spenser's conception of Red Crosse as the Christian pilgrim encountering the Flesh, the World, and the Devil obviously requires three separate and distinct episodes. At the same time, however, Spenser is also concerned with portraying Red Crosse's failure to imitate Christ's triumph over Errour, the dual Adamic affections of the flesh, intemperance and pride. Obviously the fact that Lucifera and Orgoglio both represent pride works with the lust-pride duality Spenser wished to por-

---

Ed., pp. 427-428). Pauline Parker, *The Allegory of the "Faerie Queene"* (Oxford: The Clarendon Press, 1960), pp. 84-85, apparently combines Whitney and Padelford and comes up with the distinction that Lucifera is worldly pride and Orgoglio spiritual pride. C. S. Lewis, *The Allegory of Love*, p. 335, argues that "Pride and Orgoglio are both pride, but the one is pride within us, the other pride attacking us from without, whether in the form of persecution, oppression, or ridicule. The one seduces us, the other browbeats us." And finally Rosemond Tuve, *Allegorical Imagery* (Princeton, N.J.: Princeton Univ. Press, 1966), pp. 107-108, identifies Orgoglio as spiritual pride and Lucifera as vainglory.

On the other hand, there are those who would agree with Virgil Whitaker, "Theological Structure," p. 80, that "the text will not support such a distinction" between the two forms of pride as Whitney and Padelford attempt to make; "Orgoglio is . . . simply another personification of pride as the first cause of sin and the symbol of man's liability to sin. The distinction between him and Lucifera is required by the historical, not the moral allegory." Whitaker goes so far as to find the Lucifera and Orgoglio episodes an example of "the gravest fault in the book" (p. 84), repetitiousness. More recently, D. Douglas Waters, "Duessa and Orgoglio: Red Crosse's Spiritual Fornication," *Renaisssance Quarterly*, 20 (1967), 217 (*Duessa as Theological Satire*, pp. 69-70), argues that it is no longer "necessary to make distinctions between pride (Lucifera) and pride (Orgoglio)"; Red Crosse's being enamored of Duessa, " 'the falsehood of the pope's mass,' " simply "makes him weaker and hence more vulnerable when she 'finds' him at the symbolic fountain (spiritual fornication) than he was at the House of Pride." The two episodes, then, are the same; it is Red Crosse's response that is different.

tray in the three episodes. For the infernal triad, however, a distinction had to be made between the pride of the World and the pride of the Devil. That distinction is essentially Calvin's distinction between the second and third temptations of Adam and Christ, the second being ambitious pride, the third rebellion. Lucifera's worldly pride, or *concupiscentia oculorum*, manifests itself, as we have seen, in the cluster of vices associated with the kingdoms-temptation: *avaritia pecuniae* and *avaritia sublimitatis*; the lust of the eyes for possession of material things; ambitious pride which carries one beyond what is permitted. Orgoglio's diabolic pride, or *superbia vitae*, on the other hand, manifests itself in a furious and wrathful arrogance, an open rebellion against God and the faithful. The difference between the two forms of pride is seen in the difference between the dungeons of the two palaces. The punishment in Lucifera's dungeon is for the covetous, like Croësus, the ambitious, like Antiochus, Nimrod, and Ninus, and the lustful, like Sthenoboea and Cleopatra; that is, it is a punishment for those who desired excessively the triple glories of the world—gold, glory, and pleasure. Their punishment is, like their sin, in terms of the World; the rise of princes is penalized by the fall of princes. The dungeon of Orgoglio, in contrast, manifests the devil's violent assaults on man: those who have resisted are martyred; those who have succumbed are confined to Hell.

One can say, then, that Lucifera's pride leads her not so much to attack the godhead as to pretend to it, whereas Orgoglio is in active, violent revolt against the godhead and against the faith. He resembles closely the Devil-figures and -temptations in Milton. The portrayals of Moloch in *Paradise Lost*, Harapha in *Samson Agonistes*, and the glory-, Parthia-, and pinnacle-temptations in *Paradise Regained* all associate the Devil with violence and power; his sin is linked to his revolt against God in heaven. Accordingly, Spenser's Devil-figure has in his possession the "dreadfull Beast with seuen-fold head" (vii.18), the "great red dragon" of Revelation which drew a third of the stars of heaven and made war against God (Revelation 12:3-9). In addition, Orgoglio is portrayed, as Milton's Harapha will be, as "An hideous Geant horrible and hye, / That with his talnesse seemd to threat the sky" (vii.8); and the giants were figures of brute power and pride warring against the godhead, and were thus a type of the Devil.[34] Moreover, as John Steadman has shown,[35] the biblical giants were portrayed as men of excessive cruelty and violence. Impious, tyrannical, and contemptuous of man and God, they were therefore prototypes of a faithless heroism of mere might—as is Orgoglio, and also Milton's Satan, Moloch, and Harapha.

Spenser does, then, make a distinction between the two kinds of pride, the ambitious pride of the World and the rebellious pride of the Devil. Orgoglio therefore functions as the Devil in the sequence of the infernal triad, and is distinct from Lucifera; but in terms of the two-fold tendencies in man's "body of sin," the two are seen as different aspects of the same sin of pride. As I have already suggested, this two-fold scheme is repeated, and indeed culminates, in the Devil's stage of the triad, as Duessa leads Red Crosse to Orgoglio's pride just as before she had led him to Lucifera's. Erasmus provides a useful gloss to the developments in this episode:

> If [the soul] goes over to the side of the flesh then it must be considered as belonging to the body or the lowest component. St. Paul in his Epistle to the Corinthians brings out this very point: "Do you not know that he who cleaves to a harlot becomes one body with her, but he who cleaves to the Lord is one spirit with Him?" That expression "harlot" refers of course to the weaker

[34] On Orgoglio's indebtedness to the mythologists' interpretation of the Giants and the Titans, see C. W. Lemmi, "The Symbolism of the Classical Episodes in *The Faerie Queene*," *Philological Quarterly*, 8 (1929), 275-276, and Vern Torczon, "Spenser's Orgoglio and Despaire," p. 125. The most thorough treatment is that of S. K. Heninger, Jr., "The Orgoglio Episode," pp. 178-186.

[35] *Milton's Epic Characters* (Chapel Hill, N.C.: Univ. of North Carolina Press, 1968), pp. 177-183.

nature in man in the same sense that the second chapter of Proverbs uses the term "woman". . . . For "whoever is joined to her shall descend into hell. . . ." The flesh makes us despisers of God, disobedient and cruel.[36]

Of course this is precisely what happens to Red Crosse: joining himself with the harlot Duessa, the Flesh, he comes under the control of the Devil and is led to Hell. The Devil and the Flesh are partners in the destruction of man—intimately so; for not only is Orgoglio portrayed as a fornicator with Duessa, but also his physical being is described in terms of excessive concupiscence of the flesh. As John Shroeder has shown,[37] Orgoglio's birth out of wind and earth accords with the pseudo-Aristotelian conception of the origins of the *penis erectus*; and from this perspective his is the rebellious masculine pride of and in the phallus. But there is another reason, in addition to the characterization of Orgoglio's pride, for portraying the Devil in such fleshly terms; for Orgoglio is not only the Devil but also that tendance to *superbia vitae* transmitted to us from Adam as part of our fleshly nature. Orgoglio's titanic power, which causes all the earth to shake and to "grone full grieuous vnderneath [his] blow" (viii.8), is a metaphor to the enormous power he wields over our "erthe / that is [our] flesshe"[38]—and over the knight himself; for Orgoglio's shaking of the earth in the outer landscape reflects what is occurring in the mind of George, this "man of earth." My interpretation of Orgoglio as the Devil does not, therefore, contradict A. C. Hamilton's contention, a good one, that "In Orgoglio we *see* the image of fallen man in all its terrible reality"[39]—though one must add, not only in Orgoglio but in Duessa as well: the coupling of the Woman and the Devil, which gave us Errour, is repeated in the coming together of Duessa's *fons veneris* and Orgoglio's phallus. Here is the ori-

[36] *Handbook*, pp. 88-89.
[37] "Spenser's Erotic Drama," pp. 151-152.
[38] From the Caxton translation of *Legenda Aurea*, p. 112.
[39] *Structure of Allegory*, p. 76.

gin of our nature and our Errour. In this repulsive image we see what Red Crosse has refused to see. The illusion of Edenic innocence has led the knight who was to restore Eden to participate in everything that the Fall involved and continues to involve in man's nature. Drinking of the waters of lust, Red Crosse's reason, like the Woman's, succumbs to intemperance; and he thereby becomes vulnerable to the pride of the Devil. Divested of his Christian armor, he has only his flesh to rely upon, and Orgoglio's pride is part of his own flesh. Evil is finally unmasked, confronting the knight in its full horror without pretense. The illusion of the grove is dispelled, but painfully late. The Christian knight's imitation of the man of the spirit, Christ, is thus replaced by his imitation of the old man of the flesh, Adam. Adam, *"man of clay,"* Orgoglio, that *"monstrous masse of earthly slime"* (vii.9), and George, *"man of earth,"* are brought into conjunction; and Red Crosse, like Adam, is sent *sub lege* into Hell, from which he, like his father, can be rescued only through the grace of the new Adam.[40]

II

With his rescue by Arthur, Red Crosse Knight begins anew his quest to become St. George and to imitate Christ's victory in the wilderness over the Flesh, the World, and the Devil that his sainthood stipulates. As in a similar triadic pairing in the Cave of Mammon episode, the second triadic sequence, which portrays Red Crosse's successful *imitatio Christi*, is parallel to the order in the Adamic sequence: the Flesh (Despaire), the World (the House of Holiness), and the Devil (the dragon).

As in the first half of the Legend of Holiness, so in the second Spenser employs the conventions of the pilgrimage genre to expose his hero's and indirectly our own oversimpli-

[40] On the relation of Arthur's acts to Christ's crucifixion and Harrowing of Hell, see Hamilton, *Structure of Allegory*, pp. 77-79, and the Introduction to *Books I and II of "The Faerie Queene,"* ed. Robert Kellogg and Oliver Steele (New York: Odyssey, 1965), pp. 34-37.

fication of both human nature and the rigors of Christian life. In Deguileville, Hawes, and Cartigny, one finds only a minimal sense of the difficulties of Christian regeneration. Their emphasis is less on the process of learning than on what is learned. Spenser, however, reverses their emphasis. The pilgrim must learn not merely such matters as the three theological virtues or the seven corporal works of mercy but also the difficulties of learning, and for Spenser the process of learning and regeneration has its own temptations. Vice is not easily disengaged from virtue, and repentance contains the seeds of a power hostile to it, despair.[41] Red Crosse's acknowledgment of his corruption is essential to his regeneration, but ironically his earlier rash claim to innocence is now replaced by an opposite blindness, an inability to see any possible goodness in his nature. He has moved, then, from one distorted view of his nature to another, and both oversimplifications threaten spiritual death.

Red Crosse thus begins again his *imitatio Christi* with Una almost to recapitulate his *imitatio Adamis* with Duessa: without hope, his return to the faith threatens to return him to his earlier departure from faith. Accordingly, the Despaire episode, though it has obvious affinities with the episodes at Wandering Wood and Archimago's hermitage, is affiliated primarily with Duessa's temptation of the Flesh to disbelief of the word. Admittedly, the two figures could hardly be more different in physical appearance, the one glamorous,

[41] Cf. Thomas Becon, *The Catechism*, pp. 11-12: "The doctrine of repentance enarmeth a man against the assaults of Satan [i.e., the Devil], against the pleasures of the world, against the sting of sin [i.e., the Flesh], against the dart of desperation, and admonisheth him afterward so warily and circumspectly to live, that he fall no more into the same sins, nor be snarled again with the like snares; but rather from henceforth so frame his life, that he shall not need to be combered with the like shame and sorrow for committing the like wickedness. . . . Repentance not accompanied with faith driveth rather unto desperation than unto salvation." See also "The Dialogue between the Christian Knight and Satan," in *The Catechism of Thomas Becon . . . with Other Pieces*, p. 628 esp.

the other ascetic; but the appearance of both is false. And both offer the Flesh's temptation to false faith and false religion, though the one tempts through indulgence, the other through false mortification of the flesh. Despite differences in appearance and strategy, both have the same purpose and end: just as Duessa leads Red Crosse to faithlessness (Sansfoy) and doubt (Fradubio), then to hopelessness (Sansjoy), and finally to a despairing desire for death in Orgoglio's dungeon; so Despaire places him in doubt, hopeless of heavenly mercy, that he may wish to die.

Despaire, as much as Duessa, is a parody of Una and represents false truth; for in his insistence that Red Crosse slay himself, he offers a blasphemous parody of the Pauline doctrine of baptism as a recapitulation of Christ's crucifixion and resurrection. Despaire distorts the divine word not only, as Ernest Sirluck has shown,[42] by suppressing mercy, but also by literalizing the Pauline metaphors and paradoxes underlying baptism and restoration as they are developed in, especially, the Epistle to the Romans. This tactic of literalizing divine metaphor is altogether appropriate for a temptation that is ultimately rooted in Satan's request of Christ to make bread out of stones. Christ refuses the miracle by way of metaphor, replying that man lives not by literal bread alone but also by the metaphorical or spiritual bread of the divine word. Despaire's strategy is appropriate, too, in that he would have Red Crosse live and die by the letter of the law, whereas "we should serve in newness of spirit, and not in the oldness of the letter" (Romans 7:6); "For sin, taking occasion by the commandment [i.e., the letter of the law] deceived me, and by it slew me" (7:11).

Despaire's strategy, then, consists of not merely a blocking out but also, more precisely, a parodying of New Testa-

[42] "A Note on the Rhetoric of Spenser's 'Despair,'" *Modern Philology*, 47 (1949), 8. Despaire also distorts the Church's teachings on death; see Kathrine Koller, "Art, Rhetoric, and Holy Dying in the *Faerie Queene* with Special Reference to the Despair Canto," *Studies in Philology*, 61 (1964), 137-139.

ment doctrine. Literalizing Paul's argument in Romans, Despaire requires a literal slaying of the old man, while denying the birth of the new. Man must literally "die unto sin" (6:10), must literally "mortify the deeds of the body" (8:13) that he may be free of sin and attain eternal rest. The premise underlying Despaire's appeal, introduced in ix.38, bases itself on the Pauline dictum that "by the deeds of the law there shall be no flesh justified in his sight" (3:20) and that "the wages of sin is death" (7:23). Omitted is the remainder of the last verse: "but the gift of God is eternal life through Jesus Christ our Lord." The ensuing two stanzas offer a parody of the grace obtained through the waters of baptism. Paul argues that by the waters of baptism we are "baptized into his [Christ's] death" (6:3) that "we shall be also in the likeness of his resurrection" (6:5) and attain eternal life. This conception of baptism as a recapitulation of Christ's death and resurrection Paul repeats again and again: we are "buried with him [Christ] . . . unto death" (6:4) and "crucified with him" (6:6); for "if we be dead with Christ, we believe that we shall also live with him" (6:8). Despaire also offers "great grace" (ix.39) through the dying of the old man by water. Alluding to one of the oldest figures for baptism, the crossing of the river Jordan, he urges Red Crosse to "passe the flood," the "bitter waue," in order to obtain not life after death but "death after life" (ix.39-40). Despaire's continual insistence that Red Crosse must die in order to be freed from sin seems, in fact, specifically to allude to and literalize Paul's "he that is dead is freed from sin," omitting the next verse's amplification, "dead with Christ" (6:7-8), omitting, as Duessa did, Christ's resurrection and our resurrection with Him. Ironically, it is Paul's stance towards human capacity that underlies the whole of Despaire's argument. Despaire's insistence of man's innate sinfulness, the hopelessness of man's doing good on his own, is essentially an outgrowth of Pauline, and also Calvinist, attitudes: "For I know that in me [that is, in my flesh] dwelleth no good thing" (Romans 7:18). Despaire's temptation is an infernal sermon based on God's word, taking as its central text for the day, "For all have sinned, and come short of the glory of God" (3:23).

Despaire's profanation of divine metaphor relates him, then, to the temptation of the Flesh as Protestant theologians interpreted it, a temptation to the word itself. Another factor lending support to the association of Despaire with the Flesh is that the episode contains the essential features of temptations of the Flesh in Fletcher and Milton. The physical appearance of these later tempters to despair, it is true, seems for the most part indebted less to Despaire than to Archimago, also Bale's Satan and Malory's man of false religion who tempts Sir Bors. Nonetheless, even in terms of appearance some affinity exists between Despaire and the later figures; for Fletcher's Satan and Milton's (in *Paradise Regained*) both appear in the wilderness in the false-religious guise of old hermits; and Manoa appears in the waste of Gaza as an old man of patriarchal venerability. More decisive, however, are the correspondences in the conception of the Flesh-temptation. In Spenser, as we have seen, the dominant strategy is a distortion, which in effect becomes a denial, of the divine word; it is a temptation to disbelief which employs a measure of belief in God's law as its point of departure. Samson's situation at the beginning of *Samson Agonistes* is very much the same as Red Crosse's: his repentance assumes and manifests a belief, however imperfect, in God's *lex-talionis* justice; but lacking any sense of God's mercy, he falls into despair. The distortion of repentance into despair is, of course, not found in the stones-temptation in "Christ's Victory on Earth" or *Paradise Regained*. Nonetheless, in all four temptations, the hero is tempted to distrust divine providence. All are tempted to desert God on the grounds that God has deserted them; and all are urged in lieu of God's providence or mercy to accept from the tempter an act of false charity, a parody of divine providence and grace. Despaire's offer of "great grace" in the crossing of "the flood" takes the form of an infernal parody of the grace offered by

61

Christ through the waters of baptism; and similarly Manoa offers Samson a surrogate grace in his offer to pay his son's ransom. In both episodes, a surrogate grace camouflages a temptation to the hero to despair of true grace and to deny that repentance has any purpose beyond the satisfaction of the rigorous requirements of Old Testament law. In "Christ's Victory" and *Paradise Regained*, a comparable situation is presented, as Christ is tempted to despair of God's aid in the wilderness, to act on His own independent of the Father, and to accept infernal grace—in Fletcher, rest in the Cave of Despair; in Milton, guidance out of the wilderness.

Common to all of these temptations, and also Belial's proposal in *Paradise Lost*, is the tempter's insistence on the pointlessness of the mission because of necessity. In a work antedating and possibly influencing Spenser's Despaire episode, Bale's Satan in the stones-temptation urges Christ to deny His prophetic role on the grounds of the sheer impossibility of its attainment:

> Preach ye once the truth the bishops will ye murther.
> Therefore, believe not the voice that ye did hear,
> Though it came from God; for it is unsavoury gear,
> Beyond your compass: rather than ye so run,
> Forsake the office, and deny yourself God's son![43]

Both Bale's Satan and Despaire predicate their argument on human sinfulness: if for Bale's Satan human corruption makes Christ's prophecy meaningless, for Despaire Red Crosse's own corruption makes holiness impossible. What God wills is supplanted by what necessity demands. Correspondingly, Fletcher's Satan argues that Christ's flesh necessitates His accepting his act of mercy, rest in the Cave of Despair; Milton's Satan appeals to a multifold necessity occasioned by divine desertion, a (non-existent) hunger, God's

---

[43] *The Temptation of Our Lord*, in *The Dramatic Writings of John Bale*, ed. John S. Farmer (1907; rpt. New York, Barnes and Noble, 1966), pp. 157-158.

inconsistencies, and of course the threat of the wilderness itself; and Manoa appeals to a necessity occasioned by God's injustice or excessive justice—and all of these appeals to necessity work to undermine the hero's sense of identity, to abrogate the connection between God and their heroic identity.

The Despaire temptation, then, contains the essential complex of ideas underlying the Protestant interpretation of the temptation of the Flesh. The older, Catholic reading does not entirely vanish, however. As we have seen, Spenser fuses both readings in his portrayal of Duessa, and a comparable fusion presents itself in the Despaire episode. Despaire repeats Duessa's appeal to fleshly intemperance but by way of sloth rather than lust. What Despaire offers is the slothful alternative to the heroic ordeal: with suicide, Red Crosse will attain "rest," "happie ease," "Sleepe after toyle," "Ease after warre" (ix.40); he will escape all the ills attending this "loathsome life" (ix.44). Pleasure will be attained, pain ultimately escaped. Similarly, Belial also argues according to sloth and makes Despaire's appeal to the escape from pain; Fletcher's Satan offers Christ rest from His ordeal; Milton's offers Him the easy way out of the wilderness; and Manoa, mirroring Despaire even more closely, offers Samson the slothful alternative to true repentance, the easy way out of Gaza, and the slothful ease of an unheroic hearthside.

These numerous conceptual correspondences between Spenser's Despaire and later temptations of the Flesh, coupled with the parallels between Despaire and Duessa, provide as much evidence as can reasonably be asked for the allegorical identification I suggest. Counterparts to the House of Holiness episode, however, do not appear in any of the seventeenth-century works I will consider. Nonetheless, it is obvious enough that the episode, though it does not directly pose a temptation, is intended as a counterpart to Lucifera's temptation to the World. Like the House of Pride, and like later World-temptations, this is a composite episode, involving all virtue as the House of Pride had all sin, with the seven corporal works of mercy[44] corresponding to the seven deadly sins. The numerous parallels-in-contrast between the two houses—Malvenu and Vanity versus Humilita, the broad way versus the narrow, the vision of the dungeon versus the vision of the eternal city, the false heavenly Lucifera versus the truly heavenly Caelia, the city of man versus the city of God, for example—have been observed too frequently to require discussion here; suffice to note that these parallels make perfectly clear Spenser's intention of pairing the two episodes structurally. Accordingly, Red Crosse's experience in the House of Holiness educates him in man's proper relationship to the world. Even here, however, Spenser refuses us and the pilgrim the comparative ease of the regeneration of Deguile-ville's or Hawes's pilgrim. Virtue, perceived partially and imperfectly, can provide as much of a temptation indirectly as does vice directly, so that the reforming lore of Fidelia ironically tempts the knight to repeat the earlier error of withdrawal, a slothful *contemptus mundi*, to which Despaire had tempted him, and even with the aid of Speranza he falls into "doubtfull agonie" (x.22). The integrity of these otherworldy virtues is preserved only by rooting them in the worldly virtue of charity. Again and again the House of Holiness demonstrates the difficulty of the pilgrim's accommodating the dual claims made upon his nature as man of earth and saint. The episode, therefore, is not merely an education in virtue; it is also an education in the complexity of the pilgrim's nature. For this complexity, the genre's vices-and-virtues homeopathy is not only an inadequate remedy but even potentially a temptation. The complexity of man's nature does not permit a correction of the worldliness of the House of Pride by a simplistic inversion of its vice into an otherworldly virtue; for while Red Crosse must renounce the World, he is in the world if not of it, and it is there that he must perform the mission of his sainthood.

[44] See Charles E. Mounts, "Spenser's Seven Bead-Men and the Corporal Works of Mercy," *PMLA*, 54 (1939), 974-980.

Throughout the Legend of Holiness, Red Crosse has attempted to simplify his identity, at times denying that he is George, at others denying that he can be Saint. Despite all that his own experience and the House of Holiness have tried to teach him, on Mount Contemplation Red Crosse once again longs to embrace the simplicity that would resolve the paradoxes of his own complexity and relationship to the world. Once again he renews his longing for innocence, and once again he expresses the desire to escape the earthly taint of fallen nature: he would now turn away from Lucifera's palace of the World and journey at once to the heavenly otherworld, renouncing the world as well as the World. The task of the hermit, therefore, becomes one of pointing not only to the celestial city but also back to the world. Red Crosse must learn to come to terms with the contradictions of his own nature, to live with the difficult paradox that it is from the "guilt of bloudy field," from the "bloud [that] can nought but sin" (x.60), that the acts of his sainthood are born. The complexity of our fallen nature is such that the man of earth that we are to crucify and that may be the source of our damnation is also inseparable from our sainthood. From this perspective, the pronouncing of the name "Saint *George*" (x.61) is what the whole work has been moving towards. It is the climax of the hero's coming to identity, for the name itself embodies the tensions and contradictions of the identity the hero has attempted to evade. Red Crosse, hearing the name pronounced, would be *sanctus* but not *georgos*. He repeats in a different form the error of his opening confrontation with Errour, and the hermit must remind him that "*Georgos*" (x.66) is inseparably linked to his name and mission. As Christ in *Paradise Regained* must learn what it means to be the Son of God, as Samson must learn what it means to be God's champion, so must Red Crosse learn what it means to be "Saint *George*." Not until the knight has mastered his desire to oversimplify the garden within is he prepared to restore the garden without. Not until Red Crosse confronts the full complexity of his identity as *georgos*, restored son of the man of clay, and *sanctus* can he go out into the world to perform the mission that fulfills the name.

The defeat of the Devil in the form of the dragon completes the baptismal *imitatio Christi* that holiness stipulates. It is totally in accord with the moral vision behind the Legend of Holiness that Red Crosse's victory over the violent *superbia vitae* of the Devil should be viewed for him as a man in the pilgrimage of life and for the race within history as only a single, tentative victory. The baptismal vow to defeat "the deuil and all his workes" as performed in the dragon-slaying is only the beginning of Red Crosse's "continually mortifying al [his] euyll and corrupt affections." The pilgrimage does not end with the defeat of the dragon, nor does it end with the betrothal to Una. The final events of the work bring with them a sense of the inevitable limitations attending human victory in this life. We are no more allowed a false sense of the course of our own life and the course of history than we are allowed a false sense of our nature; we are no more permitted in Una's Eden a false sense of an ending, an easy progress through the Apocalypse to the new garden, than we were permitted a false sense of a return to the beginning and the garden in the Woods of Errour. The course is longer and more difficult than that. Even in his victories, man daily falls, as Red Crosse's slipping into the Well of Life and the balm of the Tree of Life shows. The sacramental imagery that looks to the time when man will partake of the "water of life" and the "tree of life" (Revelation 22:1-2) serves also to remind us, in the falling of the knight, how far we are from that final victory. The victory over the dragon is only a shadow of Christ's victory over the dragon at the Apocalypse; and the betrothal of Red Crosse and Una is only a shadow of the marriage of the Lamb and the faithful at the end of history in another Eden. Though Red Crosse has done as much as man can do, imitating Christ's triumph in the wilderness over the Flesh, the World, and the Devil, imitating also His Crucifixion, Harrowing of Hell, and final victory over the dragon at the Apocalypse, Spenser would not have us embrace an easy enthusiasm, a perilous confidence that now all things have their ending. Red Crosse must venture beyond these beginning triumphs, leaving Una to mourn. The muted joy of the protagonists, qualified by the exigencies of a long pilgrimage, is extended to us as well, as we, in the final stanza, are joined with them and the narrator as "iolly Mariners" (xii.42). Jolly we may be, for from lesser things on this day greater are augured; but ours, Spenser reminds us, is a "wearie vesell" on a "long voyage," and that voyage has just begun. The lesson that concludes the pilgrimage is the lesson that began it.

2. Guyon *Microchristus*

The Legend of Temperance, like the Legend of Holiness, takes as its subject the pilgrimage of a Christian knight whose quest is the restoration of a garden; and like that book, too, its quest is conceived in terms of the baptismal vow to "forsake the deuil, . . . the world, and . . . the flesh." Unlike Red Crosse's pilgrimage, however, Guyon's is not structured around the Flesh, the World, and the Devil. Nonetheless, the infernal triad does play a crucial role in the episodes concluding the two major movements of the pilgrimage, first in the Cave of Mammon and finally in the Bower of Bliss. Both episodes operate against the backdrop of the Harrowing of Hell as well as the Temptation in the Wilderness and are therefore designed as complements to each other, with Guyon performing in the Bower of Bliss a full *imitatio Christi* as he fails to do in the Cave of Mammon. Red Crosse and Guyon are thus both *microchristi* triumphing over the Errour usurping the garden of man's mind, the one defeating the Dragon and his pride, the other the Woman and her intemperance.

Not only the events within the Cave of Mammon but also the events outside correspond to Adam's three temptations in the garden and Christ's in the wilderness;[1] and the two sequences occur in precisely the same order. The debate between Mammon and Guyon outside the Cave falls into three

[1] Everyone since Todd (cited in *The Works of Edmund Spenser: A Variorum Edition*, II, *The Faerie Queene, Book Two*, ed. Edwin Greenlaw [Baltimore, Md.: The Johns Hopkins Press, 1933], 254) has realized that Mammon's temptation of Guyon alludes to Christ's temptation in the wilderness; but it was left for Frank Kermode, in his classic essay, "The Cave of Mammon," in *Elizabethan Poetry*, ed. John Russell Brown and Bernard Harris (London: Arnold, 1960), p. 159, to suggest that "Guyon undergoes . . . a *total* temptation

parts. In the first stage, Mammon, having introduced himself in terms of Satan's and Lucifera's claim to be "God of the world and worldlings" (vii.8), offers Guyon his mountains of gold: "Wherefore if me thou deigne to serue and sew, / At thy commaund lo all these mountaines bee" (vii.9). Obviously, this temptation corresponds to Lucifera's temptation to the World in Book I and to Satan's World-temptation in the wilderness—"All these things will I give thee, if thou wilt fall down and worship me" (Matthew 4:9). It also corresponds to Mammon's first offer within the Cave to "all the wealth, which is, or was of yore" (vii.31). In the next temptation outside the Cave, Mammon, perceiving Guyon created in his own image, offers the "Vaine glorious Elfe" gold as a means to "crownes and kingdomes." Mammon's teleology

---

parallel to that of Christ in the wilderness." The essay is, however, debilitated by some serious flaws. The most important of these is that Kermode does not find a temptation to the Flesh in the episode (that, he says, is dealt with in the Phaedria episode); but without a temptation to the Flesh there is no "*total* temptation." The second major flaw is his interpretation of the Garden of Proserpina as a temptation to curiosity—a flaw resulting from his attempt to impose on the Cave of Mammon Augustine's formulation of the three temptations as "the pleasure of the flesh, and pride, and curiosity" in *Exposition on the Book of Psalms* (Oxford, 1847), I, 70. Paul J. Alpers, *The Poetry of "The Faerie Queene"* (Princeton, N.J.: Princeton Univ. Press, 1967), pp. 235-248, has seized upon Kermode's essay as an example of the fallacy of imposing a predetermined schematic consistency on the *Faerie Queene* at the expense of rhetorical-contextual meaning. Also objecting to Kermode and his expectation of a "rigorous consistency" in a poem like the *Faerie Queene* is A. Bartlett Giamatti, *The Earthly Paradise and the Renaissance Epic* (Princeton, N.J.: Princeton Univ. Press, 1966), pp. 233-234.

Since this chapter was completed, another essay, and a very good one, on the Cave of Mammon has appeared, A. Kent Hieatt, "Three Fearful Symmetries and the Meaning of *Faerie Queene* II," in *A Theatre for Spenserians*, ed. Judith M. Kennedy and James A. Reither (Toronto: Univ. of Toronto Press, 1973), pp. 19-52. Unfortunately, Hieatt's essay appeared too late for me to make full use of it, but I am happy to say that we agree on some of the major difficulties of the episode. Humphrey Tonkin's "Discussing Spenser's Cave of Mammon," *Studies in English Literature*, 13 (1973), 1-13, appeared too

echoes that of Genesis 3, between *avaritia* and *vanagloria*, the World and the Devil. This second temptation outside the Cave accords with the second temptation within the Cave to the glory of the Devil in the form of Philotime.

The third stage of temptation both outside the Cave and within is where most critical confusion has developed; but if we employ the two episodes as glosses to each other, and if we view them alongside comparable episodes in Spenser and Milton, this confusion can, I think, be dispelled. Having had the offer of the World's gold and the Devil's glory, we would expect next the offer of the Flesh. The Flesh does play a role here, not, however, as a temptation but as part of Guyon's answer to Mammon's question, "And why then . . . , / Are mortall men so fond and vndiscreet, / So euill thing to seek vnto their ayd?" (vii.14). Mammon's question is rhetorical, but it leads Guyon to an answer that anticipates what he will see in the third chamber within the Cave, the lost garden that is a mirror of the fallen mind. "Through fowle intemperaunce," Guyon replies, "Frayle men art oft captiu'd to couetise" (vii.15); and he proceeds to account for the origins of avarice in terms of man's loss of Eden:

> The antique world, in his first flowring youth,
> Found no defect in his Creatours grace,

---

late for me to reply in detail to his contention that "Mammon's cave has nothing to do with the Harrowing of Hell, being neither Hell nor harrowing, except perhaps to Guyon, and it is merely reminiscent of Christ's temptation, nothing more" (p. 13). Needless to say, if one sets up interpretative equivalences between Christ and Guyon, one will quickly discover that these equivalences do not hold; for there are also manifest differences between Christ and Guyon. This should not, however, negate the role of the Temptation in the Wilderness as a backdrop to the Cave of Mammon. The discrepancies between Christ and Guyon we perceive should force us to realize that the Temptation in the Wilderness is only one of the backdrops to Guyon's temptations; another is Adam's temptations in Eden. Guyon's experience "equals" neither Christ's nor Adam's; rather, as I hope to demonstrate, it exists in a tense and complicated relation to both Adam's fall and Christ's triumph.

But with glad thankes, and vnreproued truth,
The gifts of soueraigne bountie did embrace:
Like Angels life was then mens happy cace;
But later ages pride, like corn-fed steed,
Abusd her plenty, and fat swolne encreace
To all licentious lust, and gan exceed
The measure of her meane, and naturall first need.

Then gan a cursed hand the quiet wombe
Of his great Grandmother with steele to wound,
And the hid treasures in her sacred tombe,
With Sacriledge to dig. Therein he found
Fountaines of gold and siluer to abound,
Of which the matter of his huge desire
And pompous pride eftsoones he did compound;
Then auarice gan through his veines inspire
His greedy flames, and kindled life-deuouring fire.

(vii.16-17)

In Guyon's lost Eden, we encounter once again the dual corrupt affections of man's fallen *hortus mentis*, "pride . . . and . . . all licentious lust," "huge desire / And pompous pride." This familiar dual scheme will reappear in the Garden of Proserpina.

In the ensuing exchange with Guyon, Mammon attempts to allay his fear of unrightful attainment, but he also attempts to excite his curiosity—and certainly in this latter respect Mammon is successful. Guyon quesions, "What secret place . . . ? / Or where hast thou thy wonne . . . ?"; Mammon invites, "Come thou . . . and see"; and Guyon follows him into the Cave (vii.20). Does he sin in so doing? critics ask. I think, if we compare the event leading Guyon into the Cave with the events that led Guyon to encounter Mammon in the first place, that our answer must be no. In the opening description of Guyon feeding himself "with comfort / Of his owne vertues, and prayse-worthy deedes" (vii.2), we may suspect a tendance to pride; and we may suspect also, along with Harry Berger, Jr., that in addressing Mammon Guyon shows a tendance to *curiositas*.[2] But we only suspect; and in our initial reading of the episode, we probably suspect nothing at all. We tend to see the hero as he sees himself; and for the most part we are too preoccupied, as Guyon himself is, with seeing Mammon and his marvels to pay much attention to our own responses to Mammon. Like Guyon, we are fascinated by the scene; and it is as easy for us as it is for him to see that the scene is evil. What we see does not tempt us, but what we ignore is that the locus of temptation lies in not only what is seen but our own seeing it. Focusing on the evil objects of the outer world, we become blind to our own evil. Our eyes are open wide to the spectacle but closed to ourselves. The Cave of Mammon is, therefore, another of Spenser's "good temptations," which force us as well as Guyon to experience the limitations of our own nature. What makes this temptation so treacherous is that it takes the form of a resistance to temptation. While we resist the temptation of the eyes to avarice, we are simultaneously manifesting our vulnerability to it. What we learn later is that what draws Guyon and us into the Cave mirrors the same inner weakness that binds Tantalus and Pontius Pilate to Mammon.

[2] *The Allegorical Temper* (New Haven, Conn.: Yale Univ. Press, 1957), pp. 18ff.; I am profoundly indebted to this study. M. P. Parker, *The Allegory of the "Faerie Queene"* (Oxford: The Clarendon Press, 1960), pp. 130-131, accuses Guyon of "the defect of self-complacency [which] is exactly what would lay a soul open to the temptations of worldliness." Berger's and Parker's attribution of these two sins, curiosity and pride, to Guyon can, I think, be verified by a structural reading of the episode. Kermode, pp. 167-168, argues that in following Mammon into the Cave Guyon is simply imitating Christ, who permitted Himself to be tempted; Maurice Evans, "The Fall of Guyon," in *Spenser*, ed. Harry Berger, Jr. (Englewood Cliffs, N.J.: Prentice-Hall, 1968), p. 90 [originally published in *ELH*, 28 (1961), 215-224], argues that Guyon has yielded to pride, a failure "to realize the limitations of human strength," an "overconfidence in his own virtues and praiseworthy deeds"; and Lewis Miller, Jr., "Phaedria, Mammon, and Sir Guyon's Education by Error," *Journal of English and Germanic Philology*, 63 (1964), 40, simply labels it "a weakness" like that underlying Guyon's yielding to the seduction of Phaedria's words.

Guyon's demonstration of virtue becomes at the same time a demonstration of his inheritance from the fallen garden.

We must make a distinction, therefore, between actual and innate sin. Up to the point of the invitation, Guyon has successfully resisted two stages of the triple temptation, wealth and glory. The third, the Flesh, has been mentioned but not pursued. However, Mammon's invitation is the only offer of his Guyon actually accepts, and it is couched in the same imagery of sight that characterizes avarice as the lust of the eyes. In addition, it is difficult not to compare Guyon's curiosity about this underground marvell to Eve's curiosity about the source of the serpent's marvellous powers; and it is also difficult not to compare Guyon's desire to see the wealth hidden under the earth that "neuer eye did vew" (vii.19) to his own account of the desire that led to the Fall of man, the desire to see "the hid treasures" in earth's "sacred tombe" (vii.17). But having said this, can we say that Guyon has repudiated the "Sacriledge" of *avaritia pecuniae* only to sin himself in terms of a comparable "Sacriledge," Eve's and Tantalus', of *avaritia scientiae*? Can we say that Guyon has abandoned the *imitatio Christi* of his rejection of the first two offers for an *imitatio Adamis* in his acceptance of the third? I think not; and yet the gesture Guyon makes in accepting Mammon's offer is not a Christlike gesture. Guyon's acceptance of the offer is not the same thing as Christ's permitting Himself to be tempted: Christ was led by the Spirit into the wilderness, Guyon by Mammon; Christ was not motivated by curiosity, Guyon clearly is. At the same time, however, to stress Guyon's personal guilt, to say that he falls or sins at this point, makes the episode repetitive not purposefully but absurdly: if Guyon has actually sinned, there is no reason for Mammon to continue the temptation; there is no reason to eat two apples when one will suffice. Guyon does not fall in allowing Mammon to guide him any more than he fell by allowing Phaedria to guide him earlier: instead, both episodes demonstrate Guyon's penchant to sin, the corrupt affections he and all men have inherited through the Fall. Guyon's acceptance of Mammon's invitation is, therefore, ironically an illustration of his own answer to Mammon's question, Why do men seek gold if it is such an evil? The answer, as Guyon has told us, is to be found in the Fall; and now he unwittingly demonstrates the truth of his account for us, as he is drawn by his own fallen nature to see Mammon's hidden kingdoms and to confront in the Garden of Proserpina a mirror of his own mind and the corrupt affections that have led him to the garden.

In this context, Guyon's acceptance of Mammon's offer becomes the turning point in his education in temperance. This temptation, more than any other he has experienced, is like those Milton's Christ and Samson experience: for Guyon as for the reader, it is a "good temptation," providing the means for the hero's confronting his own nature and identity. We may say that Guyon's characterization, and therefore Spenser's artistry, is deficient, or we may say that Guyon's character is deficient; and for those who believe the latter, Guyon's deficiency throughout the book has been an inability to see the full reality of evil. Guyon is a *naif*; a courteous young man, polite, well-brought-up, well-schooled, of a good family, but innocent—as his opening encounter with the Satanic Archimago and Duessa points out—to the diabolic roots of evil and the fallen dimensions of his own nature. Guyon has acted like an unfallen Adam around whom the garden had fallen. The cool distance Guyon has preserved from the outer world is, from this perspective, less a sign of perfect temperance than imperfect self-perception, a false and self-deceiving distancing of himself from the taint of the fallen. Describing the Fall of man, he relates it to the avaricious, to the obviously intemperate, as though his own virtue were exempt from the Fall. And yet the Phaedria-Mammon sequence has been initiated by a demonstration of the weakness of his own nature when he leaves behind the Palmer (the Palmer, as the fact that he is a pilgrim would suggest, represents not Reason or Prudence alone but Reason restored by grace). Boarding Phaedria's boat, Guyon to some extent has already succumbed to his concupiscence, when he experiences, too late, what would seem to be a cry of conscience in his being "loath to leaue his guide behind" (vi.20):

> Yet being entred, [he] might not backe retyre;
> For the flit barke, obaying *to her mind,*
> Forth launched quickly, as *she did desire* . . .

(vi.20; my italics)

Although Guyon goes on to resist Phaedria, as he will Mammon, it is precisely his succumbing to Phaedria's will, through a lightning-swift separation from his Palmer, that makes that resistance necessary. Even a highly controlled man like Guyon is vulnerable, through the Fall, to passions beyond his control. It was, in part, to demonstrate the fallen limits of Guyon's nature that Spenser has him journey, in the two episodes in which he is unaccompanied by the Palmer, to two versions of the fallen garden, Phaedria's bower and the Garden of Proserpina: in the first place, even though in both gardens his resistance is ostensibly impeccable, he is there for the wrong reasons, reasons which, in fact, are rooted in his fallen nature; in the second place, in both gardens he demonstrates the limits of his Palmerless nature, for in these gardens (unlike the Bower of Bliss, where the Palmer accompanies him), he can resist but not reform a landscape that is at least a partial reflection of his own fallen nature. Both Edenic episodes, then, even though on one level they demonstrate Guyon's Christlike virtue, also demonstrate the Adamic limits of that virtue; and accordingly both Phaedria's and Mammon's gardens mirror Guyon's own connections to the fallen garden. (In this respect, these two episodes are similar to the Edenic episode outside Orgoglio's castle, where Red Crosse, without his dwarf and armor, and without Una, ultimately becomes powerless before his own fallen nature.) Accordingly, in Phaedria's garden Guyon encounters the impress from Eden on the concupiscible appetite; in Mammon's garden, the impress from Eden on the irascible appetite. And he will learn at the end of the Phaedria-Mammon sequence that the Edenic inheritance is his own. Guyon must learn what he found difficult to understand when Ruddymane's hands could not be washed clean, that baptism does not return man to Eden, that there remains even in the baptized Christian something of that evil against which he contends. In the final episode within the Cave, Guyon's confidence in an absolute moral disjunction between himself and his opponents gets its rebuke. Like Red Crosse Knight before him, he must confront the complications of his own nature; and like Red Crosse Knight in another Hell, he must descend to the bottom of Mammon's cave to gain the knowledge Christian virtue requires, that he like his combatants is a "wicked man" (viii.1), that he himself is fallen. That, in fact, is precisely the posture in which he will find himself at the end of the episode. The final event outside the Cave therefore foreshadows the final event of the episode as a whole: Guyon's unknowing demonstration outside the Cave of his fallen nature in his acceptance of Mammon's invitation will be repeated on a more dramatic scale at the end of the temptations within the Cave, as he faints and falls to the earth.

The Garden of Proserpina, from a number of perspectives, parallels and completes the third stage of Guyon's encounter with Mammon outside the Cave.[3] Most obviously, it provides

[3] Professor Kermode, pp. 161-165, has suggested that the Garden of Proserpina illustrates "inordinate or blasphemous curiosity," and that it is "a temptation to vain learning"; and Paul Alpers, pp. 240-248, in his attack on this reading, has accused him of succumbing to that temptation. In the introduction to his *Shakespeare, Spenser, Donne: Renaissance Essays* (New York: Viking, 1971), p. 9, Kermode announces that he is "unrepentant" about the essay, accuses Alpers of "trivializing" the episode, and reprints the essay essentially unchanged. I have no desire directly to enter their dispute over whether Spenser is an esoteric poet, or whether he should be read by remaining on the surface of the verse; my analysis should make my own eclectic position clear. Their disagreement is, however, informative. Kermode's argument for his reading is briefly this: the Hesperidean golden apples were, for the mythographers, "emblems of astronomical knowledge" ("whatever they signify it is not avarice"); Tantalus, in that he reported to men the secrets of divine knowledge,

the temptation of the Flesh omitted outside the Cave. All evidence, it seems to me, indisputably points to the Flesh as the controlling idea allegorically for the episode. Guyon opened his reply to Mammon's question, Why do men seek riches? by asserting that "through fowle intemperaunce / Frayle men are oft captiu'd to couetise" (vii.15). Accordingly, at the Garden of Proserpina, Mammon offers Guyon the fruit and the stool, the first for his hunger, the second for rest. The narrator specifically interprets the significance of the offer for us in language that echoes Guyon's outside the

---

represents "a type of blasphemous or intemperate knowledge." Pontius Pilate does not fit so easily into Kermode's scheme, and he confesses "to feeling less certain here"; but he concludes that "His question, 'what is truth?' would in the circumstances fall under Augustinian *curiositas*; and he abuses knowledge." Alpers, however, returning to the mythographers, discovers that the apples were also associated with avarice, an association he finds "more natural and relevant." (It should be noted that Augustine's *curiositas* is the avarice for knowledge.) Like Kermode, Alpers encounters problems with Pontius Pilate, who does not seem to be paired with Tantalus in terms of avarice. Alpers, however, has it a bit easier than Kermode because for him "our criterion of consistency" is false; and we are urged to "cease to worry about [Pilate's] lack of connection with riches and recognize that Spenser is directly concerned with heroic psychology and attitude." Finally, Alpers argues, almost parenthetically (for he is not eager to see Christ's Temptation in the Wilderness as the controlling reality behind the Cave of Mammon), that Mammon's offer of the apples and silver stool is analogous to Satan's temptation of Christ to turn stones into bread. I confess that for me both readings suggest the limitations of their particular approach to Spenserian allegory. If Spenser is an esoteric poet, as Kermode claims, it will not be established through a scheme that was part of every sixteenth-century Englishman's baptism. Moreover, Kermode undeniably twists the episode to fit his gold-ambition-curiosity scheme; but his failure here is not in his expectation of consistency but in his imposition of the wrong consistency. For all his impressive erudition, Kermode simply does not sufficiently take account of the multiple possibilities of the scheme he is using. At the same time, Alpers' denying of consistency and his sudden shifting of the plane of interpretation from avarice to the problem of the heroic seriously undermine the integrity of his reading. (See also Hieatt, p. 41, who, replying to both Alpers and Kermode, concludes that although "The Garden of Proserpina

77

Cave: "All which he did, to doe him deadly fall / In frayle intemperance through sinfull bayt"; and the narrator remarks later in the same stanza that Guyon "Ne suffred lust his safetie to betray" (vii.64). Moreover, if we compare this episode to its counterparts elsewhere, as Professor Kermode has urged us, that counterpart is found not in Milton's learning-temptation but in the first episode of his sequence of allegorical glories, a sequence indebted to the Cave of Mammon, namely the banquet and its appeal to Christ's temperance. The banquet is portrayed as a counterpart to Satan's offering the apple to Eve; Christ is also invited to sit and eat; and the location of temptation is also a false Eden in which the hero

---

continues the representation of the intemperance of avarice," "the Garden proper extends the concepts of prideful possession of money and what it buys, and of quickly won lofty status in the world, to the final intemperance of human desire for or infringement upon the realm of the divine." On this, Hieatt and I agree; he does not, however, proceed to relate the episode to the Flesh as well, as I think both the episode itself and its parallelism with the third episode outside the Cave require.)

Other critics of the Garden of Proserpina are equally divided. According to Janet Spens, *Spenser's "Faerie Queene"* (London: Arnold, 1934), p. 125, "In the first two chambers the evil of the desire of worldly wealth and power is exhibited, in the third the burden of its possession"; for Parker, *Allegory of the "Faerie Queene,"* p. 133, the episode presents "a more deadly temptation a touch of which was in the self-complacency which engendered the whole experience; the temptation to find his riches in himself by seeking his own will and desire"; for Kathleen Williams, *Spenser's "Faerie Queene": The World of Glass* (London: Routledge and Kegan Paul, 1966), pp. 60-61, the episode represents "aspiring ambition like Philotime's" (Tantalus) and "ambitious blasphemy" (Pontius Pilate); for Theodor Gang, "Nature and Grace in *The Faerie Queene*: The Problem Reviewed," *ELH*, 26 (1959), 15, Tantalus represents avarice, while Pilate is a type of practical politician; for J. Holloway, "The Seven Deadly Sins in *The Faerie Queene*, Book II," *Review of English Studies*, 3 (1952), 18, the whole episode depicts gluttony; and for Ernest Sirluck, "*The Faerie Queene*, Book II, and the *Nicomachean Ethics*," *Modern Philology*, 49 (1951), 90, the silver stool suggests "if anything, sloth" and Tantalus greed, "but Pilate, who represents injustice and hypocrisy, starts yet another strain."

is tempted to ignore the full impact of the Fall, to act as though Eden were restored. And if another counterpart is needed, it can be found in the first of the allegorical kingdoms offered Christ in Fletcher's "Christ's Victory on Earth," an episode also indebted to Mammon's triadic sequence; and the parallel, once again, is intemperance.

But to say that the allegorical thrust of the Garden of Proserpina is the Flesh is to say what should have been clear all along; for our criterion of consistency is only at times false and usually because of the wrong terms of consistency. If Phaedria's garden images forth intemperance of the concupiscible appetite, we can expect, not unreasonably, that Mammon's garden will image forth intemperance of the irascible appetite, as in fact it does.[4] In the Cave, Guyon is followed by a fury that is the ugly embodiment of the excess of the irascible appetite; and in the Garden, he confronts anger embodied in Tantalus' cursing of the gods, self-directed anger (despair or grief in Aquinas)[5] in Pilate's cursing of himself. Both episodes, moreover, offer a false satisfaction of desire; both, not merely the bower of Phaedria, offer a parody

[4] In the Cave of Mammon, the excess of the irascible appetite leads to irrational and savage cruelty. Recognition of this excess underlies Guyon's objection to Mammon's offer of glory outside the Cave:

> Witnesse the guiltlesse bloud pourd oft on ground,
> The crowned often slaine, the slayer cround,
> The sacred Diademe in peeces rent,
> And purple robe gored with many a wound;
> Castles surprizd, great cities sackt and brent . . .
>
> (vii.13)

The excess of Mars's *ira* underlying Mammon's avarice is manifested in his reaction to Guyon's refusals of his offers. Outside the Cave, upon Guyon's refusal of glory he "wex[es] wroth" (14); within the Cave, again after Guyon's refusal of glory, Mammon "roughly him bespake" (63). The fiend that follows Guyon, grating "his gnashing teeth" (34), holding "his cruell clawes, / Threatening with greedy gripe to do him dye, / And rend in peeces with his rauenous pawes" (27), allegorizes the excessive *ira* that motivates Mammon and will possess and destroy Guyon should he succumb to avarice.

[5] *Summa Theologica*, II, i, Q.40.

of temperance, a false restoration of the appetite's desires by holding out the prospect of desire's rest. If the excess of the concupiscible appetite in Phaedria's false Eden leads to an anesthesia of desire rather than sexual satisfaction, in Mammon's false Eden Tantalus' thirst and hunger are never satisfied, as he "labour[s] so in vaine" (vii.59), and Pilate, washing his hands compulsively, also loses "his labour vaine" (vii.61). Underlying both Edenic gardens is the dilemma of the fallen *hortus mentis* itself: the fallen mind is inflicted with the insatiability of its own desires.

From this perspective, Mammon's garden is the inevitable culmination of events preceding it. As Mammon informed Guyon earlier, his is gold that has never been seen or touched. Obviously this is a special kind of gold, for much gold has of course been touched by man. Under the guise of offering gold, Mammon is offering avarice. Mammon tempts men to symbolic desires that can never be satisfied by real goods. He tempts men to pursue what they cannot have or, as in the court of Philotime, can never be satisfied with. In the Garden of Proserpina and the figures of Tantalus and Pilate, we see the source of the appetite's anguish: through Eve-Proserpina's intemperate seizing of the apple, her sons are doomed to repeat her error, to get nothing, absolutely nothing, in return except frustration or, as in Phaedria's garden, a momentary numbing of desire. We are born heirs to our parents' insatiable desires; and unrestored, we perpetually re-enact, like Tantalus and Pilate, the desperate attempt to satisfy the insatiable. Desiring too much, nothing sates; and we are cursed by our own desires. The Cave of Mammon is thus not simply a figure of Hell, though of course it is that; it is a real, psychological Hell of the self-torment and frustration of desire that, through the Fall, has become like Acrasia herself, uncontrollable. It is a Hell in which fallen desire becomes its own punishment. In Mammon's false Eden, we see why none of the intemperate characters of Book II is ever satisfied; why the opening half of the work is peopled with characters like Atin, Occasion, and Furor, who, pursuing desires that have no rest, stir up insatiable desires in others, forcing them to re-enact their own frustration. Spenser's Cave of Mammon is not, then, a moralistic exemplum for a simplistic repudiation of all gold, glory, and pleasure. Rather, it is a repudiation of the kind of mind, imaged forth in the Garden of Proserpina, that makes these goods meaningless. Mammon's temptation is less to the indulgence of desire than to the further corruption of desire. It is a temptation to desire that must be rejected to preserve what integrity, which is to say what satisfaction, desire may have in a fallen world.

Mammon's offer to Guyon of the apples and the stool is therefore not a temptation to satisfy desire so much as it is a temptation to desires that can never be satisfied. The object of the appetite's movements, its passions, as Aquinas (if he is needed) can inform us,[6] is rest. In offering Guyon Tantalus' apples, Mammon offers apples, like his gold, which can never be had, which can never sate desire; in offering the stool "To rest thy wearie person, in a shadow coole" (vii.63), he is offering not simply rest for a man weary from a three days' journey, but a fraudulent illusion of the resting, or satisfying, of the desire the apple provokes. If we view the relationship of the apple to the stool as an emblem of Mammonic desire, we will have no real need of the Eleusinian mysteries to explain the offer of the stool. Its significance is perfectly clear from Mammon's strategy throughout the episode of teasing Guyon's desire, offering it rest and satisfaction, while leading Guyon to the torment of the damned whose desires have no rest. Mammon's garden thus answers his own question outside the Cave, Why do men seek riches if they are an evil? The answer is Acrasia, Proserpina, Eve: through the Fall, man can no longer fully resist evil; he is subject to the tyranny of his own desires.

---

[6] See, for example, *S.T.*, II, i, Q.23: "Nor, when once good is obtained, does there remain any other movement except the appetite's repose in the good obtained" (Art. 3); "When the good is obtained, it causes the appetite to rest, as it were, in the good obtained" (Art. 4).

The Garden of Proserpina verifies Guyon's account outside the Cave of the origins of avarice in the Fall, but it goes beyond this to verify his account of the two root causes of avarice in Eden, intemperance and pride, in the form of the two co-dwellers in Cocytus, Tantalus and Pilate. Tantalus embodies the presumption of the old Adam. Presuming on his favor with the gods, he profaned the holy secrets of divine knowledge by offering them to mortals, and he stole nectar and ambrosia from the gods; Adam also broke a divine injunction apropos knowledge, and he too seized what was allocated for the gods and forbidden man. Both Tantalus and Adam, then, manifest the pride that presumes against, and to, the godhead. Not only the legends surrounding Tantalus but also the text itself suggests as much. Reproached by Guyon as an "Ensample . . . of mind intemperate,"

> Then gan the cursed wretch aloud to cry,
> Accursing highest *Ioue* and gods ingrate,
> And eke blaspheming heauen bitterly,
> As authour of vniustice, there to let him dye.
>
> (vii.60)

Tantalus, continuing to blaspheme heaven, repeats the presumption that damned him. He has become the judge of gods—and so has his co-dweller in Cocytus, Pontius Pilate:

> I *Pilate* am the falsest Iudge, alas,
> And most vniust, that by vnrighteous
> And wicked doome, to Iewes despiteous
> Deliuered vp the Lord of life to die,
> And did acquite a murdrer felonous;
> The whiles my hands I washt in puritie,
> The whiles my soule was soyld with foule iniquitie.
>
> (vii.62)

Spenser has purposefully revised the biblical account of Pilate: "When Pilate saw that he could prevail nothing, but that rather tumult was made, he took water, and washed his hands before the multitude, saying, I am innocent of the

blood of this just person: see ye to it" (Matthew 27:24).
Spenser portrays Pilate not as denying his guilt as Tantalus
does but as almost hysterically displaying his guilt. His repentance of sin, however, leads to no more rest than Tantalus'
repetition of his sin; for if Tantalus distrusts divine justice,
Pilate distrusts, or is ignorant of, divine mercy. His repentance, as much as Tantalus' refusal to repent, is "vaine"
(vii.61); his acknowledgment of sin is corrupted by the very
vanity and presumption of which he ostensibly repents. Even
his goodness is corrupt. Pilate's initial sin in Jerusalem took
the form, like Tantalus', of the old Adam's presumption, only
it manifested itself in terms of Adam's traditional role as the
judge and crucifier of the new Adam. Tantalus ironically now
does what Pilate repents of, judging the gods; while Pilate's
presumption now takes the form of a perverse *imitatio
Christi*: in his vain washing of his hands, Pilate, acting as the
agent of his own mercy, presumes to the role of the minister
of mercy, the "Lord of life," he crucified. The *superbia vitae*,
or *avaritia sublimitatis*, that led the devil to presume to the
godhead thus links Pilate and Tantalus to each other and to
Mammon ("God of the world and worldlings I me call").
The relationship of Pilate and Tantalus to the temptation of
the Flesh should now be clear: in both figures, intemperance
of the irascible appetite (and in Tantalus the concupiscible
appetite as well) is linked to presumption. In a word, the
Garden of Proserpina verifies Guyon's account of the dual
Edenic origins of avarice, man's "huge desire / And pompous pride."

If the Garden of Proserpina verifies Guyon's account of
avarice and the Fall, it also serves to do what he failed to do,
to relate him to that account. The episode thus not only answers Guyon's question outside the Cave about the source of
Mammon's riches; it also manifests his own Adamic tendance
to evil which has led him through the Cave to the Garden.
Guyon's resistance of evil leads him to the illusion of innocence. It has set up for him false moral polarities, which
from the very beginning of the episode have led him to ignore

the fallen mirroring of subject and object—in the opening
description of him; in his approach to Mammon; in his rejection of Mammon's gold for "Faire shields, gay steedes,
bright armes" (vii.10)—to which Mammon replied, not entirely unjustly, by calling him "Vaine glorious Elfe" (vii.11);
in his motivation for entering the Cave and its resemblance
to his own account of the motivations of the Fall and avarice;
in his "feed[ing] his eyes" (vii.24) throughout the Cave; in
his rejection of Mammon's gold within the Cave, an echo of
the vainglory of his resistance outside the Cave, on the
grounds that he wishes "to be Lord of those, that riches
haue" (vii.33); in the narrator's ambiguous description of
him as a "greedy pray" (vii.34); in his request to leave the
forge in order "to follow mine emprise" (vii.39), which
leaves ambiguous which adventure Guyon has in mind, his
proper venture or the present one, though it is the latter he
pursues. In the most interesting of these mirrorings, Guyon
rejects the wealth of the forge with "bold mesprise" (vii.39).
The word "mesprise," which bears the meanings both of "disdain" and of "mistake," aptly summarizes the ambiguities of
Guyon's resistance, not only here but throughout the Cave.
Ironically the boldness of Guyon's resistance of evil leads him
to mirror the disdain underlying pride in the next chamber, to
which Mammon leads him in order "him further to entise"
(vii.39). Guyon's disdain, proper for the temperate hero, is
precisely what enables Mammon to entice him to the court
of Philotime and to lead him to continue to ignore his right-
ful "emprise." Accordingly, Mammon must stop Guyon's
battle with Disdain, pacifying "him [the referent is ambigu-
ous] with reason" (vii.42). Curiously, Mammon assumes the
role of Guyon's own reason. The significance of this odd
reversal would seem to be that Mammon recognizes that what
makes Guyon vulnerable to him is in fact the disdain or
"mesprise" of his reason and temperance. The disdain of
Guyon's resistance of evil verges upon ensnaring him in the
vainglory he repudiates; Guyon's disdainful sense of an absolute polarity between himself and the corruption of Mam-

mon's world is, along with his curiosity, precisely what keeps him in that world, continuing pointlessly to see and reject things he has no intention of accepting. "All thine idle offers I refuse" (vii.39), Guyon has said; but he fails to see his own fallen image mirrored in his virtuous words of resistance; for if the offers are idle, the resistance is, too. Nor is he capable of seeing that in his "All that I need I haue" dwells not only the virtue of his resistance but also his pride in that virtue; that in this context of a display of virtue, his description of Mammon's world, "With such vaine shewes thy worldlings vile abuse" (vii.39), raises the mirror to himself and his own weakness. His Christlike assertion of virtue reveals the Adamic limits of that virtue.

The paradox governing the Cave of Mammon is that Guyon's imitation of Christ's triumph over the old Adam in the wilderness brings him closer, both spatially and spiritually, to the old Adam himself and his lost garden; not only the landscape but also Guyon's physical movement through the landscape is symbolic. The seemingly innocuous reactions outside the Cave that led the knight to Mammon thus lead him, like Red Crosse Knight in Wandering Wood, through a labyrinth to the Adamic source of his own error. Erring, Red Crosse encountered in a lost Eden his own Errour; curious of knowledge, prideful in his Palmerless virtue, Guyon confronts in another lost Eden Tantalus and Pontius Pilate, the one mirroring his and Adam's *avaritia scientiae* or curiosity, the other his vain self-sufficiency—the two tendencies that led him to approach Mammon and that have led him through the Cave to the Garden. Just as Red Crosse focused on the trees rather than on his own erring mirroring of the trees, Guyon has focused on what he sees, ignoring his Adamic mirroring of the objects fascinating his eyes for his Christlike resisting of them. The success of his resistance blinds him to the fallen, Adamic affections he demonstrates in the very act of resistance itself. The ultimate outcome of his *imitatio Christi* is to show him as fallen; for his imitation of Christ is, like Pilate's, corrupted by the old Adam he tries to renounce.

The moral history Guyon had outside the Cave so complacently applied to others—the avaricious, the vainglorious, the lustful—is shown in the Adamic mirror of the Garden to apply to himself as well. Guyon is not exempt: at the end of the labyrinth is the fallen self he in vain has evaded.

Ironically Guyon's imitation of Christ's triumph in the wilderness over the old Adam manifests his own need for grace as the son of Adam. And from this perspective, too, the Garden of Proserpina is the culmination of the events of the episode. Throughout the temptations, Mammon has himself performed a perverse *imitatio Christi*: the triple offer within the Cave is designed as an infernal parody of the overflowing grace of God:

> God of the world and worldlings I me call,
> Great *Mammon*, greatest god below the skye,
> That of my plenty poure out vnto all,
> And vnto none my graces do enuye . . .
>
> (vii.8)

And in the third exchange outside the Cave, Mammon refers to his "offred grace" (vii.18). Within the Cave, Mammon says, "Such grace now to be happy, is before thee laid" (vii.32), and Guyon replies, "I n'ill thine offred grace" (vii.33); and after Philotime is offered, Guyon refuses "so great grace" (vii.50). Readers are sometimes puzzled as to why Mammon shows Guyon the arduous struggle and death of the masses of men who have attained and lost, or never attained, the glories of the world. One wonders why Spenser introduced these hardly tempting images if he wished to portray the chambers as temptations. The reason is not that Spenser sacrificed psychological plausibility to moralization. These images are in fact part of Mammon's strategy. Underlying them is this argument: "All men have aimed for wealth; you, Guyon, are a man like other men; I can get it for you wholesale." What Mammon holds out to Guyon and to all men is the prospect of an exemption from the common condition of man if they will worship him. His offer of "graces" is, therefore, a perversion of the exemption from the generic fallen condition offered by Christ in, as Paul phrases it in Romans 5:15, "the free gift" of His grace. Mammon is the world's god, and he offers the world's grace; and accordingly, his strategy is to convince man that he will find Edenic bliss in "the worldes bliss" (vii.32). He offers, that is, a parodic grace to fallen desire: in his flood of goods, man's fallen, intemperate thirst is to be sated. Mammon tempts man to resolve the problem of fallen desire by offering more goods for more desires. In fact, of course, Mammon's offer is fraudulent: for under the guise of offering more goods, he is tempting man to more desire for goods. Through his surrogate grace, Mammon seduces man to believe that the outer world can provide what grace, to some extent, provides: the world's goods will satisfy the insatiable lusts of the fallen mind, returning it to the lost harmony of desire and rest. Mammon's offers lead to Eden; for in his parody of Eden, he offers intemperance under the guise of offering that perfect balance of desire and rest that was temperance in Eden. In accordance with this counterfeit imitation of what only grace can achieve, Tantalus and Pontius Pilate are the victims of Mammon's treacherous sacraments of grace:[7] Tantalus' desire for the fruit and the water involve him in a parody of the Eucharist (appropriately, he asks Guyon, "Of grace I pray thee, giue to eat and drinke to mee" [vii.59]); and Pilate's washing of his hands is a parody of baptism. And correspondingly, in the offer of the apples and the stool, Mammon tempts Guyon in this false Eden to a false restoration of the inner garden and a false return to Eden.

The grace Mammon offers is predicated on a modification of the outer rather than the inner world, on the objects of desire rather than desire itself; and the strategy of this false grace mirrors Guyon's own weakness. Guyon rejects what Mammon offers, and the two would seem to be at antipodes,

[7] Originally noted by Northrop Frye, *Fables of Identity, Studies in Poetic Mythology* (New York: Harcourt, Brace and World, 1963), p. 80.

but the intemperance of the one and the temperance of the other ironically manifest the same error: the one in accepting the outer world, the other in rejecting it, both deny the need for divine grace and its continuous operation on the garden of the mind. Guyon's virtue is rooted in the same corrupt assumptions as Mammon's vice: both attempt to circumvent the full implications of the Fall on human nature. The limits of Guyon's virtue are mirrored in the limits of Mammonic vice, and in the Garden is the source of their community.

After three days in the Cave, Guyon faints and falls to the earth.[8] The illusion of innocence is broken. The faint of the

[8] On the reasons for Guyon's faint, older critics were inclined to be more gentle than most of the modern, ascribing the faint to physical causes (e.g., Leicester Bradner, *Edmund Spenser and the "Faerie Queene"* [Chicago: Univ. of Chicago Press, 1949], p. 129), or the exertion of resisting temptation (e.g., Kitchin, *Var. Ed.*, II, 411). Modern critics are divided. Among Guyon's gentler critics, Sirluck, p. 91, argues that the faint is a result of "purely physical causes"; Gang, p. 16, contends that a "very great effort of renunciation" has weakened Guyon; Robert Hoopes, " 'God Guide Thee, Guyon': Nature and Grace Reconciled in *The Faerie Queene*, Book II," *Review of English Studies*, 5 (1954), 20, concludes that the faint illustrates "the limits of human nature" and the need for grace; Kermode, "The Cave of Mammon," p. 168, claims that Guyon's faint is related to Christ's weakness after his initiation when angels came to minister unto Him; and Alpers, p. 274, maintains that the faint "is the culminating expression of our awareness that there *are* limits to human strength" and "is the result of the inherent strains of knowing an evil." Among Guyon's sterner critics, Berger, p. 19, maintains that the faint is related to "an unprofitable curiosity," a desire "to feed on his virtues," and the incompleteness of his own virtue; A. C. Hamilton, *The Structure of Allegory in "The Faerie Queene"* (Oxford: The Clarendon Press, 1961), p. 101, argues that the faint is a "spiritual death," a "fall . . . given in moral rather than spiritual terms"; the prostrate Guyon is an "emblem of man's body dominated by the irascible and concupiscent affections"; Evans, p. 91, asserts that the faint is part of the fall of the hero through driving his virtue so hard that he cannot resist Pyrochles and Cymochles: "His fall is due to Pride: he has failed to realize the limitations of human strength and . . . is overconfident in his own virtues and praiseworthy deeds, so

hero is by no means inconsistent with his ostensible *imitatio Christi*; it is rather the inevitable culmination of the Adamic weakness he has manifested throughout the ordeal. Accordingly, the image of Guyon prostrate on the earth is an image of man's bondage to the flesh, to the old Adam within who is "of the earth, earthly" (I Corinthians 15:47). It would be false, however, to see in this image a full *imitatio Adamis*; if Guyon's resistance is not the same thing as Christ's, neither is his fall the same thing as Adam's. Any attempt to force Guyon's experience into a neat analogue with either Adam's fall or Christ's triumph should be dispelled by the ambiguous portrayal of him at the beginning of the canto: he has fallen to the earth, and that suggests his connection to Adam; but he is also ministered to by angels, and that of course suggests Christ's triumph. Although structurally the Cave of Mammon is clearly a counterpart to Red Crosse's fall in Orgoglio's Hell, its moral counterpart in Book I is to be found more in Arthur's fall in his battle with Orgoglio and in Red Crosse's two falls in his battle with the dragon. What Guyon's faint suggests is that Christ's resistance in the wilderness can be approximated by man without grace, but only His resistance and not the full debelling of the devil; and even the virtue of Christlike resistance seems inextricable from man's Adamic inheritance, so that (to quote Hooker's observation

that he squanders his virtue"; Carl Robinson Sonn, "Sir Guyon in the Cave of Mammon," *Studies in English Literature*, 1 (1961), 26-28, suggests that the slumbering Guyon is an image of "spiritual impotence," "the spiritual death of self-reliance": Guyon can reject submission to the world but he "cannot choose God"; and finally, Miller, "Phaedria, Mammon, and Sir Guyon's Education by Error," pp. 41-42, claims that the Cave is "a projection of [Guyon's] psychic state" and his faint a sign of failure since in the Cave he has demonstrated the vice of deficiency, boorish insensibility (whereas in the Phaedria episode he demonstrates the vice of excess, licentiousness): "Guyon faints not only because he has ignored his bodily needs, but also because he has assumed a psychological stance which abhors the body and any pleasures which may be derived from it"; "Guyon's firm resistance to Mammon's offers is the very thing for which we must blame him."

again) "Our very virtues may be snares unto us." Ambiguous though this resistance is, a distinction between resistance of temptation and a full triumph over the demonic seems to underlie the repetition of the two triads in the Cave of Mammon episode. Outside the Cave all that is required of Guyon is an imitation of Christ's triumph in the wilderness. Within the Cave, however, Guyon is required not only to imitate that triumph but also the Harrowing of Hell. In his imitation of Christ in the wilderness, Guyon succeeds, at least as far as fallen nature relying on its own powers can succeed; in his imitation of Christ's Harrowing of Hell, he unequivocably fails. This contrast depends on the distinction between Christ's two missions. In the wilderness, Christ as the new Adam demonstrated Himself as the perfect man, without the assistance of His divinity; or as Satan will point out in *Paradise Regained* at the beginning of the pinnacle-temptation, Christ has shown His powers as "th'utmost of mere man" (IV.535). But in the Harrowing of Hell, Christ performed a supernatural mission, one that could be accomplished only by the sufficient sacrifice of the *deus homo* on the cross—namely the defeat, not merely the resistance, of Satan and the rescue of Adam and his descendants from Hell. Accordingly, Guyon as *homo* can, though imperfectly, imitate Christ's resistance of evil in the wilderness through the powers of his reason; but without the Palmer, without the direct assistance of grace, Guyon cannot as *homo* imitate the total triumph of the *deus homo* over the original taint of the flesh and over the devil. The House of Alma functions as a gloss to Guyon's condition. Although it embodies perfect temperance, its powers are limited to resistance; and its own virtue must be supplemented by grace, which requires that Arthur, imitating Christ, defeat Maleger, "our old man," the inherited corruption of the flesh.[9] So, too, the angel, the Palmer, and

[9] On Maleger, I follow the suggestion originally made by A.S.P. Woodhouse, "Nature and Grace in *The Faerie Queene*," in *Elizabethan Poetry*, ed. Paul J. Alpers (New York: Oxford Univ. Press, 1967), pp. 365-366 [originally published in *ELH*, 16 (1949), 194-

Arthur must come to the rescue of the prostrate Guyon; and just as Arthur must defeat Maleger at the House of Alma, so must he defeat Pyrochles and Cymochles in their attack on Guyon.

The conflation in the Cave of the Temptation in the

228], and elaborated upon by Hamilton, *Structure of Allegory*, pp. 102-104. The "baptism" of Maleger is not, however, Guyon's first baptism, or the House of Alma's, or Arthur's; rather, it represents the same need we witnessed in Red Crosse's battle with the dragon for the continuous operation of grace in the cleansing of the heart and the mortification of the old Adam. (But for an interpretation de-emphasizing the religious aspects of the episode, see Lewis H. Miller, Jr., "Arthur, Maleger, and History in the Allegorical Context," *University of Toronto Quarterly*, 35 [1966], 167-187.) From the beginning of his quest, it seems to me, Guyon is a baptized Christian knight: he speaks of the cross on Red Crosse's shield as "The sacred badge of my Redeemers death" (i.27); and the Palmer, congratulating Red Crosse on becoming "a Saint with Saints," remarks that he and Guyon "Must now begin, like race to runne" (i.32). (A.D.S. Fowler argues, however, in "The Image of Mortality," *Huntington Library Quarterly*, 24 [1961], 91-110, that the Mortdant-Amavia-Ruddymane episode represents Guyon's baptism.) Like Red Crosse, Guyon, though a baptized Christian, must in the course of his quest learn what it means to be a Christian, which means that he must confront the Fall and the full extent of its impress on his own nature and image. Both knights act as though baptism had restored them to original innocence, and therefore they become blind to their continuous need for the intervention of grace. Guyon's denial of his Adamic inheritance ironically binds him all the closer to Adam and limits his imitation of Christ, which becomes fully possible only after he has experienced in his faint the limits the Fall has imposed on him. The knowledge of his own wickedness and evil is for Guyon, as for Red Crosse, the necessary preliminary to any full victory over evil; and only after Guyon has this knowledge can he do anything a representative of pagan or classical temperance could not do. Before his faint, Guyon's victories have been at best tentative: he defeats Furor, only to unbind him; his confrontation with Cymochles leads nowhere; he leaves Phaedria where he found her, as he does Mammon. His quest is a learning experience, but not only in his virtue but also in his own nature; and the lesson Guyon has been taught is his own continuous need for grace. Not until that lesson is learned is Guyon prepared to fulfill his quest as an instrument of grace.

Wilderness with the Harrowing of Hell is thus an outgrowth of the central distinction drawn in Book II: classical or purely human temperance can restrain the flesh, it can hold the devil at bay, though precariously; but only through Christ can man be redeemed from the flesh, and only through the intervention of Christ's grace can the devil, within and without, be defeated. The wilderness provides the locus for the ultimate reaches of classical or natural ethics; the Harrowing of Hell provides the locus for the uniquely Christian triumph over the flesh and the devil. Events in the Bower of Bliss episode, which parallels and contrasts with the Cave of Mammon, point emphatically to this distinction and to the emergence of Guyon as *microchristus*; for in the final canto Guyon completes a total *imitatio Christi*, one including *both* His triumph in the wilderness and His triumph in Hell.[10] As in the Cave of Mammon, Red Crosse's defeat of the dragon, and Christ's own Harrowing of Hell, the Bower of Bliss episode takes place in the space of three days: "Two dayes now in that sea he sayled has / . . . when appeared the third *Morrow* bright" (xii.2). Moreover, just as Guyon in the Cave, like Christ in the wilderness, resisted "all sin" in the inclusive triad of vices, so Guyon sailing through the sea of perils resists "all sin" in the form of the seven deadly sins: the Gulf of Greediness (gluttony), the Rock of Reproach (lust), Phaedria and the Wandering Isles (sloth), the Quicksand of Unthriftihead and the Whirlpool of Decay (avarice), the violence of "wrathfull *Neptune*" (wrath), the Doleful Maid (envy), and the mermaids who "fondly striu'd / With th' *Heliconian* maids for maistery" and "were depriu'd / Of their proud beautie" (pride); that is, the Flesh (gluttony, lust, sloth), the World (avarice), and the Devil (wrath,

[10] Acrasia, unlike Red Crosse's dragon, is tied up but not destroyed; but this does not mean that Guyon's triumph is the less complete. In the Bower of Bliss Spenser is dealing with two matters: first, the defeat of the *membrum diaboli* in Eden, and secondly, the nature of Christian temperance, which requires not that the appetite be destroyed (for that would make good as well as evil impossible) but that it be restrained.

envy, pride).[11] Guyon, however, goes on to surpass his resistance of "all sin" in the Cave and in the sea of perils; and in the Bower of Bliss he liberates Eden from the excess that has mastered it, and like Christ in Hell defeats the devil or, more precisely, a *membrum diaboli.* In overthrowing Acrasia-Eve, Guyon overthrows the domination of *sensus* over *mens* that (according to Guyon's myth of the Fall and the Legend of Holiness' figure of the Woman-Serpent) occasioned the Fall, along with "pompous pride." Mortdant, the old man whose reason was defaced by intemperance, is restored to Verdant, the new man of the spirit regenerate in Christ. Paralleling Guyon's restoration of Mortdant is the restoration of Acrasia-Circe's brutes to their original form. Both events imitate Christ's rescue and restoration of Adam in Hell through the grace permitted by His sacrifice. Assisted

[11] The observation that the sea of perils contains the seven deadly sins is Robert C. Fox's, "Temperance and the Seven Deadly Sins in *The Faerie Queene*, Book II," *Review of English Studies*, 12 (1961), 2-5; but the observation that the sins are organized according to the Flesh, the World, and the Devil is my own. Whether one agrees or not—and apparently B. Nellish, "The Allegory of Guyon's Voyage," *ELH*, 30 (1963), 97-104, does not—that the seven deadly sins are so precisely marked in the sea of perils is not essential to my point: the numerous images of the sins in the sea, by their range and variety, are sufficient to suggest the concept "all sin." Robert M. Durling, "The Bower of Bliss and Armida's Palace," *Comparative Literature*, 6 (1954), 334-338, discovers the Flesh, the World, and the Devil in the Bower itself: "the three sinful dispositions [of I John 2:16] . . . can be applied to the different divisions of the Bower; the pride of life to the plain, the lust of the eyes to the fountain and its bathers, and the lust of the flesh to Acrasia's grove." The prospect of having the Bower episode duplicate the double temptation of the Cave of Mammon is tempting indeed, but Durling's evidence, as he seems to realize, is incomplete; and I have none to supply. (A recent article has done much to aid our understanding of the Bower of Bliss episode; in "Spenser's Wanton Maidens: Reader Psychology and the Bower of Bliss," *PMLA*, 88 [1973], 62-68, Arlene N. Okerlund employs a concept of a rhetoric of temptation, similar to that I have used in my own discussion of Spenser, to demonstrate that "the psychological impact of the poetry compels a self-recognition and admission of our own intemperate desires" [p. 64].)

by the Palmer, Guyon imitates both of Christ's triumphs, in
the wilderness and in Hell, becoming through grace Guyon
microchristus.

Books I and II provide the preliminary to all Christian
triumph and all Christian virtues, the restoration of the
garden within.[12] They are designed as companion-pieces
demonstrating the triumph over the Woman and the Serpent
that is, as in Milton, the indispensable preliminary for the
perfection of all other virtues. Perceiving the role of Christ's
Temptation in the Wilderness and His Harrowing of Hell in
both books brings them slightly closer to each other than
we are accustomed to see them. As the Palmer announces
in his speech to Red Crosse, in the first canto, the goal of both
heroes, beginning as Christian novitiates, is sainthood:

> . . . enrolled is your glorious name
> In heauenly Registers aboue the Sunne,
> Where you a Saint with Saints your seat haue wonne:
> But wretched we, where ye haue left your marke,
> But now anew begin, like race to runne.
>
> (i.32)

The conception of sainthood in both books is the same; it is
the conception set forth in the rites of baptism: the *miles
Christi,* assisted by divine grace, sets out to imitate Christ's
triumph over the Flesh, the World, and the Devil, and to
imitate also His crucifixion of the "corrupt affections" inherited from the Fall; and finally to defeat the devil. As we
have seen time and again, the sins causing the Fall and the
sinful affections inherited from the Fall are two-fold: intemperance of the flesh and pride. It should now be clear
that the figure for original sin, the Woman-Serpent Errour,
with which Book I opened is the controlling image uniting
these two books. In accordance with the baptismal vow, the

---

[12] The fullest comparison of the two books is that of A. C. Hamilton, " 'Like Race to Runne': The Parallel Structure of *The Faerie
Queene,* Books I and II," *PMLA,* 73 (1958), 327-334.

task of the knight of each book is to restore Eden through the mastery of the two sinful affections that continue to usurp the garden of man's mind: the quest of Red Crosse is to master the pride of the Serpent, the quest of Guyon to master the intemperance of the Woman, which lost us Eden; and the chief weapon against the first is faith, against the second reason.[13]

In both books, the hero must resist the Flesh, the World, and the Devil; and this resistance culminates in a Harrowing of Hell that completes the pattern of their sainthood. It is the hero's relationship to the Harrowing of Hell that chiefly marks his success as *microchristus*. The locus of each hero's initial failure to harrow Hell is symbolic of the specific cause and effect of the Fall he must overcome: the castle of Orgoglio, pride; the Cave of Mammon, intemperance. In canto seven of Book I, Red Crosse, having succumbed to the Flesh, the World, and the Devil, is cast into the devil's, Orgoglio's, dungeon: the *imitatio Christi* of his sainthood is replaced by the *imitatio Adamis* of his fall. In canto seven of Book II, Guyon also fails, but with a difference. Unlike Red Crosse, Guyon does not imitate Adam's fall; for he possesses sufficient temperance to resist the infernal triad to which Red Crosse succumbs. But if one fails in his Harrowing of Hell while the other falls, both attain sainthood through a triumphant Harrowing of Hell. In his three-day battle in the garden, Red Crosse through faith overcomes the dragon (a symbol, like Orgoglio, of the violent, wrathful, and rebellious pride of the Devil), rescues Eden from its domination by pride, and becomes Una's "faithfull knight." And Guyon through reason assisted by grace overcomes Acrasia, the Woman and *membrum diaboli* who also has usurped Eden, rescues the garden from its domination by intemperance, restores Adam's sons from fallen brute to their original form, and thereby completes the *imitatio Christi* he imper-

---

[13] The point that "the emphasis in Book I is on faith, and in Book II, on reason" is well made by Maurice Evans, "The Fall of Guyon," p. 96.

fectly fulfilled in the Cave of Mammon. Errour is defeated; the promises of the Christian Knight's baptismal vows are kept. The circle of Spenser's scheme of Christian redemption is closed, the palmer's prayer answered, as Guyon joins Red Crosse as *microchristus*, "a Saint with Saints."

II. JOHN MILTON

3. *Paradise Lost*:
The Infernal Triad in Hell and Eden

All of Milton's longer works—*Comus, Paradise Lost, Paradise Regained*, and *Samson Agonistes*—focus on temptation; and with the possible exception of *Comus*, all of them make the Flesh, the World, and the Devil the basis of temptation. The first temptation in *Paradise Lost*, however, is surprisingly not in Eden but in Hell. The first three angels advising the infernal council, Moloch, Belial, and Mammon, represent respectively the Devil, the Flesh, and the World.[1] Pandaemonium thereby provides a comic parody of Adam's temptation in Eden and Christ's in the wilderness. The fallen angels are presented in the act of self-temptation; and as a result, the episode serves, like the later temptation in Eden and also like Satan's account of his fall later in Book II, to justify God's differing ways toward Satan and man according to His own account in Book III: "The first sort *by thir own suggestion* fell, / Self-tempted, self-deprav'd: Man falls deceiv'd / By th' other first: Man therefore shall find grace,

[1] Robert C. Fox attempts to relate the fallen angels to specific sins. In "Satan's Triad of Vices," *Texas Studies in Language and Literature*, 2 (1960), 261-280, he argues that "The vices of pride, envy, and wrath form an infernal trinity: collectively, they constitute the essence of Satan's character; individually, they are the respective vices of Satan, Beelzebub, and Moloc" (p. 276). In "The Character of Moloc in *Paradise Lost*," *Die neueren Sprachen*, 11 (1962), 389-395, Fox argues that Moloch sins against the Aristotelian virtue of courage or fortitude "by the excess of rashness or foolhardiness; Belial, by the defect of cowardice" (p. 389); and in "The Character of Mammon in *Paradise Lost*," *Review of English Studies*, n.s., 13 (1962), 30-39, he concludes that "Mammon is primarily a symbol of the vice commonly termed avarice or covetousness" (p. 30), though Mammon goes beyond the limits of that vice "to embrace the more comprehensive vice of injustice" (p. 39).

/ Th' other none" (129-132; my italics).[2] The use of the infernal triad in Hell (and also in Eden) is thus at the very heart of Milton's purpose in writing his epic, "to justify the ways of God to man."

The ancestry of Pandaemonium is in the worldly houses of "all sin" in Spenser and his medieval predecessors, also in the neo-Spenserians.[3] As the house of "all demons," Pandaemonium, in accordance with its allegorical ancestry, contains "all sin" in the form of the Flesh, the World, and the Devil. The first agent in the temptation of the fallen angels is Moloch, who embodies the sin of the Devil, *superbia vitae*, or the vainglorious and violent presumption to the godhead. The connection between this sin and the Devil was made, as we have seen, by Spenser in the Orgoglio and dragon episodes in the Legend of Holiness. The same connection is made by Milton at the beginning of *Paradise Lost*, where it is said that the devil's "Pride" led him to desire to "equal the most High" through "impious War . . . and Battle proud" (i.36-43); and it is made again, in *Paradise Regained*, when

[2] Citations from Milton's poetry are to *Complete Poems and Major Prose*, ed. Merritt Y. Hughes (New York: Odyssey, 1957).

[3] The closest analogues are probably Spenser's House of Pride, Giles Fletcher's palace of vainglory in "Christ's Victory on Earth," and Phineas Fletcher's Roman palace of Aequivocus in *Apollyonists*, II-IV. The palaces of the Fletcher brothers are both houses of the World including the Flesh, the World, and the Devil, and both are indebted to Spenser's House of Pride. The opening lines of Book II of *Paradise Lost* in fact specifically allude, as Merritt Hughes notes, to Lucifera's throne in the House of Pride: "High aboue all a cloth of State was spred, / And a rich throne, as bright as sunny day" (iv.8); but it should also be noted that this passage is imitated by Giles Fletcher as well: "High over all, *Panglories* blazing throne' (st. 56). Nonetheless, it is Phineas Fletcher's house of the World that seems closest of all to Milton's in that it portrays a council considering Rome's strategy against Protestantism and portrays Rome as Hell, the bishops as fallen angels plotting against Eden-England. The fact that both Spenser's and Phineas Fletcher's worldly houses are associated with Rome gives more credence to the suggestion of R. W. Smith, "The Source of Milton's Pandaemonium," *Modern Philology*, 29 (1931), 187-198, that Pandaemonium is based on St. Peter's.

Satan upon Christ's refusal of the offer of glory and power "stood struck / With guilt of his own sin, for he himself / Insatiable of glory had lost all" (III.146-148). Accordingly, Moloch, whose name in Hebrew appropriately means "king" and who is described as "Scepter'd king" (43), proposes the devil's original means, violence, for attaining the divine kingship: "His trust was with th' Eternal to be deem'd / Equal in strength" (46-47); and his whole proposal revolves around the use of "Satanic strength" (*PR* I.161) as a means to the godhead.

Belial, whose name in Hebrew means "profligacy," represents the Flesh. When he makes his first appearance in the poem, he is characterized principally in terms of lust and perverted sexuality:

> *Belial* came last, than whom a Spirit more lewd
> Fell not from Heaven, or more gross to love
> Vice for itself . . . .
> . . . .
> In Courts and Palaces he also Reigns
> And in luxurious Cities, where the noise
> Of riot ascends above thir loftiest Towers,
> And injury and outrage: And when Night
> Darkens the Streets, then wander forth the Sons
> Of *Belial*, flown with insolence and wine.
> Witness the Streets of *Sodom*, and that night
> In *Gibeah*, when the hospitable door
> Expos'd a Matron to avoid worse rape.
>
> (I.490-505)

He is similarly portrayed in *Paradise Regained* as "the dissolutest Spirit that fell, / The sensuallest, and after *Asmodai* / The fleshliest Incubus" (II.150-152). In Pandaemonium, as in the infernal council of *Paradise Regained*, Belial's advice is based on his susceptibility to the Flesh. As a lover of fleshly pleasure, Belial is appropriately himself appealing to the senses both in his appearance ("A fairer person lost not Heav'n" [110]) and in the power of his voice to "pleas[e]

101

the ear" (117). Moreover, Belial, like the Sirens,[4] employs the alluring power of his words and beautiful voice to give the appearance of reason while subverting reason through sensuousness and counseling "ignoble ease, and peaceful sloth" (227). In an ironic twist of the despair Protestants associated with the Flesh-temptation, Belial urges the fallen angels to abandon their mission and to despair of conquering heaven; and he extends the possibility that, through the adaptability of the senses, Hell will become more pleasant. Motivated as he is by pleasure, Belial is, more than Moloch or Mammon, terrified of pain. Accordingly, he draws vivid images of the greater pain that might result from renewed activity and revolt:

> Each on his rock transfixt, the sport and prey
> Of racking whirlwinds, or for ever sunk
> Under yon boiling Ocean, wrapt in Chains;
> There to converse with everlasting groans,
> Unrespited, unpitied, unrepriev'd,
> Ages of hopeless end; this could be worse.
>
> (181-186)

Belial's fair appearance, his Siren-like ability to subvert reason, his sloth, his sensuality, and his despair—all characterize him in terms of the Flesh.

Mammon, as the representative of the World, completes the triad of vices to which the infernal council is tempted. His name means "riches," and excessive desire for riches characterizes him in the epic list of Book I; but his preoccupation with gold is, as with Spenser's Mammon, symptomatic of his overall tendency to worship the things of the World. Not

---

[4] On the traditional portrayal of the Sirens' seduction of man from the heroic quest to idleness through mellifluous eloquence, see John M. Steadman, "Dalila, the Ulysses Myth, and Renaissance Allegorical Tradition," *Modern Language Review*, 58 (1962), 560-565. Steadman has a fine discussion of rhetoric in Hell in *Milton's Epic Characters: Image and Idol* (Chapel Hill, N.C.: Univ. of North Carolina Press, 1968), pp. 241-262.

simply greed but an overriding concern for the worldly and the material underlies his denial of heaven's value for the fallen angels and his proposal to "seek / Our own good from ourselves, and from our own / Live to ourselves" (252-254). Mammon's proposal to imitate heaven in Hell suggests not so much an interest in the heavenly as an indifference to it; for like Lucifera and Panglorie, what Mammon perceives as heavenly is purely material and worldly. Heaven's light is easily imitated for Mammon, whose eyes even in heaven were "downward bent" (I.681), since for him its light is merely the luster of gold:

> As he [God] our darkness, cannot we his Light
> Imitate when we please? This Desert soil
> Wants not her hidden lustre, Gems and Gold;
> Nor want we skill or art, from whence to raise
> Magnificence; and what can Heav'n show more?
>
> (269-273)

For Milton's Mammon, as for Spenser's Lucifera and Mammon, the light of God and the light of gold are one and the same.

Moloch, Belial, and Mammon are thus not just the "human" types they are usually considered to be; they are also allegorical types: Moloch, encouraging the council to repeat the devil's violent and vainglorious presumption to the godhead; Belial, encouraging the council to a slothful acceptance of the pleasures Hell can offer the senses; and Mammon, encouraging the council through riches to find heaven in Hell—together these three image forth the concept of "all sin," the three lures of the Devil, the Flesh, and the World, or vainglory, fleshly pleasure, and avarice. Readers who, along with Addison and Johnson,[5] find the

---

[5] Addison finds Sin and Death "a very beautiful and well-invented allegory" but thinks that "persons of such a chimerical existence are [not] proper actors in an epic poem" (No. 273; in *The Spectator*, ed. Alexander Chalmers [New York: Appleton, 1864], III, 362-363); but in No. 309 he praises Milton's portrayal of Moloch, Belial, and

John Milton

presence of allegory in *Paradise Lost* a blemish may not find
this discovery a happy one. Nonetheless, the allegorical
triad is by no means out of place in this the most openly
allegorical book of the poem—a book in which virtually
every event and figure has an allegorical dimension of one
sort or another, from the opening triad in the council to
Satan's voyage in which he encounters Sin and Death and
Chaos and Old Night.[6] All of these allegorical episodes and

Mammon. Johnson, finding a conflict between the "real and sensible"
and the "only figurative," is more severe: "This unskilful allegory
appears to me one of the greatest faults of the poem" ("Milton," in
Lives of the Poets, ed. Arthur Waugh [London: Oxford Univ. Press,
1952], I, 129).

[6] The infernal triad is only one of the allegorical triads of Book II.
Satan, Sin, and Death form, as B. Rajan, *"Paradise Lost" and the
Seventeenth Century Reader* (London: Chatto and Windus, 1947),
p. 50, suggests, "a kind of infernal Trinity in contrast with its heavenly counterpart." The epic games are also, I believe, organized triadi-
cally, according to the three traditional *vitae* of classical ethics. The
section as a whole falls into four parts: (1) the epic games themselves, in which the participants are compared to armies and their
"vast *Typhoean* rage" (539) to Hercules'—lines 523-546; (2) the
poets, whose "Song charms the Sense" (556)—lines 546-556; (3)
the philosophers "on a Hill retir'd" (557)—lines 555-569; (4) the
explorers—lines 570-628. The first and last parts are devoted to war-
riors, heroes, and explorers, or the active life; the second, to the
voluptuous life; the third, to the contemplative life. The emphasis on
the active life in Hell serves to relate events within Hell to Satan's
false-epic voyage out of it. It is also consistent with Milton's portrayal of the fallen angels as exemplars of the false heroic (in this
respect, it should be noted that Milton will again relate the false
heroic to rage, in his famous account of it in IX.13-19). There is,
incidentally, the possibility here, as there is in the Parthia-Rome-
Athens sequence, that the infernal triad co-operates with the three-
vitae formula, with the active life according with the Devil, the
voluptuous life with the Flesh, the contemplative life with the World
(*avaritia scientiae*). Be that as it may, there is clearly much more
allegory in Book II—indeed, I think, in all of *Paradise Lost*—than
we are accustomed to suppose. Whether this means that Book II is an
earlier book than the rest, or whether it means that Milton never
departed as much as we tend to believe from the allegorical habit of

characters are insular; they are not integral to a continuous allegorical framework. It is in character with Milton's use of allegorical schemata and overtones in *Paradise Lost* that, after a portrayal of figures against the backdrop of the Flesh, the World, and the Devil, these overtones are apparently dropped with the appearance of Beelzebub. This is not to say that the triadic allegorical episode is an intrusion; rather it points to Milton as a poet of eclectic and continuously shifting poetic modes, ranging from the personifications of naive allegory to episodes seemingly untouched by any allegorical overtones whatsoever. Milton introduces the infernal triad in Pandaemonium largely, one suspects, not as part of a systematic framework but as a means of calling attention to a point of major thematic and structural importance for the work: through the association of Moloch, Belial, and Mammon with the Devil, the Flesh, and the World, Milton creates a mock counterpart to the central temptation of the work, in Eden, and also a mock counterpart to the second Adam's Temptation in the Wilderness, but with the devils as their own tempters; in so doing, Milton portrays in Pandaemonium the never-ending self-temptation of the Satanic mind, which is precisely what damns it, excluding it from any possible extension of mercy. He also universalizes the significance of Hell and, as with allusions to future events like Exodus and the tower of Babel, establishes Hell as the locus and archetype of "all sin" as it will manifest itself throughout history. The triad points specifically to Eden and the importation of "all sin" into human experience. Beelzebub speaks, and the proposals of Moloch, Belial, and Mammon are rejected for Satan's own plan to subvert Eden. Nonetheless, while the specific proposals are rejected, the sins they embody are not; for they reappear in Satan's execution of his scheme in Book IX.

---

thinking manifested in the Trinity MS, is difficult to say for certain (indeed both may be true)—but I myself incline, as my analysis of the schematic structure of *Paradise Lost*, IX, *Paradise Regained*, and *Samson Agonistes* suggests, to the latter position.

The Pandaemonium episode is the first of several instances I will adduce in the course of this study of Milton's tendency —a not surprising one in light of his indebtedness to Spenserian and neo-Spenserian allegory—to schematize his materials. In contrast to Spenser, Milton's allegorical over- tones are less insistent, detailed, and pervasive; and if one speaks of allegory in Milton, one speaks of not so much of a detailed structuring and organizing of precisely symbolic images as of a conceptual structuring of passages or, in *Samson Agonistes* and *Paradise Regained*, of entire works. No such overarching schematic structure characterizes *Paradise Lost* as it does the two companion poems of the 1671 volume, but one must still be constantly alert to local use of schemata and patterns. One of those local uses of a scheme, indeed the most critical one in the poem, occurs in Milton's use of the infernal triad to provide an interpretive framework for his portrayal of the Fall.

At the heart of the meaning and structure of *Paradise Lost* is, of course, Milton's announced purpose of justifying "the ways of God to men." As Milton clearly establishes in the opening lines of the poem, those ways are, in this poem as well as *Paradise Regained* and *Samson Agonistes*, dual: first, the justice underlying the "loss of *Eden*"; second, the mercy permitting "one greater Man / [to] Restore us, and regain the blissful Seat" (I.4-5). The portrayal of the Fall, responding as it had to to these dual ways, required of Milton that he make two distinctions crucial to his justifying God's ways in *Paradise Lost*: the first distinction is between Satan's primary sin, *superbia vitae*, and man's, *concupiscentia carnis*; the second, between the self-temptation of Satan and the temptation by suggestion of man. The infernal triad is re- introduced in Eden as a means of making these distinctions; it functions, along with the schematic construction of speeches, as a clarifying device controlling our interpretation of the Fall and ideally preventing us from a response to the Fall that would violate Milton's justifying of God's ways, either by finding God's justice overjust or unjust or by finding His mercy unconvincing.

If we are to recognize the role of the infernal triad in Milton's portrayal of the Fall,[7] we must recognize first that Milton has divided the temptation of Eve into two parts: the first part consists of Satan's two speeches wherein he attempts to persuade Eve to see the tree; the second consists of his speech before the tree. The dominant appeal in Satan's opening address to Eve (lines 532-548) is to his own sin of *vanagloria* or *superbia vitae*:

> Thee ["sovran Mistress"] all things living gaze on, all
>   things thine
> By gift, and thy Celestial Beauty adore
> With ravishment beheld, there best beheld
> Where universally admir'd: but here
> In this enclosure wild, these Beasts among,
> Beholders rude, and shallow to discern
> Half what in thee is fair, one man except,
> Who sees thee? (and what is one?) who shouldst be seen
> A Goddess among Gods, ador'd and serv'd
> By Angels numberless, thy daily Train.
>
> (539-548)

The devil is clearly attempting to provoke Eve to precisely the same "sense of injur'd merit" (I.98) that led to his own vainglorious desire to be a god attended "By Angels numberless." The appeal to the vainglory of the Devil also frames Satan's next speech (lines 568-612): it opens with an appeal to the "Empress of this fair World, resplendent *Eve*" (568), and it concludes on the same note. Within this framework of an appeal to diabolic vainglory, Satan recounts, and tempts Eve to repeat, his own avowed experience with the tree. This narration falls into two parts. The first and larger part (lines

---

[7] J. M. Evans, *"Paradise Lost" and the Genesis Tradition* (Oxford: The Clarendon Press, 1968), pp. 279-280, briefly considers and then briefly dismisses the possible role of the three-temptations formula.

571-597) involves the appeal of the tree to appetite and the intemperance of the Flesh:

> I was at first as other Beasts that graze
> The trodden Herb, of abject thoughts and low,
> As was my good, nor aught but food discern'd
> Or Sex, and apprehended nothing high:
> Till on a day roving the field, I chanc'd
> A goodly Tree far distant to behold
> Loaden with fruit of *fairest colors* mixt,
> Ruddy and Gold: I nearer drew *to gaze*;
> When from the boughs a *savory odor* blown,
> Grateful to appetite, more pleas'd my sense
> Than *smell* of sweetest Fennel, or the Teats
> Of Ewe or Goat dropping with Milk at Ev'n,
> Unsuckt of Lamb or Kid, that tend thir play.
> To satisfy the sharp desire I had
> Of *tasting* those fair Apples, I resolv'd
> Not to defer; *hunger and thirst* at once,
> Powerful persuaders, quick'n'd at the *scent*
> Of that alluring fruit . . .
>
> (571-588; my italics)

Three of the five senses are mentioned, and the heightening of the senses parallels Satan's alleged sense of rising in the hierarchy from abject beast to a beast envied by other beasts (591-593). Vainglory and the desires of the Flesh are intertwined, as, in the next stage of the speech, are vainglory and the avarice for knowledge:

> Sated at length, ere long I might perceive
> Strange alteration in me, to degree
> Of Reason in my inward Powers, and Speech
> Wanted not long, though to this shape retain'd.
> Thenceforth to Speculations high or deep
> I turn'd my thoughts, and with capacious mind
> Consider'd all things visible in Heav'n,
> Or Earth, or Middle, all things fair and good.
>
> (598-605)

The appeal of Eve's avarice for knowledge is a Faustian parody of the contemplative life and of the proper function of
right reason, for the object of Satan's capacity to see "all
things fair and good" through development of his "inward
Powers" becomes not God but Eve, as Satan, with brilliantly
insidious graciousness, subtly modulates into the dominant
key of his appeal, vainglory:

> But all that fair and good in thy Divine
> Semblance, and in thy Beauty's heav'nly Ray
> United I beheld; no Fair to thine
> Equivalent or second, which compell'd
> Mee thus, though importune perhaps to come
> And gaze, and worship thee of right declar'd
> Sovran of Creatures, universal Dame.
>
> (606-612)

The first stage of Satan's temptation is, therefore, based on a
distinctly defined appeal to the three vices of vainglory, intemperance, and avarice, with the dominant thrust of the
temptation being to his own sin, vainglorious pride. The
vainglory of the Devil is the subject of the prefatory speech;
it opens and closes the second, and is interlinked with appeals
to the intemperance of the Flesh and the avarice of the
World.

In the second stage of the temptation, Satan's speech before the tree, the appeals to vainglory and avarice are re-
tained, but they are subordinated to and intertwined with a
new emphasis, the temptation of the Flesh as the Protestants
understood it, a temptation to disbelief and doubt:

> And then there is credulity. Because when they replied
> to him that there was a threat of death, Ho! that will not
> be so.[8]

> In Adam the devil first [i.e., in the temptation to the
> " 'concupiscence of the flesh' "] brought him to a conceit
> that God envied his good, and of purpose kept him hood-

[8] Calvin, Sermon XLIX, in *Sermons sur l'harmonie évangélique*, in
Corpus Reformatorum, 46 (Brunvigae: Schwetschke, 1891), col. 610.

winked lest he should see his good, as falconers put hoods over hawks' eyes, to make them more quiet and ruly.[9]

As he [Satan] overcame the first *Adam* with unbelief of the threatening, Gen. 3.3., so doth he endeavour to overcome the second *Adam* with unbelief of the promise.[10]

Satan's speech before the tree is accordingly designed to allay Eve's fears regarding the prohibition and the penalty (647; 659-663); it is an attempt to lead Eve to a distrust of God and to "unbelief of the threatning." In the opening apostrophe to the tree ("O Sacred, Wise, and Wisdom-giving Plant, / Mother of Science . . ." [679-680]), Satan attempts to persuade Eve to distrust the true wisdom of obedience and to trust instead the false wisdom, "Science," of disobedience, to distrust God, who is wisdom-keeping, and trust instead the tree, which is "Wisdom-giving." The speech proceeds to provide Eve with various reasons for distrusting God and trusting the tree and the serpent and for "unbelief of the threatning": "Queen of this Universe, do not believe / Those rigid threats of Death; ye shall not Die" (684-685), for the serpent himself has not died (686-693); God cannot punish Eve and be just, and "Not just, not God; not fear'd then, nor obey'd" (693-702); God forbade eating of the fruit "to keep ye low and ignorant," to keep Eve's eyes dim and prevent her from being "as Gods" (703-709); death would be for Eve as for the serpent not real but metaphoric, a dying to a lesser state (710-715); the gods are not first movers or sole

[9] Lancelot Andrewes, Sermon II, in "Seven Sermons upon the Temptation of Christ in the Wilderness," *Ninety-Six Sermons* (Oxford, 1841-43), pp. 496-497.

[10] Christopher Blackwood, *Expositions and Sermons upon the Ten First Chapters of . . . Matthew* (London, 1659 [1658]), p. 94. Quoted by Barbara Lewalski, *Milton's Brief Epic* (Providence, R.I.: Brown Univ. Press, 1966), p. 178. For additional references see Elizabeth Marie Pope, *"Paradise Regained": The Tradition and the Poem* (Baltimore, Md.: The Johns Hopkins Press, 1947), pp. 55-60, and Lewalski, p. 396 (note 37).

producers, the godhead is therefore not inherently theirs (716-725); the offense is no offense, it does not hurt God nor is it "against his will if all be his" (725-728); and finally Satan returns to the suggestion that God may envy Eve's good, and that envy invalidates his celestial claims (729-730)—"these, these and many more / Causes import your need of this fair Fruit. / Goddess humane, reach then, and freely taste" (730-732). The central thrust of Satan's final speech, then, is based on the Protestant interpretation of the Flesh-temptation. Brilliant advocate that he is, the tree's attorney, in accordance with the best precepts of classical orators "renown'd / In *Athens* or free *Rome*" (670-671), has not only defended the merits of his client but also undermined the trustworthiness of his opponent.

It is no doubt true that the Fall as Milton portrays it at least to some extent involves man's replacing his proper *imitatio dei* with an *imitatio diaboli*, or as one Elizabethan homily puts it, "in stede of the ymage of GOD, [man] was become nowe the ymage of the Deuyll."[11] Eve ironically comes to perceive and reject the true God as diabolic in His spite and envy only to embrace precisely that diabolic godhead in her relationship with Adam: in her presumption Eve enters a long list of false gods, tyrannical presumers to the godhead, *membra diaboli*, spiteful, envious, and capricious, whose ways cannot be justified and whose reign over the human mind now begins in Eden. All this is true; but it is also true that Milton consistently demonstrates the *difference* in kind and degree between Satan's fall and that of our parents. In order to justify God's differing ways towards Satan and Adam and Eve, Milton had to establish, as many Renaissance theologians had, the Augustinian idea that man sinned less than the devil:

It is more serious to sin of one's own accord without outside persuasion and to persuade another, through

---

[11] *The Second Tome of Homelyes* (1563), sig. zzz4. Quoted by C. A. Patrides, *Milton and the Christian Tradition* (Oxford: Clarendon, 1966), p. 113.

envy and wiles, to sin, than to be led by another to sin. Therefore, the justice of God is preserved in punishing each of these sins. . . . Yet because man had sinned less than the devil, man has the power to regain his salvation. . . .[12]

Such a distinction, between the tempter and the tempted, underlies Milton's portrayal of the Fall. Most readers of Book IX attempt diligently to distinguish Adam's sin from Eve's, and they are right to do so; nonetheless, the difference between them in the nature and degree of their sin is much less than the difference between them and Satan. Readers like Waldock, Peter, and Empson[13] who find Milton's portrayal of the Fall lenient—however mistaken they are in whitewashing the pair—seem to me in part correct; the portrayal *is* lenient, but not as a result of Milton's sentimental sympathies causing him to lose artistic and moral control, rather as a result of a need to distinguish between the sin of those who can find mercy and the sin of those who cannot. For this reason, it seems to me, Milton does not emphasize as much as one might expect the role of Satan's vainglory in his account of Eve's motivation for eating. Although pride obviously is involved in Eve's separation from Adam as well as her acceptance of Satan's offer, it is not Eve but Satan who, in the temptation, emphasizes vainglory. Pride leads

[12] Augustine, *On Free Choice of the Will* [*De libero arbitrio voluntatis*], trans. Anna S. Benjamin and L. S. Hackstaff (Indianapolis, Ind.: Bobbs-Merrill, 1964), p. 111. Gregory makes a similar distinction in *Moralia*, iv.3 (*P.L.*, 75:642), as does Aquinas in *S.T.*, II, i, Q.80, art.3: "The devil's sin was irremediable, not only because he sinned without another's suggestion, but also because he was not already prone to sin." The idea is also commonplace in Renaissance theology; see Patrides, pp. 119-120.

[13] A.J.A. Waldock, *"Paradise Lost" and Its Critics* (1947; rpt. Cambridge, Eng.: Cambridge Univ. Press, 1962), pp. 25-64; John Peter, *A Critique of "Paradise Lost"* (New York: Columbia Univ. Press, 1960), pp. 110-137; William Empson, *Milton's God*, rev. ed. (London: Chatto and Windus, 1965), pp. 147-210.

Eve to her fall but the immediate and primary motivation for her taking of the fruit is less the sin of the Devil than that of the Flesh—in both its meanings, intemperance and distrust.[14]

[14] Book XI reflects the distinction I am making: the prideful envy of Cain is the sin of the devil; the vice of the lazar house, however, is "ungovern'd appetite" (517), "Inductive mainly to the sin of *Eve*" (519); the vice of the men of the tents is Adam's lust and "effeminate slackness" (634). See Virginia R. Mollenkott, "The Cycle of Sins in *Paradise Lost*, Book XI," *Modern Language Quarterly*, 27 (1966), 33-37.

The role of intemperance in the Fall is stressed by Rajan, p. 70, who sees the Fall primarily in terms of "the subjection of reason to appetite"; "Milton," he argues, "does not hesitate to be unconventional in order to secure his effects. He goes out of his way to draw attention to Eve's gluttony." See also, *inter alia*, Denis Saurat, *Milton, Man and Thinker* (1944; rpt. Hamden, Conn.: Archon, 1964), pp. 125-129; Edwin Greenlaw, "'A Better Teacher than Aquinas,'" *Studies in Philology*, 14 (1917), 213; Dennis H. Burden, *The Logical Epic: A Study of the Argument of "Paradise Lost"* (Cambridge, Mass.: Harvard Univ. Press, 1967), pp. 124-149; Fredson Bowers, "Adam, Eve, and the Fall in *Paradise Lost*," *PMLA*, 84 (1969) 265.

The role of pride is stressed by C. S. Lewis, *A Preface to "Paradise Lost"* (London: Oxford Univ. Press, 1942), p. 125, who states baldly that "Eve fell through Pride." M. M. Mahood, *Poetry and Humanism* (New Haven, Conn.: Yale Univ. Press, 1950), p. 221, argues that Eve sins "by an upward pull" in that she "aspires to intellectual equality wtih the angels"; Peter, *Critique*, p. 127, finds two main inducements to Eve's surrender, one praiseworthy, "her wish to be an ideal companion," the other reprehensible, "her wish to put on the quality of a goddess"; John S. Diekhoff, *Milton's "Paradise Lost": A Commentary on the Argument* (New York: Columbia Univ. Press, 1946), p. 70, while acknowledging other elements in Eve's fall, lays primary emphasis on *hybris* since "the effective point of the temptation [is] the aspiration to the Godhead"; and James Holly Hanford, *A Milton Handbook*, 4th ed. (New York: Crofts, 1954), p. 213, finds Eve falling "through vanity and curiosity for new experience."

Among other suggestions for a primary sin underlying Eve's fall are "triviality of mind" (E.M.W. Tillyard, *Milton*, rev. ed. [New York: Macmillan, 1967], p. 220), self-love (Arnold Stein, *Answerable Style* [1953; rpt. Seattle, Wash.: Univ. of Washington Press, 1967], p. 97), credulity (David Daiches, *Milton* [1957; rpt. New York: Norton, 1966], p. 205), and curiosity (Waldock, p. 39—though

Accordingly, Eve's reaction to Satan's words takes the form of sensual intemperance:

> Fixt on the Fruit she *gaz'd*, which to behold
> Might tempt alone, and in her *ears* the sound
> Yet rung of his persuasive words, impregn'd
> With Reason, to her seeming, and with Truth;
> Meanwhile the hour of Noon drew on, and wak'd
> An eager appetite, rais'd by the *smell*
> So savory of the Fruit, which with desire,
> Inclinable now grown to *touch* or *taste*,
> Solicited her longing eye. . . .
>
> (735-743; my italics)

If one reads this passage carefully, one notes immediately the structural parallel-and-contrast Milton develops between Eve's reaction to the tree's appeal to the Flesh and the serpent's alleged reaction in lines 575-588; and the scheme linking the two passages, and also contrasting them, is that of the five senses: the serpent mentions only three senses, while Eve experiences all five, the more important addition being the appeal of the serpent's suggestions to the ear ("in her ears the sound / Yet run of his persuasive words"). The contrast between these two schematically analogous passages suggests the greater role of the senses and the Flesh in Eve's fall. It also reinforces, through its addition of "sound," the Augustinian contrast between Satan's fall and man's which implicitly underlay the temptation in Pandaemonium and

---

he feels that no one word can account for Eve's motivation). However, for E. L. Marilla, *The Central Problem of "Paradise Lost": The Fall of Man*, Essays and Studies on English Language and Literature (Cambridge, Mass.: Harvard Univ. Press, 1953), p. 11, "it is hardly necessary or profitable . . . to speculate on what particular character-weakness it was which, in the framework of Milton's presentation of her case, led her to commit this all-embracing sin"; and indeed for Stanley Fish, *Surprised by Sin: The Reader in "Paradise Lost"* (New York: St. Martin's, 1967), p. 259, the reader who searches for such a cause "succumbs to still another form of Milton's 'good temptation.' "

which was explicitly made by God in Book III and repeated by the Heavenly Chorus: "him [Man] through their malice fall'n, / Father of Mercy and Grace, thou didst not doom / So strictly, but much more to pity encline" (400-402).[15]

Through schematic parallels and contrasts, Milton continues to emphasize the greater veniality of Eve's sin versus Satan's in Eve's meditation before the tree, which is based, like Satan's speech upon which it is modelled almost point by point, on the Protestant interpretation of the temptation of the Flesh: the whole meditation expresses a trust in the serpent and the tree, and a distrust of God and His injunction. Arguing that the tree is good and that the prohibition is therefore against good, Eve concludes that "Such prohibitions bind not" (759); she reconsiders the threat but overcomes her fear as the serpent had earlier urged by looking on him. Yet there is an important difference between Eve and Satan: unlike the serpent, Eve gives little consideration to the devil's vainglorious desire to "be as Gods." This is not to say that the sin of the Devil is altogether absent from Eve's motivation here (his pride is perhaps suggested by Eve's description of the fruit as "this Fruit Divine" [776]); but the aspects of the fruit Eve herself specifically mentions are its appeal to the senses (it is "Fair to the Eye, inviting to the Taste" [777]) and its "virtue to make wise" (778), that is, its appeal to *concupiscentia carnis* and *avaritiae scientiae*. At the same time, therefore, that Milton is portraying Eve's fall as in part an *imitatio diaboli*, he is also making a distinction between her and the devil by clearly downgrading in Eve's motivation the importance of the devil's own *superbia vitae* and presumption to the godhead; and in this distinction is suggested the justifiability of future grace.

[15] A similar distinction underlies Adam's and Eve's eating of the forbidden fruit and the fallen angels' repeated eating of it in Hell:

> . . . so oft they fell
> Into the same illusion, not as Man
> Whom they triumph'd, once lapst.
>
> (x.570-572)

115

As in Eve's meditation, so in the description of her eating the fruit, the emphasis falls decidedly on the Flesh. The portrayal of her eating pointedly contrasts with the schematic structure of the serpent's second speech, wherein he recounted his own experience with the tree; indeed, the two are mirror opposites to each other. Whereas vainglory framed the serpent's speech, *concupiscentia carnis* frames Eve's reaction upon eating. The description of her eating begins, as it will close, with her gluttony: Eve "Intent now wholly on her taste, naught else / Regarded, such delight till then, as seem'd, / In Fruit she never tasted" (786-788). The two other sins are added almost parenthetically. *Avaritia scientiae* is inserted conditionally as a possible heightener of the pleasures of taste: "such delight till then, as seem'd / In Fruit she never tasted, whether true / Or fancied so, through expectation high / Of knowledge" (787-790). The devil's *superbia vitae* not only comes last in the sequence but is also deemphasized by the negative phrasing, "nor was God-head from her thought" (790). All three vices are present, then; but there is, as J. M. Evans has said, "little evidence of pride at this juncture";[16] for the list of sins proceeds with diminishing stress from the lust of the flesh to the avarice for knowledge and finally to the pride of life. Once the sequence of the three lures is completed, moreover, Milton, completing the contrast with the serpent's speech and reinforcing his insistence on the primary role of intemperance in Eve's fall, concludes the description as he began it: "Greedily she ingorg'd without restraint" (791).

To assert that "Eve fell through Pride"[17] is, therefore, to impose on Milton's portrayal of Eve's fall an emphasis he clearly wishes to avoid and to blur the crucial contrast between Eve and Satan that Milton has attempted to establish through schematic parallels and contrasts. The emphasis on pride and vainglory is Satan's not Eve's. Eve emphasizes

[16] *"Paradise Lost" and the Genesis Tradition*, p. 280.
[17] Lewis, p. 125.

pride and the possibility of her being a god only after she has eaten. And even at this point, although the narrator's preface to the fallen Eve's first speech—"Thus to herself she pleasingly began" (794)—suggests the tendance to narcissistic pride that characterized Eve at her birth near poolside, the speech itself, while it expresses Eve's expectation of rising in the hierarchy by growing "mature / In knowledge, as the Gods who all things know" (803-804), ultimately turns upon her relationship with Adam and what Adam will call "The Link of Nature" (914), the love-lust attraction that binds and blinds them. Eve thus views the fruit, with the power to make her through knowledge "more equal, and perhaps, / A thing not undesirable, sometime / Superior" (823-825), as an instrument to an end, "to add what wants / In Female Sex, the more to draw his Love" (821-822). Eve's new knowledge does more than satisfy her pride; pleasing her self more, she now thinks she can please Adam more. Eve has become, as it were, another Adam, and her new identity becomes the means whereby she can appeal to *his* own narcissistic pride and love. But Eve's fallacy is that the Adam she would have herself become is Adam at his worst, precisely the Adam Raphael had chastized as potentially presumptuous of knowledge and intemperate. A horrible romantic narcissism has begun to corrupt Edenic love, and its punishment is the loss of the full identity and individuation that made that better love possible. Becoming more, both become less, become in fact distorting mirrors of each other. "Flesh of Flesh, / Bone of my Bone thou art," Adam is soon to declare; and for all the undeniable and touching love behind that declaration, we sense at once the narcissism that has corrupted that love and we recognize, too, that Adam unknowingly not only alludes to Eve's creation but also reveals her new re-creation from his weaknesses into this parody of himself. Milton cultivates a splendid tension in our responses to the two and their love, which now, as they hold up a mirror not only to each other but also to us, has become so much

117

like our own. It is on this love that Eve's first speech—as well as her next speech to Adam and both of Adam's speeches to her—concludes; for Eve's quandary as to whether or not she should offer the fruit to Adam is resolved, as her husband's will be when he must decide whether to accept it, by the bonds of nature, by a love-lust at once jealous and generous:

> . . . but what if God have seen,
> And Death ensue? then I shall be no more,
> And *Adam* wedded to another *Eve*,
> Shall live with her enjoying, I extinct;
> A death to think. Confirm'd then I resolve,
> *Adam* shall share with me in bliss or woe;
> So dear I love him, that with him all deaths
> I could endure, without him live no life.
>
> (826-833)

These words no doubt reflect the nobility of her pre-fallen love, but they are the shattered remnants of that nobility; for this is a love which, increasingly rooted in the ties of fleshly nature, will have its natural culmination in the flesh upon Adam's eating. It is a love that, in the giving, is corrupted by its possessing, becoming thereby the less worthy of the giving, the less worthy of the accepting. Eve's justification of her ways contains the penalty for those ways.

Eve's next speech, to Adam, roughly parallels her previous speech to herself; she treats her husband as an imitation of herself. She begins by advertising the powers of the fruit "To open Eyes, and make them Gods who taste" (866), and argues like the serpent to "look on mee" to support the disbelief of the threat (867-877); and her speech concludes, exactly like the one before it, by relating the elevating powers of the tree to Adam and their love. "I," she says,

> Have also tasted, and have also found
> Th' effects to correspond, opener mine Eyes,
> Dim erst, dilated Spirits, ampler Heart,

118

And growing up to Godhead; which for thee
Chiefly I sought, without thee can despise.
For bliss, as thou hast part, to me is bliss.
Tedious, unshar'd with thee, and odious soon.
Thou therefore also taste, that equal Lot
May join us, equal Joy, as equal Love;
Lest thou not tasting, different degree
Disjoin us, and I then too late renounce
Deity for thee, when Fate will not permit.

(873-885)

Not until the Fall does Milton reduce Eden to the commonplaces we bring to it, as a pastoral world of infantile naïveté
and self-ignorance. Appropriately, therefore, Eve's language
and thinking have now become strained to the point of almost
infantile silliness in an effort to be like Adam's. But, says
Waldock, "She means this";[18] and I think that, despite our
realization of her duplicity, we must still largely agree with
him. Eve has presented Adam, as the serpent did her, the
whole triadic battery of reasons for eating—the vainglorious
possibility of godhood, the avaricious desire for knowledge,
the disbelief in the threat—but she has added one, by far the
most important, which distinguishes her (and Adam) from
Satan, namely the appeal to the bonds between them. Both
of Eve's speeches after her fall, then, ultimately conclude, as
will Adam's, with an emphasis on the love-lust that binds
them. It is a fitting testimony of the very real, however flawed,
bonds that do indeed exist between them that both of
Adam's speeches share a movement and emphasis similar
to Eve's. Although Adam's first speech opens with an awareness of the horror of the event, which distinguishes him from
Eve, nonetheless Adam reaches the same conclusion Eve
reached in her first speech after the fall—and in fact reaches
it through Eve's own argument:

Should God create *another Eve*, and I
Another Rib afford, yet loss of thee

18 *"Paradise Lost" and Its Critics*, p. 63.

119

Would never from my heart; no no, I feel
The Link of Nature draw me: Flesh of Flesh,
Bone of my Bone thou art, and from thy State
Mine never shall be parted, *bliss or woe.*

(911-916; my italics)

Eve's argument for giving the fruit—her fear that God will
create *"another Eve"* (828), her resolution to share in *"bliss
or woe"* (831)—is Adam's for accepting it. Indeed Adam is
bound to Eve to the point of precise verbal echoes of a speech
he has never even heard!

The arguments Adam advances in his next speech for dis-
believing the threat are, as everyone realizes, rationalizations
for an act he has already decided to commit. How little faith
he actually places in his elaborate rationalizations is shown
by the conjunction he uses when, having enumerated reasons
for eating, he states his decision to die with Eve: Adam states
not *"Therefore* I with thee have fixt my Lot," but "However
I with thee have fixt my Lot" (952); and his speech concludes, as Eve's two speeches did and as his previous speech
did, with what most persuades him, the fleshly bond:

However I with thee have fixt my Lot,
Certain to undergo like doom; if Death
Consort with thee, Death is to mee as Life;
So forcible within my heart I feel
The Bond of Nature draw me to my own,
My own in thee, for what thou art is mine;
Our State cannot be sever'd, we are one,
One flesh; to lose thee were to lose myself.

(952-959)

And so Adam, urged on by Eve to make "This happy trial
of thy Love" (975), encouraged by her to rely "On my experience" (988), eats, "Against his better knowledge, not
deceiv'd, / But fondly overcome with Female charm" (998-
999).

For some readers, Milton's account of Adam's motivation,

120

his being "fondly overcome with Female charm," has seemed contradictory to the sympathetic leniency of the portrayal itself—as though Milton suddenly realized that his sympathetic portrayal of the Fall was causing his material to get out of hand theologically.[19] In response to this objection, it has been argued recently that Milton meant for us to have two different impressions of Adam's act—its nobility and its baseness—to allow for "interpretative possibility" in order to produce an educative drama in the reader's own mind, a "good temptation" from which he can profit by rejecting his fallen interpretation, which admires Adam, for his regenerative interpretation, which condemns him.[20] No one will deny that if one feels admiration for Adam rather than (what is very different) sympathy, one obviously imitates Adam's own simplistic evaluation of himself. But is it necessary to conclude that the reader overcomes the temptation merely by substituting condemnation for admiration? Adam and Eve will, to their profit, condemn themselves later, as God has done and will do; and yet this is not their final response to the Fall, nor is it God's. If there is a temptation here, it is a temptation to reduce a complex response to a simple one which, whether overly rigorous or overly lenient, runs counter to the complexity of the divine ways Milton set out to justify.

As I have tried to show, the reason for Milton's lenient portrayal of the Fall is based on a theological commonplace:

[19] Waldock, pp. 49-50. Other critics, while accepting Milton at his word, have had different impressions of what he meant by "Female charm." For Evans, p. 287, it is Adam's "weakness against 'the charm of Beauties powerful glance' "; for Burden, p. 163, it is "the sexual nature of Eve's appeal"; for Empson, p. 183, it is the same tendency to which Adam confessed in Book VIII; for B. A. Wright, *Milton's "Paradise Lost"* (1962; rpt. London: Methuen, 1968), p. 177, it is "the seemingly preternatural, the irresistible power Eve exercises over him; and as he had told Raphael, this is a matter not only of her physical attractions but of all she means to him as the companion of his life"—which seems to me quite nicely put.

[20] Fish, pp. 269-272.

man's fall must be distinguished from Satan's, must be portrayed more leniently, in order to justify the ways of God, that "Man therefore shall find grace, / Th' other none." Milton's use of the Flesh-World-Devil scheme has clearly been to support that distinction. The triad serves as a means whereby Milton can give clarity to his portrayal of an episode, the Fall, highly charged, even to the point of confusion, with interpretive and emotional possibilities. Milton uses the Flesh-World-Devil scheme, then, not only because of its theological value—it represents all sin and the Fall involves all sin—but because of its rhetorical value in directing and controlling the reader's response to the Fall. His argument demanded a distinction between the two falls, and the triad works to point to this distinction. Accordingly, the infernal triad underlies and calls attention to the contrast between the "temptation" in Pandaemonium, which is self-temptation, and the temptation in Eden, which is temptation by suggestion. Accordingly, too, the infernal triad calls attention to the difference between Satan's sin and man's. Milton's argument required that the parents commit a sin sufficiently great to justify the sternness of divine wrath—and how great that sin is the historical panorama of Books XI and XII amply demonstrates—but at the same time his argument also required that they not commit a sin so heinous, like the devil's, as to preclude and make artistically and emotionally unconvincing the justifiability of mercy. It is one of the commonplaces of criticism of the Fall that Eve's fall occurs through aspiring upward, Adam's through falling downward;[21] but this con-

---

[21] The best statement of this position is M. M. Mahood's, p. 221: "Eve breaks [the Chain of Being] by an upward pull, and Adam breaks it with a downward wrench. A less rational nature than Adam, Eve aspires to intellectual equality with angels. He, on the other hand, sins in full awareness of the consequences involved in the act. Passion gains the mastery of reason and he is drawn down by 'The Link of Nature' and 'The Bond of Nature.'" A similar opposition is found in other critics—e.g., Diekhoff, p. 74, contrasts Eve's "aspiration to Godhead" with Adam's "love for Eve plus his physical desire for her"; and Lewis, pp. 125-126, contrasts Eve's "Pride" with Adam's "uxoriousness."

ventional reading, though it has some claim to truth, runs the risk of undermining the argument behind the episode. For, as we have seen, one of the most remarkable aspects of Milton's portrayal of the Fall is how small a part Satan's own sin, *superbia vitae*, plays, and how large a part the lesser sins of the Flesh play; and even those fleshly sins are presented in a forbearing light as a love not fully corrupted by fallen lust. No one sin, of course, can account for the motivation of either Adam or Eve; the Fall involves all sin.[22] Nonetheless, through his use of the Flesh-World-Devil scheme and through a careful structural counterpointing of arguments, speeches, and narration, Milton has focused on the most venial of the traditional agents of the Fall, and his portrayal of the Fall is among the most tolerant and humane.

If my account of the argument underlying Milton's schematic counterpointing is true, I think one proceeds naturally to the conclusion that Milton has scrupulously attempted to preclude any simple and single response to the Fall on the part of his readers, be that response moralistic or indulgent. It is a complex event and it demands a complex response. The divine response to the Fall should be the pattern to our own, and that response is not simple or single. "In Mercy and Justice both, / Through Heav'n and Earth, so shall my glory excel," claims the Father; "But Mercy first and last shall brightest shine." The anger of justice and the mildness

---

[22] As Milton says in *De Doctrina*, I.xi: "For what sin can be named, which was not included in this one act? It comprehended at once distrust in the divine veracity, and a proportionate credulity in the assurances of Satan; unbelief; ingratitude; disobedience; gluttony; in the man excessive uxoriousness, in the woman a want of proper regard for her husband, in both an insensibility to the welfare of their offspring, and that offspring the whole human race; parricide, theft, invasion of the rights of others, sacrilege, deceit, presumption in aspiring to divine attributes, fraud in the means to attain the object, pride, and arrogance." (In *The Works of John Milton*, ed. Frank Allen Patterson *et al.*, xv [New York: Columbia Univ. Press, 1933], 181-182. All citations to *De Doctrina* are to the Columbia Edition, hereafter CE.)

of mercy conjoin in the divine response—as they must in our own. Obviously, this means that we should not fall into a whitewashing of Adam and Eve's sin through romantic sentimentality; to do so is to make Milton contradictory to himself and to the ways of God he set out to justify. But, I would insist, we also violate his argument when we go to the opposite extreme of assuming that the more severe, the more moralistic, our judgment, the more Miltonic it is. This simply is not so; it is equally unfaithful to Milton, less a response to his art and argument than an overreaction to Waldock and Empson. Both the modern unorthodox response and the conventional counter-response fail to cope with the complexity of the theological problem Milton confronted. Both sentimentality and moralistic condemnation violate the balance of the divine perspective, the wrath of its justice and the gentleness of its mercy; and both violate the complexity of the happy consequence of grace emerging from the tragic loss of Eden. To embrace either of these simplifying perspectives is to denigrate either divine justice or divine grace. If we have followed the direction Milton has given us through both the Flesh-World-Devil scheme and a careful structural pairing of speeches, the response most readers intuitively have to Adam and Eve, a mixed response, no longer seems an evasion of the intellectual and emotional complexities of the episode; on the contrary, it properly preserves those complexities. This mixed response is the theologically proper response to the Fall: both sympathetic and condemning, both forgiving and angry, it provides the fallen, human approximation of the balance of the divine perspective itself.

4. The Structure of *Paradise Regained*

In 1671 Milton grouped together two poems under the title *Paradise Regained. A Poem. In IV Books. To which is added Samson Agonistes.* He did so with good reason: the two works were companion-pieces, comprising the poet's final words on Christian heroism, and providing a Christian definition of the two great poetic modes, the heroic and the tragic.[1] Although *Paradise Regained* is a brief epic, *Samson*

---

[1] The problems involved in examining the relationship of the two poems of the 1671 volume have been admirably handled by Arthur Barker, "Calm Regained through Passion Spent: The Conclusions of the Miltonic Effort," in *The Prison and the Pinnacle*, ed. Balachandra Rajan (Toronto: Univ. of Toronto Press, 1973), pp. 3-48. However important the differences between the two poems are, my approach will work upon the assumption that the two poems of that volume were designed as companion-pieces; and accordingly it is first necessary, wherever we may go after that, to examine in what way these poems are alike. Chapter 5, "Milton's Christian Redefinition of Tragedy," will demonstrate, I hope, that the common adoption of the Spenserian double-triadic structure in *Paradise Regained* and *Samson Agonistes* extends to a common use of symbolic appearance in the temptations, to a common conception of the nature of the temptations, and indeed even to common arguments within the temptations. The extent of these resemblances would seem to insist upon a late date for both works, though Milton may well have done work earlier on *Samson Agonistes*, later revising it as companion-piece to *Paradise Regained*. The most cogent rebuttal of the arguments for an early date for *Samson* is Ernest Sirluck, "Milton's Idle Right Hand," *Journal of English and Germanic Philology*, 60 (1961), 749-785. It should be noted, however, that John T. Shawcross, "The Chronology of Milton's Major Poems," *PMLA*, 76 (1961), 345-358, argues forcefully for an early date for both *Samson* and *Paradise Regained*. See also William Riley Parker's elaboration on his earlier arguments in *Milton: A Biography* (London: Oxford Univ. Press, 1968), II, 903-917, and in "The Date of *Samson Agonistes* Again" in *Calm of Mind: Tercentenary Essays on "Paradise Regained" and "Samson*

a tragedy, both are brief heroic poems with the common subject of a hero coming to knowledge of his identity through temptation: Christ in the darkness of the wilderness, and Samson in the darkness of his own blindness, struggle against the sins to which the old Adam had succumbed, raising finally an inner Eden from a "waste Wilderness" (*PR*, I.7). Milton's readers would, I believe, have recognized at once that in addition to a similarity in subject the two works shared a similarity in structure as well; for the structure of both works emerges largely from the structure, based on Adam's temptation in Eden and Christ's in the wilderness, established by Spenser in the Legend of Holiness and imitated by Giles Fletcher in "Christ's Victory on Earth." In *Samson*, Milton's borrowing from his Spenserian heritage is confined primarily to the poem's "middle" and Samson's confrontation with Manoa, Dalila, and Harapha, or the Flesh, the World, and the Devil. In *Paradise Regained*, however, the borrowing is much more comprehensive; it extends to virtually every major structural aspect of the work. Following Spenser and Fletcher, Milton employs a linear triadic sequence in which the first day is linked to the Flesh, the second to the World, the third to the Devil.[2] Also like Spenser and Fletcher, Milton

---

Agonistes" in Honor of John S. Diekhoff, ed. Joseph Anthony Wittreich, Jr. (Cleveland: The Press of Case Western Reserve University, 1971), pp. 163-174.

[2] The pioneer study relating *Paradise Regained* to the three-temptations scheme is Elizabeth Marie Pope, *"Paradise Regained": The Tradition and the Poem* (Baltimore, Md.: The Johns Hopkins Press, 1947). The historical value of this study is unimpugnable, but its structural conclusions less so, if for no other reason than that Miss Pope finds it difficult to stick to a single structural outline. According to Miss Pope, "each day is devoted to a different *type* of temptation: temptation by necessity—the Protestant *dic ut lapides* [the first day]; temptation by pleasure—the world, the flesh, and the devil in their attractive and alluring shapes [the second day] and temptation by violence—Milton's own addition of a trial not usually included with the others" (p. 101). The temptations of the three days would seem to be to the Flesh, the World, and the Devil, respectively; but

makes the World-temptation a composite one, but he goes beyond Spenser to make the World include not only one but two temptations to the Flesh, the World, and the Devil, the first occurring in the banquet-wealth-glory sequence, the sec-

---

Miss Pope confuses matters by suggesting that since the pinnacle episode as Milton finally conceived it "did not admit of being treated as *any* sort of temptation, even by violence . . . the formal temptation by violence had to be pushed back and given independent treatment in the storm scene" (p. 99). Barbara K. Lewalski, in the finest study of the poem, *Milton's Brief Epic: The Genre, Meaning, and Art of "Paradise Regained"* (Providence, R.I.: Brown Univ. Press, 1966), contends that the three days are organized around Christ's three mediatorial roles and that, therefore, "the specific treatment of the triple equation and of the Second Adam theme" (p. 227) is relegated to the banquet-wealth-glory sequence, though she does find the second-Adam theme recurring in the learning temptation. I think one must agree with Miss Pope, however, that the first two days are directed to Christ's role as the second Adam. Otherwise it becomes almost impossible to make sense out of the pinnacle episode. This essay will attempt to bring a clearer focus to the second-Adam theme by emphasizing the Edenic context of the temptations on the first two days, which is much more precise and specific than even Lewalski and Pope have realized, and by contrasting the disguises of the first two days with the "wonted shape" of the third.

Also emphasizing a triadic structure is Burton J. Weber, "The Schematic Structure of *Paradise Regained*: A Hypothesis," *Philological Quarterly*, 50 (1971), 553-567, but he finds the neoplatonic division of the soul as the main source of the triadic patterning. James R. McAdams, "The Pattern of Temptation in *Paradise Regained*," in *Milton Studies IV*, ed. James D. Simmonds (Pittsburgh, Pa.: Univ. of Pittsburgh Press, 1972), pp. 177-192, argues ingeniously for a structure based on the principle that "the first part or episode is related to the last, the second episode to the second-to-last, and so on" (p. 172); this pattern is repeated in the temptations of the second day, with the banquet-temptation (the Flesh) complementing the Athens-temptation (the Devil or vainglory); the intervening five episodes make up "the exhibition of avarice of the temptation of the world, the third of the three categories of sin: the lures of fame, riches, Israel, Parthia, and Rome" (p. 183), with the glory-temptation pairing off with the Parthia-temptation, the avarice-temptation with the Rome-temptation, and the Israel episode at the center of the pattern. I have especially strong reservations about McAdam's asso-

ond in the Parthia-Rome-Athens sequence. Underlying *Paradise Regained* is Milton's desire to outdo his great English master and his triadic structural triumph in the Legend of Holiness. As a result, Milton goes beyond Spenser not only in the amplification of the World-temptation but also in the addition of two structural features: first, a fusion of the Flesh-World-Devil sequence of the three days with another triad, Christ's mediatorial roles as Prophet, King, and Priest;[3] sec-

ciation of Rome with riches (though riches are, of course, found there) and Athens with pride (though pride is incorporated into that temptation); for these connections, based on a rather freewheeling use of theology, ignore the central meaning underlying the Flesh-World-Devil pattern, namely the dialectic between Eden and the wilderness, the old Adam and the new.

[3] The role of the mediatorial triad had been ably handled by Mrs. Lewalski, *Milton's Brief Epic*, pp. 164-321. I agree with the connections Mrs. Lewalski makes between the three days and Christ's three mediatorial roles, but I will approach this triad from a different perspective—Satan's, in his parody of Christ's roles as prophet and king as an infernal type of Christ. Michael Fixler, *Milton and the Kingdoms of God* (London: Faber and Faber, 1964), pp. 248-269, also relates *Paradise Regained* to Christ's mediatorial roles; but he, I think mistakenly, relates the banquet rather than the pinnacle to Christ's priestly role. If one approaches *Paradise Regained* by way of its Spenserian analogues, one realizes this to be highly improbable; indeed, it violates the poem's structural symmetry and its portrayal of Christ as the perfect man on the first two days and as the *deus homo* on the third. The banquet is clearly one of the glories of the World, and Satan offers it to Christ in His role as king of nature and king of creation, not as priest. Moreover, although one may view the banquet as an infernal type of the Eucharist, there are no specific allusions in the episode to Christ's sacrifice on the cross, which is of course essential to the role, whereas there are numerous such implications, as Mrs. Lewalski (pp. 311-314) has shown, in the storm-pinnacle sequence. Howard Schultz, "A Fairer Paradise? Some Recent Studies of *Paradise Regained*," *ELH*, 32 (1965), 294-295, supports Fixler; whereas James Holly Hanford and James G. Taaffe, *A Milton Handbook*, 5th ed., rev. (New York: Appleton-Century-Crofts, 1970), p. 231, support Mrs. Lewalski.

The following are the crucial passages from *De Doctrina*, I.xv (CE, xv, 287-300) describing the three mediatorial roles:

His function as a prophet is to instruct his church in heavenly

ond, the imposition of a tetradic book structure. Milton's additions, however, are exactly that, additions; they do not supplant but supplement the structure he inherited from Spenser and Fletcher. The result is a work of a vigorously mature and seasoned artistry, a brilliant structural tour de force with everything in perfect measure and proportion.[4]

truth, and to declare the whole will of his Father. . . .

Christ's sacerdotal function is that whereby he once offered himself to God the Father as a sacrifice for sinners, and has always made, and still continues to make intercession for us. . . .

The Kingly function of Christ is that whereby being made King by God the Father, he governs and preserves, chiefly by an inward law and spiritual power, the Church which he has purchased for himself, and conquers and subdues its enemies. . . .

[4] More controversy has surrounded the structure of *Paradise Regained* than any other work of Milton's; but surprisingly few critics, with the exception principally of Mrs. Lewalski and Miss Pope, have emphasized a triadic structure, despite what would seem a clear principle of organization, the three days. Howard Schultz, "Christ and Antichrist in *Paradise Regained*," *PMLA*, 67 (1952), 790-808, contends that the events in the poem are structured according to a "quasi-allegory" of the history of Christ's church: Milton shows us "Antichrist, soon to be uncased, foisting worldliness and 'distrust' upon the infant church at first by means of hypocritical disguise; next, tempting it to traffic with superstition, money, secular power, and 'promotion,' both in the abstract and in the particular institutions of Rome and Parthia, or more significantly Rome and Protestantism [in "A Fairer Paradise?" p. 294, Schultz has since retracted the association of Parthia with Protestantism]; at last (for the poet ascended an ethical ladder in arranging these lures) offering it the specious bait of clergy learning"; the lull after the storm refers to the Millennium, the pinnacle episode to the Antichrist's being "loosed for a season after the Thousand Years" (pp. 806-807). This is a very tempting suggestion indeed; for it can and should be argued that Milton and Spenser both use the Temptation in the Wilderness to reveal the temptations that beset not only the individual pilgrim but also the church (though in Spenser, of course, the church's difficulties are dealt with primarily in a separate character); but I cannot see that *Paradise Regained* presents these difficulties in chronological order, as it can be argued that Spenser does. Many of the vices Schultz describes are, after all, the same vices Paul attacks in his Epistles. What we would seem to have, then, is simply a portrayal of the vices to which Christ's

I

At stake in the wilderness is nothing less than the divine word itself. Accordingly, not only is the first temptation a temptation to the word and Christ's prophecy, but the episodes leading into the temptation all focus on prophecy and

---

church is continually tempted rather than a Spenserian allegorical history of ecclesiastical vice. Schultz has another structural suggestion: "Satan's campaign," he says, "is divisible into three phases, according to strategy: *fraud* (deception by disguise), *snares* (lures), and *terrors* (terrors and threats first, then violence). The poet sketches the tripartite plan in 1.97 and again in 1.178" (p. 797). The problem with making Satan's different strategies the basis of the work's structure is that, contrary to what Schultz claims, the two accounts differ. The second account, which Schultz only alludes to, is not, as he claims, triadic but pentadic: "what'er may tempt, what'er seduce, / Allure, or terrify, or undermine" (1.178-179). Mason Tung, "The Patterns of Temptation in *Paradise Regained*," *Seventeenth-Century News*, 24 (1966), 58-59, works from a similar tack; he simply ignores 1.97 for 1.178-179. Alexander H. Sackton, "Architectonic Structure in *Paradise Regained*," *University of Texas Studies in English*, 33 (1954), 33-45, argues that "In the first and last encounters Satan seeks, first by persuasion and finally by force, to make Christ reveal his divine nature. The second encounter, on the other hand . . . , presents a whole series of temptations which appeal to Christ as a human being" (p. 37); and M. M. Mahood, *Poetry and Humanism* (New Haven, Conn.: Yale Univ. Press, 1950), p. 233, and Douglas Bush, *John Milton* (New York: Macmillan, 1964), p. 186, have argued similarly. It does not seem, however, that Christ's divinity is being tested in the first temptation, but rather His trust in divinity; Satan himself states on the third day that his previous temptations have been to Christ as "th'utmost of mere man" (IV.535), and Christ's performing a miracle of making bread from stones would demonstrate His divinity no more than Satan's miracle of the banquet on the next day demonstrates his. Lee Sheridan Cox, "Food-Word Imagery in *Paradise Regained*," *ELH*, 28 (1961), 225-243, strains a good point, that "Milton's primary concern throughout the poem is the nature and office of the Word Incarnate and of the word" (p. 226), when he concludes that "Milton set up the structure of the poem most exactly in the light of the food-word image. An overall view of the pattern reveals that on the first day occurs the temptation of what supports physical life, human bread; on the third day, tempta-

the word. The narrator, participating in the events he will describe, presents himself as prophet: following John the Baptist, he will reveal deeds "in secret done," proclaiming Christ to his own age as John had "many an Age" before (1.15-16); and following Christ, the word itself, he asks to be led by the same "Spirit who led'st this glorious Eremite / Into the Desert" (7-8). The three reflections on the baptism by God, Satan, and Christ all concern themselves with the meaning and verification of God's prophetic signs and word. God's purpose, as His speech in the celestial council reveals again and again, is "to verify" (133) His word. Christ's purpose, as His meditation demonstrates, is at once to perceive, embody, and reveal that word. His life both before the wilderness and within it has been a continuing meditation on the word and God's prophetic signs to discover the nature

---

tion of what supports spiritual life, divine bread; in between, on the second day, all the varying temptations, single and combined, of food supporting the life of the senses, imagination, reason" (p. 235). Another pattern is suggested, finally, by Linwood E. Orange, "The Role of the Deadly Sins in *Paradise Regained*," *The Southern Quarterly*, 2 (1964), 190-201. Orange discovers gluttony in the stones and banquet temptations, lust in Belial's proposal, avarice in the gold-temptation, pride in the glory-temptation, sloth in Satan's accusation (III.177-180) that Christ is too slow in freeing His country, envy in the Parthia- and Rome-temptations (both, he argues, are appeals through sight, and the Latin root of "envy" is "videre"), and wrath in Satan's reactions in the storm-pinnacle sequence. Although there is some evidence in Milton's *Commonplace Book* of an interest in the seven-deadly-sins formula (see Ruth Mohl, *John Milton and His "Commonplace Book"* [New York: Frederick Ungar, 1969], pp. 55-62), the formula plays, as far as I know, no role in any of his works; indeed it is rather infrequently used by Protestant writers in the seventeenth century. Moreover, the stones-temptation is not to gluttony, nor the Parthia- and Rome-temptations to envy; and curiously Orange skips over the Athens-temptation. No doubt one can find all seven sins in *Paradise Regained*, but there is no evidence whatsoever, any more than there is for the now discredited argument of Edwin Greenlaw, "'A Better Teacher than Aquinas,'" *Studies in Philology*, 14 (1917), 215, with respect to Book XI of *Paradise Lost*, that these sins appear as a structural formula.

of His identity and mission; through examination and re-examination of the divine word, He has progressed from a sense of His prophetic role ("born to promote all truth" [205]), to a sense of His kingly role (to rescue Israel), and finally to a sense of His priestly role (His "hard assay even to the death" [264])—which is precisely the order the temptations will take.[5] And Satan's purpose is to perceive and thwart the word, to discover Christ's identity, as Christ has also attempted to discover it, in terms of the relationship between the old prophecy of Genesis and the new signs at the nativity and the baptism: "Who this is we must learn" (91).[6]

[5] Lewalski, pp. 190-191, analyzes Christ's meditation in terms of His growing knowledge of His mediatorial roles; but the observation of the schematic order of the roles' appearance is my own, and would seem to confirm the Prophet-King-Priest order for the poem as a whole. Arnold Stein, *Heroic Knowledge* (Minneapolis: Univ. of Minnesota Press, 1957), pp. 38-41, emphasizes how the meditation reflects Christ's growth, fulfilled in the wilderness, towards a "collaboration of the intuitive and the discursive" (p. 41) ways of knowing.

[6] On Satan's search for Christ's identity and Christ's own gradual illumination, the most persuasive account is Barbara Lewalski's, pp. 133-321; but see also Pope, pp. 27-41; Sackton, pp. 33-45; Allan H. Gilbert, "The Temptation in *Paradise Regained*," *Journal of English and Germanic Philology*, 15 (1916), 599-611; Edward Cleveland, "On the Identity Motive in *Paradise Regained*," *Modern Language Quarterly*, 16 (1955), 232-236, and Stein, pp. 3-134. In opposition, Don Cameron Allen, *The Harmonious Vision* (Baltimore, Md.: The Johns Hopkins Press, 1954), pp. 110-121, argues that Satan only "pretends to doubt who Christ is in order to establish a mood of self-distrust in the mind of the 'exalted man'" (p. 111), and that "It is fear, cold fear, rather than uncertainty" (p. 112) which motivates Satan. Allen's reading has been supported by Thomas Langford, "The Temptations in *Paradise Regained*," *Texas Studies in Language and Literature*, 9 (1967), 37-46, and Schultz, "A Fairer Paradise?," p. 289. A.S.P. Woodhouse, "Theme and Pattern in *Paradise Regained*," *University of Toronto Quarterly*, 25 (1956), 167-182, argues that Satan "is the great romantic, the rebel not only against God, but against fact, who cannot bring himself . . . to act upon what in his heart he knows to be the truth" (p. 172); and somewhat similarly, George M. Muldrow, "An Irony in *Paradise Regained*," *Papers on Language and Literature*,

Satan's understanding of Christ's uniqueness is as limited as his understanding of the word. He can perceive Christ only through the blinding distortions of his own parody of Him throughout history; he is deceived by his own deceptions. Chiefly he sees Christ as king, but king as Satan sees himself king, as "in the head of Nations . . . / Their King, their Leader, and Supreme on Earth" (96-99). And through John the Baptist, the "great Prophet" (70) and Christ's "Harbinger" (71), he suspects Christ's role as prophet; but even this he perceives only according to his own distortion of the role. John's prophecy and baptizing Satan interprets in terms of the fraudulent promises of his own false prophecy: John only "Pretends to wash off sin" (73). Imaged in what Satan sees as pretense is precisely the role he least perceives, Christ's priesthood and expiatory sacrifice on the cross; and yet it is this role that will permit the removal of man from the exactions of the law, upon which Satan's claim to kingship over man depends; and it is this role to which all of *Paradise Regained* points. The roles of king and, to a lesser extent, prophet Satan can at least partly conceive of, if through a glass darkly; but the role which above all requires and testifies to Christ's uniqueness as the Son of God and the *deus homo* Satan merely finds absurd. Satan perceives Christ, then, largely as himself writ large, a more powerful king, a more persuasive prophet. These are the two roles Satan has imitated, parodied, and falsified throughout history, as he will continue to do in the wilderness; but for Christ's priestly death on the cross there is no diabolic parody. Accordingly, on the first two days of temptation, Satan will portray himself in disguise as a parodic approximation of Christ's roles as prophet and king; but on the third day, in the temptation to Christ's priestly role, he will appear "in

---

3 (1967), 377-380, argues that "Satan both knows and does not know the identity, and hence the power, of his opponent" (p. 377), and that although "Satan knows conceptually that the exalted man he confronts is the divine Son," knowledge of this identity "by proof or by experience" (p. 378) does not come until the third day.

wonted shape" (IV.449), without parodic disguise. Ironically, Satan will offer himself up in the wilderness as an infernal type of Christ; he will present himself as a type of Christ as much as Moses and Elijah are types, tempting Christ to fulfill and inherit his own false prophecy and kingship. Satan's use of disguise on the first two days epitomizes his strategy of seducing Christ to accept a diabolic parody of His true nature and roles. Partly out of ignorance, partly out of cunning, Satan attempts to approximate what he imagines Christ's identity to be; and in the approximation, which is in fact an extension of his parody of Christ throughout history and of evil's perennial parody of good, he offers himself up as a mirror wherein Christ can perceive the identity for which He is searching. Not unlike Dalila and Harapha, the false mirrors of the hero in *Samson*, Satan appears in parodic imitation of what he suspects Christ's nature to be in order that Christ will become an imitation of him, false prophet and false king.

In assuming the guise of hermit for the Flesh-temptation to disbelief, Satan obviously parodies the withdrawal into the wilderness of the Old Testament types of Christ, the prophets Moses and Elijah, and also of Christ's "Harbinger," the hermit and prophet John the Baptist. In accordance with his strategy of portraying himself as Christ's type, he also parodies the withdrawal into the wilderness of Christ, the "glorious Eremite" Himself; he offers himself up as Christ's infernal double:

> But now an aged man in Rural weeds,
> Following, as seem'd, the quest of some stray Ewe,
> Or wither'd sticks to gather, which might serve
> Against a Winter's day when winds blow keen,
> To warm him wet return'd from field at Eve,
> He saw approach . . .
>
> (314-319)

The narrator's conflicting interpretations of the false hermit suggest, clearly enough, the difficulty of perceiving the real

nature of the Archimagoan hypocrite; but more important
than that, they prefigure the two major ploys Satan will use
in the Flesh-temptation: the argument to charity (the hermit,
of course, parodies Christ's charity as the good shepherd)
and the argument to necessity and to self-preservation against
present and future hardship. The stones-temptation not only
is part of a schematic structure; it is itself a schematic structure. In the first stage of the temptation, Satan has two
speeches, the first arguing to Christ's necessity and Satan's
charity, the second arguing to Christ's charity and their common necessity. In the second stage of the temptation, which
follows Christ's undisguising of Satan, Satan once again has
two speeches: in the first, he argues a community between
them in terms of the greater charity of a prophecy of pure
truth; in the second, he argues a community between them in
terms of necessity forcing both of them to abandon the hard
ways of truth. The opening description of Satan, then, reveals
his strategy of placing Christ in a hall of mirrors: Satan becomes Christ the good shepherd; Christ Himself becomes
the good shepherd, but with Satan becoming the object of
His salvation; and Satan and Christ become one. But in addition to this, the opening description prepares us for the
fundamental aesthetic strategy of the work itself: ideas become structural schemes; they are valued not only for their
intrinsic substance but also for their aesthetic and architectonic possibilities. We are prepared for a dramatic conflict
based on the counterpointing and conflict of ideas. Pleasure
does not lead to instruction so much as instruction leads to
delight. *Paradise Regained* is a grand musical structuring of
ideas, wherein themes are stated, inverted, developed, un-
ravelled, interwoven.

From Satan's first words it is clear that he is tempting the
second Adam to the same distrust and despair to which he
had tempted the first.[7] Satan tempts Christ to perceive God

[7] Jackson I. Cope, "Satan's Disguises: *Paradise Lost* and *Paradise
Regained*," *Modern Language Notes*, 73 (1958), 9-11, notes that the
animals mentioned in I.812-813—"The Fiery Serpent fled, and nox-

as one of Satan's own capricious pagan deities, to see God as Satan, Satan as the true god, as he suggests that "ill chance" (321) rather than "some strong motion" (290) of the Spirit has brought Him into the wilderness. Satan is trying to persuade Christ, as he did Eve, to distrust His true god and guide and to trust a false guide. But not only is Satan setting himself up as God; he is also setting himself up as Christ Himself. In his offer to lead Christ out of the wilderness to prevent His death from "hunger and . . . drought," he parodies Christ's mission in the wilderness as *Paradise Regained* will portray it. Satan offers an infernal parody of the pattern for the human pilgrimage Christ is to establish, a pilgrimage through the wilderness of the world to the eternal banquet, where man will satisfy his spiritual "hunger" for "Fruits fetcht from the tree of life" (IV.589) and his spiritual "drought" for water from "the fount of life" (IV.590).

In the first temptation, Satan has invited Christ to accept as His guide a diabolic parody of Himself and His prophecy: Satan becomes the good shepherd and Christ the "stray Ewe." In the next stage, Satan invites Christ to become that diabolic parody of Himself: Christ will be the good shepherd but to His and Satan's mutual self-interest. Christ is tempted to become the bane of His flock and church throughout his-

---

ious Worm, / The Lion and fierce Tiger glar'd aloof"—are "the animal masks of the betrayer in *Paradise Lost*": "A Lion now he stalks with fiery glare, / Then as a Tiger" (IV.402-403), and of course Satan adopts the disguise of a serpent for the temptation in Eden. The four animals mentioned in *Paradise Regained* would seem to insist upon our seeing the stones-temptation as a temptation to Christ as the second Adam; but so do the similarities, as I will point out, between Satan's arguments here and the serpent's last speech to Eve. I suspect that the four animals mentioned in I.812-813 allude to Psalm 91:13: "Thou shalt tread upon the lion and adder; the young lion and the dragon shalt thou trample under feet." The irony behind this illusion, if it is that, is that the two verses preceding this one are paraphrased by Satan on the pinnacle, as he is about to fall under the feet of the Son of God: "For he shall give his angels charge over thee, to keep thee in all thy ways. / They shall bear thee up in their hands, lest thou dash thy foot against a stone" (Psalm 91:11-12).

tory, the bad shepherd masquerading as the good, the Satanic prophet masquerading as the true. The form this stage of the temptation takes is, then, an outgrowth of the confusion underlying the narrator's opening description of Satan: Christ will become the Satanic hermit confusing the good shepherd's charity for others with His own necessity for self-preservation:

> But if thou be the Son of God, Command
> That out of these hard stones be made thee bread;
> So shalt thou save thyself and us relieve
> With Food, whereof we wretched seldom taste.
>
> (342-345)

If earlier Satan offered Christ a parody of His grace, here Christ is invited to offer a parody of grace to Satan. Not only is Satan attempting to thwart Christ's prophetic role by having him rely on literal or physical bread rather than on the metaphorical or spiritual bread of the divine word; he is also indirectly attacking the new covenant by binding man to the letter rather than the spirit of the word. Moreover, in tempting Christ to distrust the provision of providence and to make bread "So shalt thou save thyself and us relieve," Satan— appropriately dressed as the false hermit associated by Spenser and others with Roman Catholicism—is tempting Christ to what he will tempt His church in future history, the Roman doctrine that man finds salvation through good works rather than faith.[8]

---

[8] This, it seems to me, is the central thrust of Satan's temptation to disbelief as far as Christ's church is concerned. Schultz, "Christ and Antichrist," p. 797, suggests that the chief point of Christ's refusal is that "The true church can survive and do without 'carnal reliance,' without Antichrist's 'fleshly supportment.'" Fixler, pp. 252-253, argues that "the temptation suggests that Jesus prove his right to the care of souls by demonstrating the miraculous power of transubstantiation, the same power which formed the cornerstone of the mass, the daily ritual upon which the Church of Rome was later built" and that Jesus demonstrates that "faith needs no reliance on miracles."

137

Christ's seeing through Satan's disguise initiates the second stage of temptation, which, like the first, also consists of two temptations. In the first of these, Satan attempts to shift Christ's distrust from himself to God by adopting a new disguise, one that justifies his falsehood through precisely the obedience to God and His word which Christ has just asserted. Satan is not what he appears to be, falsehood disguised as truth, but rather truth disguised as falsehood: under his disguise, he is really an image of Christ Himself. The deception itself is a deception, his falsehood itself a disguise that God, Himself the ultimate disguiser, has foisted upon him. The falsehood Christ perceives as hostile to God's word is in fact the result of Satan's obedient execution of that word. His lies, voiced in the Satanically inspired mouths of Job's friends and King Ahab's prophets, were, he claims, part of his obedience to the divine will: "For what he bids I do" (377). The Adversary becomes no adversary, rather a necessary agent in the working out of the divine will and word, which are themselves impure and corrupt, also disguised. Satan continues to cast aspersions on the word by arguing that God has used and actually abused him:

> Though I have lost
> Much luster of my native brightness, lost
> To be belov'd of God, I have not lost
> To love, at least contemplate and admire
> What I see excellent in good, or fair,
> Or virtuous . . .

>   (377-382)

On the surface Satan is claiming that, although he has lost God's love, he has not fallen so low that he cannot appreciate the pure beauty of Christ's prophecy and truth. However, Satan's language is ambiguous, so that he implies that what is good in him remains through his own salvaging, that his "native brightness" has been "lost [*in order*] / To be belov'd of God," that he has become tarnished in the act of doing the dirty work for God as His agent in falsehood. Christ

138

becomes the image of the true prophet Satan would himself
be were God's word and prophecy not itself corrupt. As in
the earlier request for Christ to feed Himself and the hermit
through a miracle, Satan again suggests a community between
them. The context has changed, but the implication of the
infernal mirror is the same: both sons are true prophets deserted by their father.

Satan's strategy of tempting Christ to see His image re-
flected in the infernal mirror becomes clearer in the remainder of the speech. Satan ironically casts himself in the role
of John the Baptist,[9] admiring a worthier—and fellow—
prophet:

> What can be then less in me than desire
> To see thee and approach thee, whom I know
> Declar'd the Son of God, to hear attent
> Thy wisdom, and behold thy Godlike Deeds?
>
> (383-386)

Satan now reworks his appeal, made in the earlier request for
a miracle, to Christ's charity. The context of the temptation has
shifted, of course, from Christ's charity as a dispenser of
physical bread to His charity as a dispenser of the spiritual
bread of truth. The image in the mirror accordingly shifts,
offering Satan's infernal approximation of that role: Satan,
too, is a dispenser of spiritual bread:

> [I] lend them [man] oft my aid,
> Oft my advice by presages and signs,
> And answers, oracles, portents, and dreams,
> Whereby they may direct their future life.
>
> (393-396)

Having argued that he is God's enforced servant in falsehood,
Satan now argues that he is man's willing servant in truth.
As before, Christ is invited to perceive His identity in Satan,

---

[9] Lewalski, p. 214, sees Satan as a Balaam-figure here, and rightly
so; but he is Balaam masquerading as a John the Baptist. Once again,
Satan is acting as the wolf in sheep's clothing.

to see Satan as a mirror and type of Himself; for both are prophets motivated by charity, dispensing words whereby men may "direct their future life." Satan is not only whitewashing his own evil; he is also using Christ's own assertion of the value of truth and charity to cast doubt upon God and thereby to depreciate the value of Christ's role as God's prophet. The underlying argument of the speech should, I think, be paraphrased like this: "God is not a god of truth alone, but works through falsehood as well as truth; I am one office, you another; but I (like you) prefer truth, and would like to be a student of 'Thy wisdom, and behold thy Godlike deeds' rather than be subject to the impure truth of the Father; moreover, I (like you) wish to be an agent of truth to aid man, rather than God's agent in falsehood, which is the role God has bade me do, and in fact I have been an agent of truth—on my own—through 'answers, oracles, portents, and dreams' [395], and, since I am (like you) a humanitarian, I have done so without self-interest." The argument is a clever revision of Satan's argument to distrust in Eden: once again Satan is portraying God in his own image, as unreliable and unjust, and "Not just, not God; not fear'd then, nor obey'd" (IX.701); and he suggests, once again as in Eden, that God—unlike the "Wisdom-giving Plant" and unlike himself—is less willing to impart truth and knowledge to man, and that to attain and impart full knowledge man and man's prophet must act independently of God. For Christ to become God's prophet is to adulterate His truth with the corruption of the divine word; He has no alternative but to become a kind of Satanic Prometheus. In his defense of his disguise as a hermit, Satan has thus subtly accepted Christ's assertion that the bread is not physical food but spiritual truth; but in applying this assertion, he casts doubt on Truth itself, transforming the divine word from a dark mystery into a sinister disguise which he, not Christ, can penetrate. In this temptation to the word and Christ's prophecy, Satan has cast himself in the role of prophet, as true interpreter of the word; and his conclusion is that the word deceives, that truth and prophecy must be independent of God, and that Christ must, to fulfill His mission as prophet, turn to the "good works" of his own diabolic prophecy.

Intertwined with the Protestant interpretation of the temptation of the Flesh as a temptation to distrust was the idea that it was also a temptation through necessity.[10] In Satan's speech before the tree, which is based primarily on the Protestant version of the temptation of the Flesh, he concludes that "these, these and many more / Causes import your *need* of this fair Fruit" (IX.730-731; my italics). Correspondingly, Satan's final speech focuses on the necessity of his falseness. The final strategy is, therefore, the logical outgrowth of all that has gone before in terms of the false hermit and prophet's two seeming motivations, charity and necessity, and the alternation of these themes in Satan's arguments. Christ has exploded Satan's pretense of a disguised truth and charity by pointing out, as Eve should have, that it is the devil and his "word" that are disguised, that it is he who would disguise himself as God, God as himself, that it is he not God who mixes "somewhat true to vent more lies" (433). Satan, finally confessing that his falsehood is in fact real, his charity fraudulent, now attempts to justify that falsehood in charity through an appeal to necessity. Misery has forced him from the ways of truth:

> Sharply thou has insisted on rebuke,
> And urg'd me hard with doings, which not will
> But misery hath wrested from me; where
> Easily canst thou find one miserable,
> And not enforc'd of time to part from truth . . . ?
> (468-472)

[10] See Pope, pp. 55-64, 101. To her references add Francis Quarles, *Judgment and Mercy for Afflicted Soules*, in *Complete Works*, ed. Alexander B. Grosart, I (1880; rpt. New York: AMS Press, 1967), 122-123.

141

Once again Satan is tempting Christ to see Himself mirrored in Satan as a false prophet but not, as in the previous speech, through a common charity—that Christ has shown to be nonsense—but through a common necessity. In the second speech of the first stage of the Flesh-temptation (the stones), Satan had tempted Christ through the necessity for physical food; here, in the second speech of the second stage, he once again threatens Christ in terms of a necessity, but a necessity this time in terms of His role as dispenser of *spiritual* food. Again parodying John the Baptist admiring a worthier prophet, Satan argues, speaking ostensibly of himself but implicitly also of Christ, that

> Hard are the ways of truth, and rough to walk,
> Smooth on the tongue discourst, pleasing to th' ear,
> And tunable as Silvan Pipe or Song;
> What wonder then if I delight to hear
> Her dictates from thy mouth? most men admire
> Virtue, who follow not her lore: permit me
> To hear thee when I come (since no man comes)
> And talk at least, though I *despair* to attain.
>
> (478-485; my italics)

Satan's warning is simply that truth is easier said than done. Testimony is found not only in his experience but also in mankind's; and the reason for this, Satan implies, using the pastoral-heroic terminology he will use for the second day's temptations, is that for most men truth is pastoral ("Silvan") self-indulgence: pastoral is not a preliminary to the heroism of the active life but a retreat from it. Men can enjoy truth in retreat, but the misery of real life forces them from it. The implications for Christ, speaking truth in His wilderness retreat, are obvious: misery, already at hand "since no man comes," may force Christ to imitate Satan and "despair to attain" the ways of truth. Satan concludes with a further threat, similar to that made by Bale's Satan when he claims that Christ should not undergo such physical torment to be God's prophet since "Preach ye once the truth the bishops

142

will ye murther,"[11] and similar, too, to that made by Spenser's Despaire when he argues the pointlessness of all action:

> Thy Father, who is holy, wise and pure,
> Suffers the Hypocrite or Atheous Priest
> To tread his Sacred Courts, and minister
> About his Altar, handling holy things,
> Praying or vowing, and vouchsaf'd his voice
> To *Balaam* Reprobate, a Prophet yet
> Inspir'd; disdain not such access to me.
>
> (486-492)

"I am," Satan intimates, "the first of the hypocrites who will violate your word. In the wilderness is set the pattern of your prophecy, for I (the hypocrite) alone am here to hear your voice 'since no man comes.'" The present situation, of the hypocrite listening to the prophet, images forth the futility of the whole ordeal. The misery of the "hard" ways of truth is not worth it all; for if God has suffered the hypocrite in "Sacred Courts" in the past, He will continue to do so in the future, as He does now in the wilderness.[12] God works no harder than mortals to assure the triumph of truth. The threat, veiled with praise and solicitous concern, is that Christ's idealism exists in pointless isolation, and that the young Jew, cast off from God and from man, is a prophet without a church and even a god, dedicated to a mission He must "despair to attain." Whether by choice or by necessity, Christ's identity as prophet is to be found in its parody, and the Satanic type will be fulfilled in Him.

[11] "The Temptation of Our Lord," in *The Dramatic Writings of John Bale*, ed. John S. Farmer (1907; rpt. New York: Barnes and Noble, 1966), p. 157.

[12] Satan would seem to be tempting Christ to confuse the visible church, which can include the hypocritical and the unregenerate as well as the regenerate, with the invisible church, which includes only the true believers and the regenerate, and which is known only to Christ (see *De D.*, I.xxiv and I.xxix; CE, XVI, 57-65, 218-249).

143

II

The reflections on Christ's mission and nature, which open Book II, act as a link between the temptation of the Flesh on the first day and the temptation of the World on the second. The meditations of Andrew and Simon and Mary look back to the first day in their expression of doubt, their fear that God's word has somehow deceived them, promised more than or something other than it would deliver; and even Christ Himself seems to feel exasperation and impatience, bordering on doubt, as He asks Himself, "Where will this end?" (245). But the patient trust in the word Christ asserted on the first day is also ultimately asserted in these meditations. At the same time, however, the meditations also look ahead to the temptations of the second day to Christ's kingship. For neither in the bower nor on the mountain is found the proper landscape of Christ's kingdom; rather it is here, in the hearts of those who would seek Him out and perceive Him, that His kingdom lies. They look for a kingdom, but they are that kingdom; it is within them. The misconception of Christ's kingship that Andrew and Simon express, of a messiah who will physically liberate and rule Israel, is of course the same misconception which Christ has felt and to which Satan will tempt Christ: what they perceive as liberation is in fact only Adamic enslavement in a different guise. Correspondingly, Mary's attempt to perceive some purposeful connection between her "Afflictions high" and her "Exaltation" (92) parallels Christ's own meditation and adumbrates Satan's strategy on the second day and his suggestion that Christ's lowness runs counter to the loftiness of the "mission high" (114) prophesied for Him. And finally, Christ's newly felt hunger obviously prepares for the banquet-temptation.

Satan's speeches in the second infernal council are a foil to the meditations of the other characters. Like them, he too is disturbed by doubt, though his doubt ironically takes the form of growing belief in Christ as the Son of God and despair over his own powers to vanquish Him. Primarily, however, this episode looks forward to the temptation of the World and Christ's kingship. Most obviously, in terms of the inner kingdom Christ is soon to demonstrate, the episode reveals a mind which, unlike the minds of Andrew and Simon, Mary, and Christ, can have no rest. In his own inner kingdom, the tyrant is himself tyrannized by desires for glory and kingship in the outer world which he can never fully satisfy. It is a mind fixed, obsessed; focused as it is on the outer world rather than itself, and seeking in the outer world alone its desires' resolution, it is a mind that admits no growth, in which no Eden can be raised. Satan's central concern, like Andrew and Simon's, is a physical kingdom, which he describes, appropriately enough, as ruled over by the four elements, the "Powers of Fire, Air, Water, and Earth" (124); and it is to such a materialistic conception of His kingdom that Satan will tempt Christ in the ensuing temptations.

Satan's first encounter with Christ has given him some intimation of Christ's uniqueness. He has learned that Christ requires "Far other labor to be undergone / Than when I dealt with *Adam* first of Men, / Though *Adam* by his Wife's allurement fell, / However to this Man inferior far" (132-135)—"If he be Man" (136) at all. In light of Satan's explicit assertion of Christ's superiority to Adam, it may at first seem curious that Belial should propose a repetition of the temptation in Eden to Adam's sensuality. One reason for Milton's including this proposal, I suspect, was to make perfectly clear, through Satan's rejection of it, that while Christ is being tempted as the second Adam, this is no reason to expect an exact replica of the temptations used in Eden. It is, then, a declaration of his own latitude in treating the second-Adam theme. Christ will have to overcome temptations similar to but much more difficult than Adam's—which is the only way of making the second-Adam theme persuasive, since it may well seem that Christ has it much easier than Adam. But Belial's proposal has another function: it looks forward to the banquet's temptation to intemperance. The relationship between Belial and Satan is, of course, an

145

infernal parody of temperance, but the banquet Satan will offer Christ will itself take the form of a parody of temperance. Belial, rendered irrational by his fleshly obsessions, requires that Satan repeat what he has already said about Christ, and reprove Belial: "thou weigh'st / All others by thyself" (173-174). But one is inclined to reply to Satan in his rebuke, "Tu quoque!"; for Satan proposes to tempt Christ in his own terms, "manlier objects" (225) of aspiring pride. Satan's conception of temperance is comically distorted. Solomon, he claims, fell into intemperance because he "aim'd not beyond / Higher design than to enjoy his State" (202-203). As before in the Flesh-temptation, Satan sees Christ as Himself; and in Satan's parody of Christ's inner kingdom, it is not reason but pride that controls the appetite: the higher vice restrains the lower.

The temptation Belial has proposed is Circe's: sense seduces reason, and "amorous Arts, enchanting tongues" (158) "lead / At will the manliest, resolutest breast" (167-168).[13] Ostensibly Satan rejects the Circean temptation as unfit for Christ's more manly character; but in fact Satan does not so much reject the strategy of Circe as expand it, so that Christ is tempted not only, indeed not primarily, to Belial's effeminate unheroic life but also, and primarily, to the masculine false-heroic life, the aspiration for "honor, glory, and popular praise" (227), which is the World. Like Circes of the World before him, Spenser's Lucifera and Fletcher's Panglorie, also like Milton's own Dalila, Satan appears before Christ in courtly disguise as a wealthy man of the world:

[13] On the relationship of the Circean temptation to the seductive songs or words of the Sirens, see John M. Steadman, "Dalila, the Ulysses Myth, and Renaissance Allegorical Tradition," *Modern Language Review*, 57 (1962), 560-565; also Merritt Y. Hughes, "Spenser's Acrasia and the Circe of the Renaissance," *Journal of the History of Ideas*, 4 (1943), 381-399. Comus, it should be recalled, speaks of hearing "My mother *Circe* with the Sirens three" (253), and employs "Wit and gay Rhetoric" (790) to seduce the Lady's reason; so, too, Belial in *Paradise Lost* and Dalila in *Samson Agonistes*.

> . . . suddenly a man before him stood,
> Not rustic as before, but seemlier clad,
> As one in City, or Court, or Palace bred . . .
>
> (298-300)

The Circean image is like its predecessors purposefully ambiguous: in what will be a temptation to Christ's kingship,
has Satan come as king or courtier? has Satan come to serve
a king or to place a king in service? This ambiguity is an
ironic foreshadowing and mirroring of Christ's paradox about
His own kingship, that the true king is in fact a servant. Indeed, the ambiguity of the disguise underlies all of Satan's
offers of service to Christ on the second day, until finally,
after the temptation to Rome, Satan reveals himself for what
he is. If in the disguise of the first day, Satan offered himself
up as the diabolic parody of Christ's prophecy, in this disguise he offers himself up as the diabolic parody of Christ's
kingship.

The disguise Satan has adopted for this new series of temptations implies an opposition of mutually exclusive contraries,
of the pastoral and contemplative life, parodied by the hermit, and the heroic and active life, parodied by the urban
courtier-king. It implies what Satan will continually suggest
to Christ in the ensuing temptations and what was the fear
underlying the meditations opening Book II, that the mean
estate of pastoral runs contrary to the heroic high estate
prophesied for Christ. Accordingly, Satan will attempt to convince Christ that His rustic unworthiness, His simplicity, and
His lack of worldly knowledge make Him unprepared for
higher achievement; that Christ, without Satan's assistance,
is and will be little more than a country bumpkin whose "life
hath yet been private, most part spent / At home, scarce
view'd the *Galilean* Towns" (III.232-233). In fact, of course,
the opposition between pastoral and heroic, low estate and
high, the active life and the contemplative life, is false. The
real opposition, as Christ is to demonstrate, is between true
pastoral and false, true heroic and false. In keeping with

147

Satan's strategy of opposing pastoral and heroic, it is significant that, while Satan's disguise suggests the courtly false
heroic, the setting (which is apparently one of his own devising) is false pastoral:

> Up to a hill anon his steps he [Christ] rear'd,
> From whose high top to ken the prospect round,
> If Cottage were in view, Sheepcote or Herd;
> But Cottage, Herd or Sheepcote none he saw,
> Only in a bottom saw a pleasant Grove,
> With chant of tuneful Birds resounding loud.
> Thither he bent his way, determin'd there
> To rest at noon, and enter'd soon the shade
> High rooft, and walks beneath, and alleys brown
> That open'd in the midst a woody Scene;
> Nature's own work it seem'd (Nature taught Art)
> And to a Superstitious eye the haunt
> Of Wood Gods, and Wood Nymphs . . .
>
> (285-297)

The absence of "Cottage, Herd or Sheepcote," marks of the
simplicity of true pastoral, is significant; for this "pleasant
Grove" of singing birds and restful shade is in reality a garden of the senses, deluding the reason into false ("Super-
stitious") beliefs, and tricking the eye into accepting it as
something other than what it is. The setting for the first sequence of temptations on the second day thus embodies the
same distortion of pastoral Satan employed in his last speech
in the stones-temptation: the pastoral world, like the truth
the good shepherd and prophet enunciates, is mere sylvan
self-indulgence; the contemplative life is in reality a refined
version of the voluptuous life. Accordingly, the setting is a
counterpart to the false-pastoral gardens of the voluptuous
life associated with Renaissance Circes, which the hero encounters as a preliminary temptation before a temptation on
a mountain. It is also, as Fletcher describes his Garden of
Vain-Delight through which Christ passes on his way to

Panglorie's castle on top of a mountain, a "false Eden."[14]
Reinforcing the connection between the setting and Eden,
Milton notes that in this spot Christ was "determin'd . . . /
To rest at noon," which was of course the time of the temptation in Eden.[15] Appropriately enough, it is within this
counterpart to the lost garden that the first (i.e., banquet-
wealth-glory) sequence of temptations, directed primarily to
Christ's inner kingdom, the paradise within, takes place; the
setting is a parody of the inner *"Eden* [to be] rais'd in the
waste Wilderness" (I.7). Appropriately too, it is within this
false Eden that Christ will define both true pastoral and true
heroic, rejecting the false pastoral Eden of nature's banquet
of the senses and the false heroic of gold and glory, and affirm-
ing the garden of the mind that is the true pastoral landscape
and the necessary prerequisite to true kingship and heroic
glory.

As in Milton's predecessors, and as in *Samson Agonistes*,
the ensuing temptation to the World and Christ's kingship is
a composite temptation. Milton outdoes his predecessors,
however, by including in the World-temptation *two* versions
of the infernal triad: the first sequence, as Barbara Lewalski
suggests, is devoted to Christ's inner kingdom, with the banquet corresponding to the Flesh, the gold-temptation to the
World, and the glory-temptation to the Devil; the second

[14] "Christ's Victory on Earth" (marginal note to st. 50), in *The
Poetical Works of Giles and Phineas Fletcher*, ed. Frederick S. Boas,
I (Cambridge: Cambridge Univ. Press, 1908). All citations to
Fletcher are to this edition.

[15] Albert R. Cirillo, "Noon-Midnight and the Temporal Structure
of *Paradise Lost*," in *Critical Essays on Milton from "ELH"* (Baltimore, Md.: The Johns Hopkins Press, 1969), pp. 210-233, indicates
that "Noon was morally the most dangerous time of day. The resulting prevalence of *luxuria* and the awakening of the sensual appetite
in dreams made midday an hour of extreme sexual temptation" (p.
218). Although Cirillo does not suggest it, it would seem that noon
carries precisely the same significance in *Paradise Regained*, as it
does in *Samson Agonistes*.

149

sequence, I believe, continues the temptation of Christ as the second Adam but within a new context, Christ's public kingdom, with the Parthia-temptation corresponding to the Devil, Rome to the Flesh, and Athens to the World.[16] All six temptations are in quite specific ways designed as replies to the temptations in Eden; and the beauty of these passages resides in large measure in the intellectual subtlety of the connections being made.

Though Satan claims otherwise, the banquet-temptation is of course a temptation to the Flesh and Eve's intemperance; and the banquet itself is a counterpart to Eve's apple:[17]

[16] In this reading I accept Lewalski's suggestion that the first triadic sequence is primarily concerned with "the definition and display of Christ's kingship over self" (p. 219), and that the temptations to Parthia and Rome are "principally concerned with the challenge to and the full revelation of Christ's kingly office" (p. 256). I cannot, however, follow her separation of Athens from the kingdoms-sequence, which mars the triadic symmetry of the World-temptation; nor can I accept her contention that Milton relegates "the specific treatment of the triple equation and of the Second Adam theme" (p. 22) to "the wholly original banquet-wealth-glory sequence" (p. 223), since I see the Parthia-Rome-Athens sequence repeating and completing the second-Adam theme within the new context of Christ's public kingdom. With regard to the structure of the temptations on the second day, Pope argues that "In a sense . . . Milton may be said to present a combined temptation of the world, the flesh, and the devil since the three sins which typify them—gluttony, vain glory, and avarice—all appear on the same day" (p. 101). How Pope manages this is something of a mystery. "The kingdoms themselves—the countries he [Satan] actually shows Christ from the mountain," are, she claims, treated "as the simple temptation of *the world*"; the banquet-temptation is the Flesh, and the glory-temptation the Devil. But where does this leave the wealth-temptation? And if the wealth-temptation is the temptation of the World, what does one do with Pope's claim that the kingdoms equal the World? See also Schultz, "Christ and Antichrist," p. 797n.; Woodhouse, "Theme and Pattern," p. 176; and Irene Samuel, *Plato and Milton* (Ithaca, N.Y.: Cornell Univ. Press, 1947), p. 71.

[17] Where one places the banquet-temptation is crucial to one's conception of the structure of temptation on the second day. If we approach the banquet-wealth-glory sequence by way of Spenser and

> Alas how simple, to these Cates compar'd
> Was the crude Apple that diverted Eve!
>
> (348-349)

The banquet-temptation, however, is more complex than that in Eden not merely because it offers more food but because it offers it in a more convoluted and indirect way. In presenting Christ with a banquet table laden with food and attended by lovely boys and nymphs, Satan would seem to be follow-

---

Fletcher, it becomes perfectly clear that the banquet must be part of the World-temptation as are comparable temptations to the Flesh in the House of Pride, the Cave of Mammon, and Panglorie's house of vainglory. Gilbert, pp. 603-605, was the first to point out that the banquet is not a repetition of the stones-temptation but is really the first of the allegorical glories. However, Theodore H. Banks, "The Banquet Scene in *Paradise Regained*," *PMLA*, 55 (1940), 773-776, contends that the banquet is best regarded as "a link between the first temptation and the second" (p. 773), which begins with the temptation to gold; but his argument is based on the misconception that the stones-temptation grows out of Christ's desire for food; nonetheless, Jacques Blondel, *Le Paradise reconquis, Etude critique* (Paris: Aubier, 1955), pp. 52-53, has substantially agreed with him. Pope, pp. 70-79, argues against Gilbert on the grounds that "If the banqueting scene is really part of the temptation of the kingdoms, it ought logically to conform to the same pattern as the glories of the world. But this is by no means the case. The feast is not associated with any particular realm, nor is it in any way related to the winning or exercise of purely human and temporal sovereignty, like the other glories of the world" (pp. 70-71); and she suggests that the temptation is "an independent episode" (p. 74), which "can be fairly described as the Protestant equivalent of the old *gula* temptation" (p. 79). Pope is right to insist on the role of intemperance in the banquet but wrong to deny the banquet's relationship to Christ's sovereignty, for Christ is offered the banquet as a form of temporal sovereignty over nature in His role as *rex naturae*. Moreover, the strategy of the temptation, though Satan subtly conceals it, is identical to the strategy of the following two temptations. The fact that there is no teleology between the banquet and the offer of wealth, as there is between the wealth- and glory-temptations, should not in the least be surprising: there is no such teleology in Genesis 3. Nonetheless, E. L. Marilla, "*Paradise Regained*: Observations on Its Meaning," *Studia Neophilologica*, 27 (1955), p. 183n., and Schultz, "A Fairer Paradise?,"

ing precisely the version of the Circean temptation as a direct appeal to sensuality that Belial had earlier suggested and Satan rejected; he would also seem to be merely repeating, though on a larger and grander scale, the temptation to Eve's intemperance. Accordingly, the banquet has its counterpart in the Circean banquets of the senses found in classical and Renaissance epic and, of course, Milton's own *Comus*; and as Frank Kermode has shown,[18] all five senses are involved in the banquet-temptation, as they were, as we have seen, in Eve's fall. The similarity is accurate but deceptive; for in order to play Circe to Christ, Satan has adopted a "manlier" disguise. Consequently, he deviously tempts Christ to interpret the banquet not as a temptation to the unheroic effeminacy of intemperance but rather as an offer of kingship and heroic glory:

> All these are Spirits of Air, and Woods, and Springs,
> Thy gentle Ministers, who come to pay
> Thee homage, and acknowledge thee thir Lord.
>
> (374-376)

This table "in regal mode" (340) is the lowest of the material kingships Satan will offer Christ, a kingship over the elements of air, earth, and water (Satan's own element, the highest, fire, is omitted and reserved for the glory-temptation). Christ is thus tempted to accept as His identity Satan's own diabolic parody of His role as the Creator and *rex naturae*, and in so doing to be enslaved to His own nature. In this respect, the underlying irony of the banquet-temptation is that Satan would have the Creator to be subject to

---

p. 295, have agreed with Pope. Fixler, pp. 255-261, also repeats this error of making the banquet a separate episode, but on the grounds that Christ is being tempted to His priestly not His kingly role. Finally, Frank Kermode, "Milton's Hero," *Review of English Studies*, 4 (1953), 317-330, pursues the old argument that the banquet is a repetition of "the initial appeal to Christ's hunger," but for new reasons, that "the first temptation is canonical, the second a quasi-allegorical development of it which is essential to the structure of the poem" (pp. 323-324) as a foil to the celestial banquet.

[18] "Milton's Hero," p. 324.

His own creation. But another irony operates here as well: the temptation to temperance takes the form of an infernal parody of temperance. It is an extension of the parody of temperance in the infernal council. The inner kingship of reason over appetite and one's own nature, which is true temperance, is translated into and replaced by an outer kingship over nature and the elements; temperance's control over man's inner nature is replaced by a control over outer nature. Consequently, the banquet-temptation has precisely the same strategy as the two temptations that follow it: it attempts to substitute external kingship for inner kingship.

The offer of gold as a means to glory obviously corresponds to Satan's offer to Eve in Eden of the knowledge of good and evil as a means to the glory of the godhead; it is, therefore, a temptation to the World. In keeping with the homeopathy of Christ's resistance, one would expect Eve's avarice to be countered by charity. That does in fact happen, but in a more complicated fashion. Ironically, it is Satan, in another of the distortions of his mirror, who counters Eve's avarice by an ostensible act of generosity; his offer of gold, then, is an infernal parody of the second Adam's correction of Eve's avarice by charity. In order for Christ to counter Satan's Christlike correction of avarice by charity, it is not enough for Him merely to repudiate gold. He must progress to a higher charity, repudiating not only *avaritia pecuniae* but also its counterpart, *avaritia scientiae*. He must counter Eve's avarice in seizing knowledge with His own charity in dispensing truth; He must counter the kingship she attempted to seize with the higher kingship of the inner kingdom of the man "who reigns within himself" (466):

> But to guide Nations in the way of truth
> By saving Doctrine, and from error lead
> To know, and knowing worship God aright,
> Is yet more Kingly . . .
>
> (473-476)

Merely renouncing gold, or even false knowledge, may give Christ a victory over Adam but no substantial victory over

Satan. That victory is possible only through Christ's raising, by means of His truth, a new Eden in the wilderness of man's mind, which is "Anarchy within" (471). Christ's charity in bestowing the truth of His own inner kingdom does more than counter Eve's avarice in seizing knowledge; by removing man's mind from Satan's dominion, it provides the essential preliminary for the victory of His own kingship over Satan's.

As the temptation of the Devil, the offer of glory completes this first triadic sequence: if in Eden Satan argued that knowledge would lead to the glory of the godhead, Satan now argues that Christ's truth will lead to glory. Of the three temptations in this sequence, this is the most brilliant in its strategy of a kaleidoscopic shifting and merging of identities. Once again Satan tempts Christ to become an imitation of himself by perceiving His image in the infernal mirror: Satan attempts to divert Christ's imitation of God into an imitation of the devil by confusing the "Godlike Virtues" (21) of His glory with Eve's and the devil's vainglorious attempt to "be as Gods."[19] This infernal equation of true glory and vainglory leads to another equation; two things equal to the same thing are equal to each other: Christ and Satan are one. Christ recognizes the deception in the mirror, as He condemns seekers of glory as men who "swell with pride, and must be titl'd Gods" (81). Satan's offer of glory has also involved a parody of God's offering glory to man; the very offer of glory is part of the vainglory of Satan's fraudulent *imitatio dei*. True glory, Christ must reply, comes from God alone; and He proceeds to counter Eve's seizing of glory through knowledge with His own sacrificing of His glory in a martyrdom "For truth's sake" (98).

In the first stage of the glory-temptation, Christ refuses Satan's offer of glory on the grounds that it involves a fraudulent imitation of God. Satan shifts his tack accordingly: it is

[19] On the Renaissance conception of the hero as the "Godlike man," see John M. Steadman, *Milton's Epic Characters* (Chapel Hill, N.C.: Univ. of North Carolina Press, 1968), pp. 23-43.

Christ, in His refusal of glory, and not himself who is the fraudulent image of God. As in the stones-temptation, Christ's "Godlike Virtues" make Him ungodlike: "Think not so slight of glory; therein least / Resembling thy great Father" (109-110). The threat, a formidable one, is that human virtue has no divine sanction or pattern, that in fact it runs counter to the very nature of God Himself, and that Christ's virtue places Him in a relationship not as the Son to God but as Prometheus to Zeus. The implication of Satan's final speech is that this ostensible Son of God is more in revolt against the Father than the Adversary himself; and that if Christ is to become a son of God, He will find that identity in and through Satan himself, who, like the Father, requires "Glory from men, from all men good or bad" (114). The more Christ is like Satan the more He is like the Father. This is very clever strategy, for it throws all three identities into total confusion: Satan and God mirror each other, God being Satanic, Satan godlike, with Christ the virtuous pariah cast ironically in the role of His Father's Promethean adversary. The only possible reply is the one Christ makes: that Satan misperceives God as he misperceives the nature of glory; that there is no absolute disjunction between God and human virtue; that for God as for man, glory is a means to a selfless end. The episode has thus worked from many angles to throw the identity of true glory into confusion and to throw Christ into confusion as to where to discover the pattern for His glory and identity. The result of Christ's reply, however, is to turn on Satan himself the mirror Satan has perversely used against Christ. The sequence appropriately concludes with Satan, "struck / With guilt of his own sin" (146-147), shocked by the horrible recognition of his own image in the mirror of Christ's words.

III

The glory-temptation completes the first Flesh-World-Devil sequence in the temptation to the World; but it has also laid the groundwork, in its development of the relationship of Christ's inner kingdom to His public mission and glory, for the second sequence and its consideration of the proper means to this mission. The Israel episode, which immediately follows the allegorical sequence and prefaces the temptations on the mountain, must be regarded not as a separate temptation but rather, as Mrs. Lewalski suggests,[20] as an induction to Satan's offer of the three kingdoms. The fact that the three kingdoms are all offered on the mountain, just as the three glories were all offered in a false-pastoral retreat, would seem to insist upon this approach. To do otherwise is to violate the symmetrical structure of the World-temptation, in which the Parthia-Rome-Athens sequence is organized like the first sequence around the infernal triad.

Throughout the Israel episode, and indeed throughout the kingdoms-temptation as a whole, recurs the ambiguity surrounding Satan's disguise as parodic king: he comes appearing to serve, when in fact he has come to be served. Urging Christ to zeal in freeing "Thy Country from her Heathen servitude" (176), he appears in the role of a zealous courtier urging on a sluggish and reluctant king. Satan goes so far as to suggest that Christ's kingship may be to his advantage:

> . . . to that gentle brow
> Willingly I could fly, and hope thy reign,
> From that placid aspect and meek regard,
> Rather than aggravate my evil state,
> Would stand between me and thy Father's ire
> (Whose ire I dread more than the fire of Hell)
> A shelter and a kind of shading cool
> Interposition, as a summer's cloud.
>
> (215-222)

Identities once again are thrown into almost surrealistic confusion, as Satan distorts Christ's role as mediator between God and man (or His church) to apply to Christ's mediating between him (Satan) and God: Christ ironically is cast in

---

[20] *Milton's Brief Epic*, p. 261.

the role of Satan's savior, just as before He was Satan's prophet and king.[21] Satan then proceeds to return to the strategy underlying the previous temptations: once again, he offers himself up as a type of Christ and an infernal mirror, this time in terms of Christ's role as mediator. Revising the matter of mediatorial service from Christ's serving him to his serving Christ, Satan now offers to act as Christ's mediator between Him and the World: he will instruct Christ, whose "life hath yet been private" (232) and inexperienced, in "The world" (236). Satan thereby sets up a diabolic parody of Christ's mediatorial role as prophet and teacher, just as later on the mountain he will, in his offer of the kingdoms, set up a parody of Christ's mediatorial role as king as Christ Himself has already defined it: "to give a Kingdom hath been thought / Greater and nobler done, and to lay down / Far more magnanimous than to assume" (II.481-483). Satan's stance in this sequence as false king and false prophet thus parodies the two mediatorial offices which are at stake in the kingdoms-sequence; for while Parthia and Rome are offered as a means of attaining kingship of Israel, Athens is shown as a means of Christ's becoming Israel's prophet-king.

The Israel episode also serves to make clear that the temptation of Christ as the second Adam is not dropped:

> The world thou hast not *seen*, much less her glory,
> Empires, and Monarchs, and thir radiant Courts,
> Best school of best experience, quickest *insight*

[21] In keeping with the irony underlying this exchange, Satan's imagery echoes the Canticles, 1:6 and 2:3 especially, and should probably be understood in terms of Christian exegeses of the Canticles in which Christ becomes the shade of grace protecting man, here Satan, from the burning rays of *sol iustitiae*. The Canticles were commonly interpreted as an allegory of Christ's love for, and marriage with, the church. In this context, what Satan would seem to be suggesting is that the Old Testament prophecy of Christ's marriage to His church will be fulfilled with him as Christ's spouse, his kingdoms as Christ's church. A full survey of these exegetical traditions can be found in Stanley Stewart, *The Enclosed Garden* (Madison, Wisc.: The Univ. of Wisconsin Press, 1966), chs. 1 and 3, esp.

In all things that to greatest actions lead.

. . . .

But I will bring thee where thou soon shalt quit
Those rudiments, and *see before thine eyes*
The Monarchies of th'Earth, thir pomp and state,
Sufficient introduction to inform
Thee, of thyself so apt, in regal Arts,
And regal Mysteries. . . .

(236-249; my italics)

"Insight / In all things" as a means to "greatest action," the
opening of the eyes to "Mysteries" as a preparation to kingship: the progression should be familiar. It was made in the
temptation to gold, and it will culminate in the kingdoms
sequence with Athens, where knowledge will be offered as a
means to power. It was made also in the *concupiscentia oculorum* temptation in Eden: "your eyes shall be opened and
ye will be as gods knowing good and evil" (Genesis 3:5).
We are prepared for another triadic temptation to the World.
The second-Adam theme is thus by no means dropped; it is
simply given a new frame of reference, the public kingdom
rather than the inner kingdom, with Parthia the temptation
of the Devil, Rome the Flesh, and Athens the World.

In offering Parthia, Satan offers the kingdom of the Devil.
This is the earthly kingdom that most resembles Satan's own
conception of the ideal kingdom. As the kingdom of glory
and brute force, it is, like Moloch, the giants of Book XI of
Paradise Lost, and Harapha, the embodiment of the devil's
"own sin," and accordingly it is the one he himself prefers:
"the *Parthian* first / By my advice" (363-364). In the allegorical glory-Devil temptation, Satan offered Christ the glory
of such conquerors by force as Alexander, Scipio, and Pom-
pey; and Christ rejected the offer chiefly in terms of His inner
kingdom, on the grounds that conquerors are themselves inwardly enslaved: they repeat the Fall, falling first into "pride"
(81) and then into "brutish vices" (86), or intemperance,
just as the devil himself fell first into pride and then into lust

for Sin. In the Parthia-temptation, Christ applies to a public context the conclusions He reached in the previous glory-Devil-temptation to His private kingdom: if glory enslaves the conqueror, it obviously cannot do in the outer world the opposite of what it does in the inner world and liberate a nation inwardly enslaved.

Rome, though it is linked not only with intemperance but also with wealth and power, has as its central thrust and import a temptation to the Flesh. To associate this temptation with either riches or power primarily is to confuse the real end of the temptation with the heroic terminology Satan uses to camouflage its essential appeal; for like the banquet to which it is the public counterpart, Rome offers a temptation to the Flesh and unheroic intemperance cloaked, as in fact the nation itself is, in the guise of the heroic and kingly. In this respect it is significant that for all their differing attitudes towards Rome, Christ and Satan do agree on one point: Rome has fallen through intemperance. The city is portrayed by Satan as combining Parthian power with beauty and "Civility" (83), but the price of civility is for Satan high: in contrast to Parthia, which in the prime of its power has "From the luxurious Kings of *Antioch* won" (III.297) its empire, Rome is in the twilight of its civilization and is controlled by precisely such a "luxurious King," Tiberius, who is

> Old, and lascivious, and from *Rome* retir'd
> To *Capreae*, an Island small but strong
> On the *Campanian* shore, with purpose there
> His horrid lusts in private to enjoy,
> Committing to a wicked Favorite
> All public cares . . .
>
> (IV.91-96)

Satan holds the same contempt for the fleshly intemperance of Rome's head that he earlier expressed for the intemperance of Belial; and his suggestion that Christ's "Regal Virtues" (98) should enable Him to replace the intemperate king as head of the Roman state involves the same distorted concep-

159

tion of temperance Satan displayed with Belial: pride rather than reason controls the unruly desires of the public kingdom as it does the appetite of the private kingdom. Satan's protest against Tiberius' intemperance is, in actuality, an effort to disguise the fact that Christ is once again being tempted to the intemperance of the Flesh, couched, as in the banquet-temptation, in heroic terms. In the banquet-temptation, the kingship over outer nature parodied the inner kingdom's kingship of reason over appetite. In the Rome-temptation, the nature of the temptation shifts slightly because the context has changed to Christ's public kingdom. Instead of Christ's being tempted to succumb to His own hunger and thus accept intemperance as part of His private kingdom, He is now tempted to accept an intemperate nation as His public kingdom. Despite this difference, in both Flesh-temptations Christ is tempted to intemperance under the guise of His being a king; and here as in the banquet-temptation, the kingship offered Him is a parody of reason's kingship over the appetite. In His rebuttal, Christ shows Himself aware that this temptation also conceals a temptation to repeat Eve's intemperance and that it implies, though ever so much more indirectly than the banquet, an illegitimate appeal to His hunger:

> Nor doth this grandeur and majestic show
> Of luxury, though call'd magnificence,
> More than of arms before, allure mine eye,
> Much less my mind; though thou should'st add to tell
> Thir sumptuous gluttonies, and gorgeous feasts
> On *Citron* tables or *Atlantic* stone,
> (For I have also heard, perhaps have read)
> Their wines of *Setia*, *Cales*, and *Falerne*,
> *Chios* and *Crete*, and how they quaff in Gold,
> Crystal and Murrhine cups emboss'd with Gems
> And studs of Pearl, to me should'st tell who thirst
> And hunger still . . .
>
> (110-121)

In tempting Christ to the Flesh in the form of Rome, Satan, it should be clear, continues to tempt Christ as the second Adam. Indeed, as if to reinforce the continued presence of this theme, Milton has alluded to Eve and Eden in introducing the Rome-temptation:

> . . . and the persuasive Rhetoric
> That sleek't his tongue, and won so much on *Eve*,
> So little here, nay lost; but *Eve* was *Eve*,
> This far his over-match . . .
>
> (4-7)

Christ Himself recognizes the continuing tempting of Him as the second Adam in the Parthia- and Rome-temptations when He dismisses Satan's offer of "The Kingdoms of the world" (163) as "this attempt bolder than that of *Eve*" (180).

From one perspective, the offers of Parthia and Rome form a structural unit of their own. The one representing the pride of the Devil, the other the intemperance of the Flesh, they represent together the two principal corrupt affections to which fallen man is heir. This degenerate progression in vice from pride to intemperance is true for the unregenerate individual soul—it is true for Satan and Samson, for example; it is also true for the history of nations and for the race as a whole. The Parthia-Rome sequence, then, is a paradigm of human history, and it bears comparison with a similar version of history in *Paradise Lost*, Book XI, where history is schematically portrayed as a continuing alternation between the Devil and the Flesh: Cain and the prideful envy of the Devil; the lazar house and the men of the plains, Eve's and Adam's intemperance of the Flesh, respectively; the giants and the vainglory of the Devil (and also, to a lesser extent, the "luxurious wealth" [788] of the World); and finally, the people of Noah and intemperance of the Flesh. This is also the pattern of degeneration in the Parthia-Rome sequence: Parthia, for Satan, is in the prime of her power through pride, Rome in her decline through intemperance. Christ has a different view of the moral decline of Rome: its decline is not, as Satan views it, from false-heroic pride but from heroic temperance to unheroic and effeminate intemperance:

> For him [Tiberius] I was not sent, nor yet to free
> That people victor once, now vile and base,
> Deservedly made vassal, who once just,
> Frugal, and mild, and temperate, conquer'd well,
> But govern ill the Nations under yoke,
> Peeling thir Provinces, exhausted all
> By lust and rapine; first ambitious grown
> Of triumph, that insulting vanity;
> Then cruel, by thir sports to blood inur'd
> Of fighting beasts, and men to beasts expos'd,
> Luxurious by thir wealth, and greedier still,
> And from the daily Scene effeminate.

(131-142)

The history of Rome's decline is literally a progression through "all sin," from the ambitious and cruel pride of the Devil, to the wealth of the World, and finally to—what is its immediate significance to the structure of the work and in its second-Adam theme—the intemperance of the Flesh. Rome therefore not only concludes this paradigmatic sequence but also in its own history recapitulates it.

Although as a paradigm of the history of fallen nations Parthia and Rome form a structural unit of their own and are as a result set apart slightly from the Athens-temptation, they also form an ultimately more important unit with Athens. Ostensibly Satan sets Athens apart from "The Kingdoms of this world," which are "transitory" (209-210). In reality, the separation is more strategic than real; for Athens is in fact a kingdom of the world, and it is also transitory. The Athens-temptation climaxes the strategy of the previous two temptations to subvert the inner kingdom by offering Christ unworthy public kingdoms: with Parthia and Rome, Satan attempted this subversion through the two *vitae* of the World, *vita activa* and *vita voluptuosa*, respectively; in the Athens-temptation, Satan attempts to subvert the inner king-

dom through what might seem to be its own terms by offering a way to kingship traditionally thought otherworldly, *vita
contemplativa*. From another perspective, too, Athens is the
logical culmination of this triadic sequence: Satan's ostensible
motive from the beginning of the kingdoms-sequence has
been a desire to teach Christ worldly knowledge. With Athens
this offer takes its fullest and most distorted form, as Satan
now offers worldly knowledge in the guise of unworldly
knowledge, a parody of the word it is Christ's function as
prophet to dispense. From this perspective, the Athens-temptation completes Satan's attempt to thwart the two mediatorial roles of Christ, the kingly and the prophetic, that Satan
perceives dimly and has parodied throughout history and
indeed continues to parody here in the kingdoms-sequence as
he becomes Christ's prophet and teacher in order that he may
also become Christ's king.

Finally, of course, as a temptation to the World Athens
completes the infernal triad of kingdoms shown Christ on the
mountain. To be sure, the temptation subsumes as well the
refined pleasures of the grove of Academe, also the pride of
the Stoic philosophers; but the central thrust of the temptation is clearly to knowledge either false or inferior, and just
as clearly the temptation operates against the backdrop of
Genesis 3:5. The second day's temptation to the World appropriately ends with a temptation to the World disguised as
the unworldly, with the sin of the World now being not
avaritia pecuniae but solely *avaritia scientiae*.[22] In complet-

[22] Lewalski, pp. 123-127, suggests a number of precedents in biblical epics for the learning-temptation; but ultimately the source is
Augustine, who, in his *Exposition on the Book of Psalms* (Oxford,
1847), I, 70-71, makes curiosity one of the three vices to which
Christ is tempted. Although Augustine associates curiosity not with
the kingdoms-temptation but with the pinnacle-temptation, the Edenic
counterpart would seem to be, as in Milton's learning temptation,
Eve's avarice for knowledge. On the avarice for worldly knowledge
as one of the three temptations according to medieval commentary,
see Donald R. Howard, *The Three Temptations* (Princeton, N.J.:
Princeton Univ. Press, 1966), pp. 43-56. It is noteworthy that Her-

ing the triad, Athens also completes the second-Adam theme. The teleology of Genesis 3:5 is preserved as it was in the World-temptation of the first sequence, only here knowledge alone becomes the means to glory. The Edenic teleology frames the actual offer itself: "Be famous then / By wisdom" (221-222), Satan begins; and he concludes,

> These rules will render thee a King complete
> Within thyself, much more with Empire join'd.
> (283-284)

This advice was given before, of course, in Eden. Christ, in rejecting the Stoic and Satanic perversion of His inner kingdom, makes the Edenic context of Satan's offer clear:

> The Stoic last in Philosophic pride,
> By him call'd virtue; and his virtuous man,
> Wise, perfect in himself, and all possessing
> Equal to God. . . .
> (300-303)

> And in themselves seek virtue, and to themselves
> All glory arrogate, to God give none. . . .
> (314-315)

The closest pagan approximation of Christ's own inner kingdom is in actuality a repetition of Eve's sin of seeking to be "Equal to God" through knowledge. The Stoics' "contemning all / Wealth, pleasure, pain or torment" (304-305) parodies Christ's own performance in the wilderness; their renunciation of the world ironically takes the form of the sin of the World.

The uncompromising severity of Christ's repudiation of pagan, fallen knowledge has struck many as unpleasant. As

---

bert in "The Pearl" takes "the ways of Learning" as one of the three glories of the World, the other two being honor and pleasure; and Marvell in "A Dialogue between the Resolved Soul and Created Pleasure" places knowledge last in an unusual sequence of four glories of the World, the other three being the familiar lust, gold, and glory.

the second Adam, however, Christ must repudiate all that Eve had accepted; but what Satan offers Him is, as Satan's strategy throughout all the temptations would lead us to expect, a secular and mundane parody of His own role as the second Adam. The irony underlying the Athens-temptation is that the height of pagan knowledge imitates Eve's error while seeming to imitate the second Adam's own overcoming of it. Consequently, Christ must affirm the true contrary of Eve's embracing knowledge for glory, not the Stoic parody of that contrary, namely the true wisdom of obedience, "Where God is prais'd aright" (348). If we understand the Edenic background of the Athens-temptation, if we understand that Satan offers fallen knowledge, gotten by the light of fallen nature, that Christ might fall, then we understand that there can be no compromise; for this is where it all began.

IV

The controversy over the structural function of the storm episode seems itself something of a needless tempest.[23] The obvious procedure is to compare it with its only counterpart within the work, the night between the first and second days of temptation. The events of both nights reinforce the previous day's temptation while preparing for the next day's temptation. The dream on the first night, like the "ugly dreams"

[23] Allen, p. 115, Cleveland, p. 234, Lewalski, pp. 303-321, and Northrop Frye, *The Return of Eden* (Toronto: Univ. of Toronto Press, 1965), p. 138, regard the storm as either an interlude between the kingdoms-temptation and the pinnacle-temptation or a preliminary to the pinnacle-temptation. However, Pope, p. 99, suggests that "the formal temptation by violence had to be pushed back and given independent treatment in the storm scene." Steadman, *Milton's Epic Characters*, pp. 90-101, suggests that the storm episode completes the kingdoms-temptation by presenting an adversity-temptation to counter the prosperty-temptations of the second day. Dick Taylor, Jr., "The Storm Scene in *Paradise Regained*: A Reinterpretation," *University of Toronto Quarterly*, 24 (1955), 359-376, also has argued that the storm is part of second day's temptations and that "there is no connection between the storm scene and the pinnacle scene through violence" (p. 371).

(IV.408) on the second, would seem to be Satan's attempt to work upon Christ's "Organs of . . . Fancy, and with them forge / Illusions as he list, Phantasms and Dreams" (*PL*, IV.802-803), as he did in Eden with Eve. Although all that the text says is that Christ "dreams, as appetite is wont to dream" (II.264), the dream would seem to be as much a product of Satan's art of illusion as the pastoral setting and banquet of the World-temptation. The dream is a misleading prophetic sign, and as such it is an extension of Satan's parody in the Flesh-temptation of Christ's prophetic role and his claim to have helped man direct his "future life" "by . . . dreams" (I.394-396). At the same time, of course, the dreams of the appetite also look ahead to the banquet's temptation to intemperance. Correspondingly, the dreams and disturbances on the second night also look backwards and forwards. As part of Satan's effort to convince Christ that God is displeased by His refusal of Satan's offer of glories and kingdoms, these false signs obviously look back to the World-temptation. But as phenomena attempting to "terrify" (IV.496) Christ to Satan's will through violence and adversity rather than allurement, they look ahead to the pinnacle-temptation. In fact, the connection between the violence during the night and on the pinnacle is made quite explicit:

> . . . ill wast thou shrouded then,
> O patient Son of God, yet only *stood'st*
> *Unshaken*; nor yet stay'd the terror there.
>
> (419-421; my italics)

The violence in the night looks ahead, therefore, to the uniqueness of the Devil-temptation on the pinnacle; for while Satan has used threats before, he has not used violence. In addition, as Mrs. Lewalski has shown,[24] both the violence of the storm and the violence of Satan's removing Christ to the top of the temple suggest Christ's priestly role, His crucifixion and His submitting Himself to, and overcoming, Satanic vio-

---

[24] *Milton's Brief Epic*, pp. 309-313.

lence. The subject of the temptation to which the storm points is, then, in respect to the work as a whole, as unique as the strategy of temptation; for although there have been intimations before of Christ's priestly role, they have been only that, intimations.

The manner of Satan's appearance on the third day reinforces the day's specialness and uniqueness. On the previous two days, Satan has appeared in disguise in accordance with a strategy of fraud; on the third day, in accordance with his direct, violent assault on Christ, "Out of the wood he starts in wonted shape" (449)—the "shape" (*PL*, x.574) "visibly impair'd" (IV.850) and "fierce" (IV.871) which Satan is permitted to resume in Book X after he has been transformed into a snake.[25] In addition, his starting out of the woods openly as the devil in all his ugliness fits well with his new strategy of terrifying Christ. His revealing himself as he is, the fallen angel who warred against the Son in heaven, suggests also the uniqueness of the third day's temptation as a special test to discover if Christ is indeed the divine Son against whom he once warred:

> . . . opportunity I here have had
> To try thee, sift thee, and confess have found thee
> Proof against all temptation as a rock
> Of Adamant, and as a Center, firm;
> To th'utmost of mere man both wise and good,
> Not more; for Honors, Riches, Kingdoms, Glory
> Have been before contemn'd, and may again:
> Therefore to know what more thou art than man,
> Worth naming Son of God by voice from Heav'n,
> Another method I must now begin.
>
> (531-540)

This is more than an attempt to frighten Christ, for the distinction Satan draws here between the coming temptation and

[25] Pope, p. 50, argues that Satan's "wonted shape" is "his 'usual disguise' rather than 'ordinary form,'" but Satan has no single "usual disguise" but many disguises.

the previous ones has much the same validity as that drawn by Spenser in the Cave of Mammon: "mere man" may resist the devil but only Christ as the *deus homo*, or man ingrafted in Christ, can debel him. Similarly, in *Comus* the Lady can resist all of Comus' temptations, but until she receives the water of grace cannot be freed from his dominion. Christ's resistance of the Flesh, the World, and the Devil and His assertion of His prophetic and kingly roles on the first two days do not in themselves necessarily testify to His divinity, however much they may ultimately presuppose it. Christ's defeat of the devil and His assertion of His priestly role, however, do unequivocally testify to divinity. For, as Milton says in *De Doctrina*, Christ, "Being God-man . . . offered himself in that capacity"[26] as a worthy propitiation for our sins. The reason Milton placed the pinnacle episode last, then, was not only, as Miss Pope suggests,[27] to lighten the load of the argument by a spectacular conclusion, but also, and more important, to give climactic emphasis to the role which makes the other two possible; for without the sacrifice on the cross of the *deus homo*, Christ's kingship and prophecy are merely empty promises, and He Himself at the most a superior Moses or Elijah. The whole movement of *Paradise Regained* points to the cross and the sacrificial humiliation of the *agnus dei*.[28]

On the first two days Satan has attempted to allure Christ into becoming an imitation of himself, false prophet and false king; on the final day, in accordance with his direct attack on Christ as the Son of God, Satan repeats the violence of his earlier attack on the Son in heaven, as he attempts literally to force Christ to be like him and fall morally and physically from the pinnacle as he himself had fallen morally and physi-

[26] *De D.*, I.xvi; CE, xv, 303.

[27] *"Paradise Regained": The Tradition and the Poem*, pp. 97-99.

[28] E. L. Marilla, "Milton on the Crucifixion," *Etudes Anglaises*, 22 (1969), 7-10, has some valuable remarks correcting the old but still highly influential opinion of Denis Saurat that the crucifixion played only a negligible role in Milton's theology.

cally from a high place. Satan forces Christ physically into a cul-de-sac which would apparently offer Him no alternative but to sin. If He stands on His own powers by a miracle—and Satan's "to stand *upright* / Will ask thee skill" (551-552; my italics) in its punning suggests the moral dilemma he has forced Christ into—Christ would seemingly commit the same sin of distrust of God's assistance as He would have had He changed stones into bread. And if He casts Himself down, He would commit the sin opposite to distrust, which is presumption, an excessive reliance on God's favor. Satan's strategy seems airtight, but he (and most critics have followed him in this) has overlooked the obvious but essential point: once Christ realizes His divinity, performing a miracle becomes no sin as before. It is thus not necessary to argue that Satan does not take seriously the first of the two alternatives in order to avoid having Christ accept one of Satan's alternatives by standing;[29] nor is it necessary to argue that Christ avoids both alternatives by standing as "mere man" as a kind of steeplejack stunt because "if Christ did a miracle to stop himself from falling, it would mean he distrusted God just as surely if he had done a miracle to stop himself from starving."[30] These two extremes of interpretation, around which all others can be said to cluster, result from misunderstanding or ignoring the difference between the situation on the third day and the situation on the previous two days. On the first two days Christ, as the second Adam, must perforce respond to the temptations as "mere man" without the advantage over Adam of divinity, so that performing a miracle to save Himself would indeed be distrusting God's will and providence. But on the pinnacle the context of temptation has been completely altered, for Christ is now being tempted as more than "mere man." Christ's realization of His divinity eliminates the whole issue of dis-

[29] Gilbert, p. 609. Woodhouse, "Theme and Pattern," p. 181, and Bush, p. 193, follow Gilbert; and, with some modification, so do Pope, p. 95, Cleveland, pp. 235-236, and Stein, p. 127.

[30] John Carey, *Milton* (London: Evans, 1969), p. 128.

trust of God because any question of a conflict between His will and the Father's *ipso facto* is eliminated; for "the Father's will was identically one with his own."[31] When Christ replies "Tempt not the Lord thy God" (561), He is speaking of both God the Father and that measure of the godhead that He Himself is.[32] The demonstration of Christ's divinity on the pinnacle lies, therefore, not in His performing a miracle of not falling physically, for that He could have done as merely *a* son of God and that Satan himself can do; rather, it consists of His "stand[ing] *upright*," that is, standing without falling morally, which He could do only upon the completion of His role as the second Adam and the realization of His divinity.

If the pinnacle-temptation is Christ's unique triumph as the *deus homo*, the work nonetheless concludes by returning us and Christ to the world of man and human experience.

[31] *De D.*, I.xvi; CE, xv, 305. Milton is speaking of Christ on the cross, but the relationship between the Father and Christ would of course be applicable to Christ on the pinnacle.

[32] The majority of modern critics—Pope, pp. 103-105; Woodhouse, p. 181; Cleveland, p. 235; Bush, p. 193; Lewalski, pp. 316-318; Frye, p. 138; and Kenneth Muir, *John Milton* (London: Longmans, Green, 1955), p. 138—agree that Christ is claiming divinity in these words. In opposition, Dick Taylor, Jr., "Grace as a Means of Poetry: Milton's Pattern for Salvation," *Tulane Studies in English*, 4 (1954), 57-90, argues that Christ obediently maintains to the end the human terms of the trial, resisting the temptation to use His miraculous powers, so that "God immediately enters with his grace . . . and performs himself the miracle that holds Christ standing aloft" (p. 88). Langford, pp. 42-43, also argues that the Father is referred to in Christ's words and that Christ's resistance of this temptation to "a proud, reckless assertion of [His] identity" "involves no means not available to all the sons of Fallen Adam"; for if it did, it would destroy the value of Christ's role as man's example. Jon S. Lawry, *The Shadow of Heaven* (Ithaca, N.Y.: Cornell Univ. Press, 1968), pp. 334-335, while he admits that "claims of divinity are present," feels that "The Son has intimated that part of his nature is divine throughout"; and he denies that the difference between this temptation and the previous ones arises "from a mysterious identification of the Son with, or as, God." Stein, pp. 127-128, denies that Christ is claiming divinity, but concludes that once Christ has preserved the discipline of His "moral and intellectual example," "the miracle of theophany" can then occur.

Which is as it must be; for in the wilderness is set the pattern for our own pilgrimage which we begin with baptism.[33] "His weakness," God prophesied in the celestial council, "shall o'ercome Satanic strength / And all the world, and mass of sinful flesh" (I.161-162). The order of the triad as God arranges it is the reverse of the order as Christ experiences it, and deliberately so, for God's order is identical to the order of the baptismal vow of the "chosen Sons," whom Christ has "come down to reinstall" (IV.614-615). The banquet and concluding chorus function to insist upon our participation in the triumphs we have witnessed, to see the combat against Adam as our battle. For us as for Christ in the wilderness, there is an unceasing "struggle against the *flesh* and the Spirit . . . and against the *world* and *Satan*";[34] and if our struggle imitates His, so does our triumph: "There is also a victory to be gained. Rev. ii. 7. 'to him that overcometh will I give to eat of the tree of life' . . . Over the *world* . . . Over death [i.e., of the *Flesh*] . . . Over *Satan*."[35] Accordingly, as a token not only of His victory over the Flesh, the World, and the Devil, but also of our own, Christ eats from

> A table of Celestial Food, Divine,
> Ambrosial, Fruits fetcht from the tree of life,
> And from the fount of life Ambrosial drink . . .
>
> (587-589)

Figuratively, this is the Lord's Supper:[36] the fruits from the tree of life are "the living bread" (John 6:51), which is Christ's flesh; the water from the fount of life is the "living

[33] As Thomas Stroup, *Religious Rite and Ceremony in Milton's Poetry* (Lexington, Ky.: Univ. of Kentucky Press, 1968), p. 169, indicates, at Christ's baptism as at all future baptisms all three persons of the Trinity are present.

[34] *De D.*, I.xxi; CE, XVI, 19 (my italics).

[35] *De D.*, I.xxi; CE, XVI, 21 (my italics).

[36] Steadman, *Milton's Epic Characters*, pp. 82-89, admittedly with evidence from *De Doctrina* to support him, denies the sacramental import of the *arbor vitae*; but the coupling of "the living bread" and the "living water" in the passage would seem almost certainly to suggest the Lord's Supper.

water" (John 4:10), which is His blood. *Paradise Regained* is thus framed by the two sacraments which are the "tokens of the sealing covenant of grace"[37] and which make possible our own victory—baptism at the beginning, the Lord's Supper at the end. The beginning and the end of the poem are brought together as an image of the course of our own pilgrimage: if baptism points to the beginning of our pilgrimage in the wilderness of the world, our redoing of Genesis and the Fall, the Lord's Supper points to the end of the pilgrimage, to Revelation and the Apocalypse: "To him that overcometh will I give to eat of the tree of life, which is in the midst of the paradise of God."

V

The structure of *Paradise Regained* is composed largely of recurring triads, but containing and encompassing the triadic structure is the tetradic division of the work into books. One would gather, however, from their silence on the matter, that most readers believe that the division is either arbitrary or at least not particularly meaningful; or that, at best, it contributes to a "staggered effect" to prevent the symmetry of the poem from becoming "too emphatic" and "mechanical."[38] Yet surely an artist like Milton, who would be the last to embrace an arbitary structure, and who was so attentive to the structural importance of even minor details, would hardly neglect the meaningfulness of the whole itself. What I have to say in the following brief account of the poem's tetradic structure is, I should make clear, only the skeletal essentials of that structure; any poetic structure is infinitely more fluid, more flexible, than the expository outline a critic may give it.

---

[37] *De D.*, i.xxviii; CE, xvi, 219.

[38] Woodhouse, "Theme and Pattern," pp. 170-171. E.M.W. Tillyard, *Milton*, rev. ed. (New York: Macmillan, 1967), p. 273, states baldly that "in studying the structure of *Paradise Regained* we should forget the division into books." Lewalski, pp. 330-331, and Lawry, pp. 302-345, have made conscientious, if not entirely convincing, attempts to account for the tetradic structure.

This qualification granted, one may begin by suggesting what is at least a reasonable possibility, that Milton chose to contain the three days of temptation within four books in order to provide a structural mirror of the nature of the *deus homo* Himself: three (*deus*, the spiritual) and four (*homo*, the corporal, the mortal). The whole poem, after all, points to, and prepares us for, the climactic disclosure of Christ as the *deus homo* and the repetition of His initial confrontation with the devil. Book I announces, and is organized around, the central theme of the work and of Christ's temptation in the wilderness as Protestants perceived its significance, the verification of the divine word. Accordingly, the book opens with a counterpointing of perspectives on the relationship of the divine word and prophecy to the baptismal scene, and it concludes with a temptation of Christ as prophet. Book II is principally concerned with Christ's inner kingdom. Appropriately, the book opens with a counterpointing of perspectives on Christ's high estate, and these reflections all provide approximations, intimations, or parodies of the inner kingdom Christ will define by the end of the book in the gold-temptation. The essential preliminaries for Christ's combat with the devil, namely reliance on the word and establishment of the inner kingdom, are developed in the first two books. Book III brings us one step closer to this climactic combat. Indeed, it is the book of the devil and his glory; and within it, Christ examines the public role of the inner kingdom. The book opens with the allegorical glory-Devil temptation and, after the Israel link, concludes with another glory-Devil temptation, this time to a public kingdom, in the form of Parthia. Book IV climaxes the poem's movement with the actual combat itself; but even more than that, it provides a climactic recapitulation of all the major structural and thematic motifs of the work. Christ's role as the second Adam or perfect man is fullfilled in Book IV in the Athens-temptation, and His role as the *deus homo* is established on the pinnacle. But in addition to this, it seems entirely probable that Milton intended the three temptations in this book to correspond to Christ's

173

three mediatorial roles just as in the three days of temptation, though the correspondences between the three roles and the three sins would differ in this sequence: Rome can be seen as a continued temptation to Christ's kingship, with Rome as the false church; Athens, a renewed temptation to His role as prophet; and the pinnacle, a temptation to His role as priest. Nor is this all: Milton also structured the final book as a recapitulation of the Flesh-World Devil triad organizing the three days. In fact, the order of the three temptations in Book IV is precisely the same as the order for the three days. Rome represents the Flesh; Athens, the World; and the pinnacle, the Devil. The pinnacle-temptation may be the grand finale of the three days of temptation, but the fourth book is itself a grand finale, a masterful bringing together of all that has gone before.

VI

Despite the additions of the framework of four books and the mediatorial triad that Milton brought to the structure he inherited from Spenser and Fletcher, that structure nonetheless recognizably constitutes the principal basis for the structure of *Paradise Regained*, as it does also for *Samson Agonistes*. Though the additions give Milton's structure a new intellectual dimension and complexity, the fundamental outlines of the double-triadic structure remain essentially unaltered. Indeed, almost all of the artistic machinery of the poem—the infernal and celestial councils, Satan's hermit disguise, the wilderness, the *locus amoenus*, the Circean banquet, Satan's portrayal as a Circe of the World, the progression from a false-pastoral Eden to a mountain, the storm, and the celestial banquet—all of these, in addition to the poem's triadic structure, emerge from Spenser, Fletcher, and, to a lesser extent, the great Italianate epics of Ariosto and Tasso.[39] A clear line of literary development

[39] My emphasis on the Spenserian background is not meant to deny claims made for more obvious influences on the work like the Book of Job and the shorter epics of the Middle Ages and the Renaissance,

culminates in *Paradise Regained*, which we are now in a position to see more clearly.

Not Book II and the Cave of Mammon but Book I and Red Crosse's pilgrimage of life contain Spenser's major contributions to the conception and structure of *Paradise Regained*.[40] Structurally, the two works are almost iden-

---

which Lewalski, pp. 102-129, has examined in considerable detail. Many features of the work, moreover, have an exceptionally rich ancestry which cannot be reduced to a single tradition—for example, Satan's hermit disguise, which Merritt Y. Hughes, "The Christ of *Paradise Regained* and the Renaissance Heroic Tradition," *Studies in Philology*, 35 (1938), 256, locates in Malory (as well as in Spenser and Fletcher), and which Pope, p. 44, locates in a number of works in the visual arts as well as literature. Despite these qualifications, the Spenserian tradition seems to me to provide the essential literary background of the work. The storm scene, however, has no direct analogue in either Spenser or Fletcher; but Steadman, *Milton's Epic Characters*, pp. 97-101, has suggested a number of possible analogues in classical and Renaissance epic, the most important of which are found in *Gerusalemme Liberata* and Gratiani's *Il Conquisto di Granata*. John E. Seaman, "The Chivalric Cast of Milton's Epic Hero," *English Studies*, 49 (1968), 97-107, explores the relationship of *Paradise Regained* to some of the traditional features of Homeric and Virgilian epic.

[40] Frye has some interesting but brief remarks comparing the Legend of Holiness and *Paradise Regained* in *The Return of Eden*, pp. 118-119, pp. 125-126, as does, in passing, W. N. Knight, " 'To Enter Lists with God': Transformation of Spenserian Chivalric Tradition in *Paradise Regained*," *Costerus: Essays in English and American Language and Literature*, 2 (1972), 80-108; but the most thorough comparison of the two works is by John Major, "*Paradise Regained* and Spenser's Legend of Holiness," *Renaissance Quarterly*, 20 (1967), 465-470. Some of the connections Major draws—e.g., those between Christ's stones-temptation and Despaire, Christ's kingdoms-temptation and Lucifera, the pinnacle episode and the dragon—my readings can, though for different reasons, support. In the main, however, the possibility of Spenserian influence on *Paradise Regained* has been considered in terms of Book II (see, e.g., Greenlaw, " 'A Better Teacher than Aquinas,' " p. 205; Hughes, "Introduction" to *Paradise Regained*, pp. 474, 478; Hanford and Taaffe, pp. 223-224; and Lawry, p. 294), though Archimago is commonly suggested as a source for Satan's disguise on the first day. Largely, it seems to me,

tical in their use of the Flesh, the World, and the Devil. The order of temptation is the same in both, and both works portray the World-temptation as a composite Circean episode including "all sin." Although the physical appearance of Satan in Milton's Flesh-temptation as "an aged man in rural weeds" resembles Archimago, "an aged sire in long black weeds yclad," more than Despaire, Despaire is also portrayed as a mock-religious figure; and his arguments to disbelief, as I noted in an earlier chapter, resemble those in Milton's temptation. Not only is Milton's World-temptation, like Spenser's, triadic, but also in both the subsidiary triad occurs in the same order as the principal triad. (The second triad in Milton's World-temptation does not, of course, have the same order as the main sequence; but the idea for a second triad may well have been suggested by the Cave of Mammon episode, or Milton may have thought it his own invention.) And finally Milton, like Spenser in his Orgoglio- and dragon-temptations, conceives the sin of the Devil as pride expressed through physical might and violence.

For Milton as for Spenser, Christ's Temptation in the Wilderness was above all a temptation to the divine word: the Legend of Holiness begins and ends with Una, the word, as the pilgrim's guide; *Paradise Regained* begins with a temptation to the word, and the three days of temptation conclude with Christ's assertion of the word's supremacy: "Also it is written, / Tempt not the Lord thy God" (iv.560-561). In addition, both works portray the pilgrim's progress as be-

---

the influence of Book II on *Paradise Regained* is confined to the influence of the Cave of Mammon on the banquet-wealth-glory sequence. Christ's arguments in the wealth- and glory-temptations are, as everyone realizes, heavily indebted to Guyon's in his rejection of gold and glory outside the Cave. But in addition the banquet-temptation would seem to be indebted to the Flesh-temptation within the Cave (see Ch. 2). If this is so, it would suggest that Milton read the episode as a double temptation of Guyon, which would tend to confirm my reading of the episode, as of course the similarity of his overall structure in *Paradise Regained* and *Samson Agonistes* tends also, I believe, to confirm my structural reading of the Legend of Holiness.

ginning with baptism, proceeding to a temptation in the
wilderness, and concluding with a triumph over the Devil
that alludes at once to the Crucifixion, the Harrowing of Hell,
and Christ's final victory over the dragon at the Apocalypse.[41]
That is to say, the conception of the pilgrimage in both works
is identical with that in the baptismal rites—a combat against
the old Adam and the Flesh, the World, and the Devil,

[41] Milton quite explicitly borrows from Spenser's description of
the fall of the dragon:

> So downe he fell, and forth his life did breath,
> That vanisht into smoke and cloudes swift;
> So downe he fell, that th'earth him vnderneath
> Did grone, as feeble so great load to lift;
> So downe he fell, as an huge rockie clift,
> Whose false foundation waues haue washt away,
> With dreadfull poyse is from the mayneland rift,
> And rolling downe, great *Neptune* doth dismay;
> So downe he fell, and like an heaped mountaine lay.
>
> (xi.54)

> But Satan smitten with amazement fell
>
> . . . .
>
> So after many a foil the Tempter proud,
> Renewing fresh assaults, amidst his pride
> Fell whence he stood to see his Victor fall.
>
> . . . .
>
> So struck with dread and anguish fell the Fiend,
>
> . . . .
>
> So Satan fell. . . .
>
> (IV.562-581)

I am preceded in this observation by Major though I am not indebted
to him for it. Major finds in Milton's passage a "bit of stylistic evidence" (p. 467) to suggest Milton's indebtedness to Spenser; but it is
more than that for Milton as for Phineas Fletcher, who also imitates
Spenser's stanza in describing Christ's combat with the dragon in *The
Purple Island* (XII, st. 59). In both passages the suspension and the
anaphora capture the effect of a fall from great heights, and in so
doing both passages look back to the first defeat of Satan when he
fell "headlong flaming from th' Ethereal Sky / . . . to bottomless
perdition" (*PL*, I.45-47) and look ahead to the final defeat of the
dragon at the end of history. Accordingly, both passages allude to
Revelation 18:2: "Babylon the great is fallen, is fallen."

culminating in a banquet prefiguring the marriage supper of the Lamb and the faithful.

Linking the Legend of Holiness to *Paradise Regained* and also to *Samson Agonistes* is Giles Fletcher's "Christ's Victory on Earth,"[42] which borrows from Spenser to portray Milton's own subject, Christ's Temptation in the Wilderness. In its overall conception of the temptation, Fletcher's work bears a smaller resemblance to Milton's than does Spenser's: Fletcher's work does not seem to have been conceived as a paradigm of the Christian pilgrimage. Structurally, however, it seems to have been at least as influential as Spenser's work. Fletcher, it is true, unlike both Spenser and Milton, follows the Matthew rather than the Luke order of temptation. Nonetheless, Fletcher like Milton adopts and revises Spenser's double-triadic structure. The linear triad for the three days receives a Protestant reading as in Milton and, to a substantial degree, Spenser: the temptation of the Flesh is to despair, the temptation of the Devil (the tower) is to presumption, and the temptation of the World (the kingdoms) is to vainglory. And the kingdoms-World temptation consists of an orthodox version of the Flesh, the World, and the Devil, which permits Fletcher, like Milton, to include a temptation to Christ's temperance without having to conceive the stones-temptation in Catholic terms as a temptation to temperance and thereby an example of the virtue of fasting. In Fletcher's house of the World, three separate stories are devoted first to pleasure (the Flesh), then gold (the World), and finally ambition (the Devil); the order of temptation is identical to Spenser's order in the House of Pride and to Milton's in the sequence of allegorical glories. Presiding over the three kingdoms is Panglorie, who is, like Milton's Satan in the World-

[42] Opinions on the extent of Fletcher's influence on Milton range from Hughes's contention that "Only in Milton's imagery is there an occasional reflection of Fletcher's allegory" ("Introduction," p. 480) to Frye's contention that "Milton's most obvious source . . . , apart from the Bible itself, was Giles Fletcher's poem" (*The Return of Eden*, p. 125).

temptation, a courtly Circe-figure. Many of the features associated with her—the false-pastoral Garden of Delight through
which Christ passes on His way to her palace, the herd of
men changed into beasts, the palace on top of the mountain,
her enjoyment of her own beauty in the mirror-like columns
of crystal, and her carpe-diem rosebuds song—could be indebted to any one of several Circes. But her major predecessor would seem to be Lucifera, especially in the description
of her "blazing throne" and the comparison of it to "Phoebus
lamp" (st. 17), her paternity by Satan, and her request
(though never articulated in Spenser) of Christ to "bend
thy knee to mee" (st. 59). Fletcher thus follows Spenser
in making the connection (and as far as I can tell Spenser
was the first to make this connection) between the Renaissance Circe's high-situated palace and Christ's temptation
on the mountain; and Milton would seem to be following both
of them but especially Fletcher. Milton also follows Spenser
and Fletcher in making a false-pastoral Eden a preliminary
encounter for the hero before the temptation on the mountain.
Fletcher's influence is no doubt stronger here, but nonetheless
Fletcher himself was probably reworking Spenser's Fradubio
episode, which is based on the Astolfo episode of *Orlando
Furioso* and which leads into the temptation of the World.
All three English poets, then, would seem to be adapting
canto 6 of *Orlando Furioso*, and probably also canto 15 of
Gerusalemme Liberata, to Christ's temptation on the moun-
tain to the kingdoms of the World.

Fletcher's temptation of the Flesh also borrows from
Spenser while it anticipates Milton. This episode is divided
into two sections: an invitation to change stones into bread
followed by an invitation for Christ to rest in the Cave of
Despair. The episode draws heavily from the episode at
Archimago's hermitage and the Cave of Despaire. The dis-
guise Satan assumes is essentially that of Archimago and
Milton's Satan; he is, like them, "an aged Syre" (st. 15).
The stones-temptation itself has no Spenserian analogue, but
it may have given Milton a suggestion for his handling of the

temptation. Fletcher's Satan, like Milton's, tempts Christ to despair and distrust through a charity of good deeds without faith and through a confusion of charity with the necessity for self-preservation:

> But oh, he said, and therewith sigh't full deepe,
> The heav'ns, alas, too envious are growne,
> Because our fields thy presence from them keepe;
> For stones doe growe, where corne was lately sowne:
> (So stooping downe, he gather'd up a stone)
>   But thou with corne canst make this stone to eare,
>   What needen we the angrie heav'ns to feare?
> Let them envie us still, so we enjoy thee here.
>
>   (st. 22)

Both Fletcher's Satan and Milton's tempt Christ to see His mission in terms of an alliance with Satan and mankind against celestial powers who show towards man not charity but envy and hostility. The stones-temptation completed, Satan moves to the Cave of Despair. Instead of Christ's offering an act of false charity to Satan, Satan, like Spenser's Archimago and Despaire, and also like Milton's Satan, offers an act of false charity to Christ, inviting Him into the Cave of Despair that "thear he might baite the day, and rest the night" (st. 29). The episode is replete with allusions to, paraphrase of, even open plagiarism from Spenser's Cave of Despaire. Although there is not, of course, a cave of despair in *Paradise Regained*, Fletcher's Satan's manipulation of the themes of charity and necessity in the Flesh-temptation may possibly underlie the strategy of Milton's Satan in his offer to be Christ's guide.

The most substantial difference between Fletcher and Milton lies in their portrayal of the temptation of the Devil; and in the context of so many resemblances, the difference becomes revealing of Milton's own intentions in *Paradise Regained*. Although both poets associate the Devil-temptation with presumption, Fletcher is more simplistic: he makes the temptation solely one of relying excessively on God's

180

assistance. No doubt in part this was because he was using the Matthew order and wished to keep the obvious relation-in-contrast between the presumption of the second temptation and the despair of God's assistance in the first. Fletcher, however, does not develop the element of fear and violence, nor does he emphasize the precariousness of the site. Indeed, apart from the association of the temptation with presumption, the only important resemblance between the two is that Fletcher's Satan "tombled headlong to the flore" (st. 38) as Christ is borne up by angels. The difference between the two temptations, emerging as it does from a choice of a different order of temptation, reflects, I believe, Milton's desire to have all of the temptations in *Paradise Regained* point to Christ's priestly and sacrificial role and to have his poem culminate with Christ triumphing in that role with all of its implications. As a result, Milton could achieve not only a more artistically satisfying conclusion but also a much more tight connection between the Temptation in the Wilderness and the triumph on the cross than Fletcher had achieved.

Paradise Regained is therefore born of a marriage between Spenser and Fletcher, with the presiding assistance—primarily in the infernal and celestial councils, the banquet and the storm episodes—of classical but mainly Italian Renaissance epic. For all the other literary influences on this poem, the most important are found in Milton's native Spenserian tradition. No work of Milton's is more indebted to Spenser than *Paradise Regained*; and no two works of Milton are more indebted to Spenser than *Paradise Regained* and *Samson Agonistes*. If in *Paradise Lost* Milton attempts to outdo Virgil and the tradition of classical epic, if in *Samson Agonistes* he attempts to outdo the Greek tragedians, in *Paradise Regained* he has attempted to outdo Fletcher and his English master, for him the most important writer within his own native literary tradition, Edmund Spenser.

5. *Samson Agonistes*:
Milton's Christian Redefinition of Tragedy

Old definitions do not apply well to Milton. Never one to leave tradition where he found it, for him the genres of pagan literature became a vehicle whereby he could explore and re-answer the central questions they embodied; and this exploration led inevitably to a Christian redefinition of those genres. In the Nativity Ode, for example, Milton takes the conventions of the Virgilian messianic eclogue to celebrate not a secular messiah as Virgil had done but the true Christian Messiah, who alone could bring to fulfilment the golden age Virgil's pastoral longs for; and in "Lycidas," Milton employs the conventions of the pastoral elegy to examine the questions emerging from the death of a good shepherd and resolves them ultimately in terms of the promise offered man by the good shepherd, Christ, who alone can bring to fulfilment the consolation for death the pagan pastoral elegy hopes for. The rebirth of the world as described in the Nativity Ode and the rebirth or resurrection of the individual soul as described in "Lycidas," while portrayed within the literary conventions of pagan literature, are shown to be possible only in Christian terms. The same is true of heroism, as *Paradise Lost* demonstrates; for though the poem works within the conventions of pagan epic, this is epic transformed and re-examined according to a new and greater argument in which the heroic values of traditional epic are modified by the more truly heroic values of the Christian saint, which are, like the rebirth of the world and the rebirth of the soul in the two earlier poems, realizable only through Christ and His grace.

There is nothing for controversy in what I have just said. These are commonplaces all of us agree upon, and yet, curiously, when we reach Milton's tragedy we balk. We ask ourselves, Is *Samson* a classical tragedy? Is it a tragedy at all, for is it possible to have such a thing as Christian tragedy? —which is, inevitably, to impose old definitions on Milton's work.[1] Surely the first question must be, How is Milton him-

[1] By far the most influential treatment of *Samson* as tragedy is that of Una Ellis-Fermor, *The Frontiers of Drama*, 2nd ed. (London: Methuen, 1964), pp. 17-33, who argues that Milton has written "a play that belongs to the rare category of religious drama, a kind which, by the nature of some of its basic assumptions, cannot be tragic" (p. 17), since "religious drama . . . is almost invariably positive [and] the only type of conflict that this subject can offer for the use of drama is that of a heroic contest rising to exultation and passing on, in a few rare cases, into beatitude" (p. 23). In contrast, William Riley Parker, *Milton's Debt to Greek Tragedy in "Samson Agonistes"* (1937; rpt. New York: Barnes and Noble, 1969), pp. 189-242, avoids the problem of considering the work as a Christian tragedy by de-emphasizing the Christian elements in it: Parker argues that *Samson* is very much a Hellenic tragedy in its spirit, which is "serious," "thoughtful," "didactic," "religious," and "sublime" (pp. 198-199), and that "Milton also believed in unmerited suffering" (p. 218); and he agrees with E.M.W. Tillyard, *Milton*, rev. ed. (New York: Macmillan, 1967), p. 283, that "'There is a sense of waste in the play which arouses tragic feelings'" (p. 241). A.S.P. Woodhouse, "Tragic Effect in *Samson Agonistes*," *University of Toronto Quarterly*, 28 (1959), 205-222, questions Parker's approach and suggests that *Samson* be considered a Christian tragedy just as *Paradise Lost* is considered a Christian epic: from the human perspective *Samson* is tragic since "suffering, though it may be a means of grace, is suffering still, and death, though it be the price of such a victory, and though it even come as a release from suffering, is still death" (p. 220). Ann Gossman, "Milton's Samson as the Tragic Hero Purified by Trial," *Journal of English and Germanic Philology*, 61 (1962), 528-541, suggests that Milton reconciled Christian spirit and classical form by treating the Greek *hamartia*, or tragic flaw, as sin. Anthony Low, "Tragic Pattern in *Samson Agonistes*," *Texas Studies in Language and Literature*, 11 (1969), 915-930, argues that "a series of negative characteristics . . . contribute significantly to the tragic effect. For in Milton's play, Samson, though a hero, is also presented as an outcast, as a scapegoat, and as a kind of monster" (p. 916); and that the "progressive isolation of the hero is characteristic of many of the greatest tragedies [and] is simultaneously admirable and pitiable; admirable in religious terms, but tragic in human terms"

self defining and redefining tragedy? Hebraic though its subject is, classical its form, Milton's tragedy, like the two other great genres he had worked with in the past, pastoral and epic, ultimately attempts to contain all of its elements within a Judæo-Christian synthesis. As in the past so here, the pagan genre is converted to the Christian end of justifying the ways of God to man; and since for Milton these ways included mercy as well as justice, tragedy would naturally have to

---

(p. 918). John M. Steadman, "The Tragic Glass: Milton, Minturno and the *Condition Humaine*," in *Th'Upright Heart and Pure*, ed. Amadeus P. Fiore (Pittsburgh, Pa.: Duquesne Univ. Press, 1967), pp. 101-115, maintains that Samson's tragedy is a mirror-exemplum to the human condition, whereby "we learn to distrust worldly prosperity and to endure evil with a patient mind" (p. 105). Irene Samuel, "*Samson Agonistes* as Tragedy," in *Calm of Mind*, ed. Joseph Anthony Wittreich, Jr. (Cleveland: The Press of Case Western Reserve University, 1971), pp. 235-257, denies that *Samson* is the tragedy of a saint or martyr and its hero "a model of divinely illumined conduct" (p. 252); motivated by revenge to destroy Philistia, Samson is, like other tragic agents, the victim of a *hamartia*, egomania, he cannot fully escape from, even in his final act, despite the growth he has made. John T. Shawcross, "Irony as Tragic Effect: *Samson Agonistes* and the Tragedy of Hope," in *Calm of Mind*, pp. 289-306, argues that while on one level *Samson* is a tragedy of the wastage of the good of the individual man through blindness, on another it "is the tragedy of hope which repeatedly dogs man, blinding him to realities, to full recognition of self, to lasting achievement" (p. 296); for us, as for Samson's fellow people, "The tragedy of hope is that hope replaces truth and action" (p. 303), a wastage of our own potential for good. Although all of the preceding works have useful things to say, the most valuable considerations of *Samson* as tragedy are those of Barbara K. Lewalski, "*Samson Agonistes* and the 'Tragedy' of the Apocalypse," *PMLA*, 85 (1970), 1050-1062, and Sherman H. Hawkins, "Samson's Catharsis," in *Milton Studies, II*, ed. James D. Simmonds (Pittsburgh, Pa.: Univ. of Pittsburgh Press, 1970), pp. 211-230. Lewalski, relating *Samson* to the commentaries of Pareus and others on the Book of Revelation, concludes that "The Saints' story . . . is a tragedy of suffering and struggle" (p. 1054), and that "The true tragic impact of the play is carried by the suffering and death of Samson and what it says about the condition of human life until the Apocalypse. . . . For Samson as for all the Elect the realization is a tragic one that there is no effective deliverance from external bondage

involve not only the defeat and loss that justice requires but also, as Milton's authority Pareus said of Revelation, some "sure comfort of an happy issue out of . . . calamities,"[2] so that the Christian tragedian could say what the pagan could not justifiably say, that "All is best" (1745), and could claim, therefore, what the pagan could not justifiably claim, the "calm of mind" (1758) of a full and true tragic catharsis. The catharsis of the passions, claimed by Aristotle as an end of tragedy, could for Milton find its true fulfilment only in Judæo-Christian terms in which an awareness of the justice of God leads to the merciful recovery and regeneration of the soul. This is what we witness in *Samson*. It is also what we witness in the closing books of *Paradise Lost*.

For the Renaissance, tragedy and epic were not necessarily mutually exclusive genres. Giraldi Cinthio, for example, while arguing that the *Iliad* and the *Odyssey* are both examples of tragedy, the first of tragedy ending unhappily, the second of

---

save by death (though there is from the internal bondage of sin), and that in the fallen world the deliverers whom God raises up achieve no lasting liberations because they are constantly betrayed by the people's corruption and their own sinfulness" (p. 1061); and my reading largely supports her conclusions. According to Hawkins, in his splendid essay comparing *Samson* with the final books of *Paradise Lost*, Milton and Pareus share a common conception of tragedy as involving consolation as well as grief. My reading supports Hawkins' central point that Samson's "catharsis is the tragic or dramatic counterpart of what theology calls repentance and regeneration" (p. 216). Also briefly relating Samson to Pareus is Lynn Veach Sadler, "Typological Imagery in *Samson Agonistes*: Noon and the Dragon," *ELH*, 37 (1970), 195-210. Northrop Frye's "Agon and Logos: Revolution and Revelation," in *The Prison and the Pinnacle*, ed. Balachandra Rajan (Toronto: Univ. of Toronto Press, 1973), pp. 135-163, appeared too late for me to take advantage of it; but we agree on a number of essential points, not the least of which is that "*Samson Agonistes* is a Christian conquest of the Classical genre of dramatic tragedy" (p. 135).

[2] David Pareus, *A Commentary upon the Divine Revelation of the Apostle and Evangelist John*, trans. Elias Arnold (Amsterdam, 1644), p. 15.

tragedy ending happily, cites as the common opinion that the *Iliad* furnishes an example of tragedy, the *Odyssey* an example of comedy.[3] Milton, in the very subject of his epic, the losing and regaining of paradise, found the patterns of tragic and heroic experience. At the beginning of Book IV, as we and Satan are about to view for the first time the future protagonists and landscape of the Fall, Milton asks for the voice heard by St. John, warning of the Apocalypse:

> O for that warning voice, which he who saw
> Th' *Apocalypse*, heard cry in Heav'n aloud,
> Then when the Dragon, put to second rout,
> Came furious down to be reveng'd on men,
> *Woe to the inhabitants on Earth!* that now,
> While time was, our first Parents had been warn'd
> The coming of thir secret foe . . .

(1-7)

With these words Milton places the Fall in the context of the Book of Revelation—the work which Milton twice cites, in the *Reason of Church Government* and in the Preface to *Samson*, with "the grave authority of *Paraeus*,"[4] as an example of tragedy. And at the beginning of Book IX, as Satan is about to enter paradise, Milton explicitly proclaims his subject as tragic:

> I now must change
> Those notes to Tragic; foul distrust, and breach
> Disloyal on the part of Man, revolt,
> And disobedience: On the part of Heavn'n,
> Now alienated, distance and distaste,
> Anger and just rebuke, and judgment giv'n,

[3] "On the Composition of Comedies and Tragedies," in *Literary Criticism: Plato to Dryden*, ed. Allan H. Gilbert (1940; rpt. Detroit, Mich.: Wayne State Univ. Press, 1962), pp. 258-259.

[4] *The Reason of Church Government*, in *Complete Prose Works of John Milton*, ed. Don M. Wolfe (New Haven, Conn.: Yale Univ. Press, 1953), I, 815.

That brought into this World a world of woe,
Sin and her shadow Death, and Misery
Death's Harbinger . . .

(5-13)

The prologue does not, however, as one might expect, stop at
this point, but moves immediately into a discussion of the
false and the true heroic:

Sad task, yet argument
Not less but more Heroic than the *wrath*
Of stern *Achilles* on his Foe pursu'd
Thrice Fugitive about *Troy* Wall; or *rage*
Of *Turnus* for *Lavinia* disespous'd,
Or *Neptune's ire* or *Juno's*, that so long
Perplex'd the *Greek* and *Cytherea's* Son . . .

(13-19; my additional italics)

Not sedulous by Nature to indite
Wars, hitherto the only Argument
Heroic deem'd, chief maistry to dissect
With long and tedious havoc fabl'd Knights
In battles feign'd; the better fortitude
Of Patience and Heroic Martyrdom
Unsung . . .

(27-33)

I would quote these passages, *loci classici* that they are, with
some embarrassment, were it not for the fact that their
significance to all that follows in the remaining books has
been so much ignored. The reason why Milton would discuss
tragedy at this point seems obvious enough, but it is less
obvious why he would discuss the heroic and also why he
would discuss it in conjunction with the tragic. We can begin
answering these questions by making a simple but very important observation: Milton has schematized his material;
all of the events Milton cites as examples of the false heroic
have a common denominator, and that is *ira*, wrath. The

187

heroism of wrath—unlike God's "Anger and just rebuke," which, though it pronounces the judgment that permits tragic woe to enter the world, is nonetheless justifiable—is unanswerable and unjustifiable, simply because it is rooted in the excesses of fallen nature, human and angelic, an excess of the irascible appetite. This heroism is inferior not because it is more active (for Milton action is, of course, neither intrinsically heroic nor intrinsically unheroic), but because its actions are motivated by a mind enslaved by fallen intemperance. Accordingly, Milton once again schematizes his material: true heroism counters the intemperate wrath of fallen heroism with the virtue traditionally opposite wrath, "the better fortitude / Of Patience";[5] the "Heroic Martyrdom / Unsung," moreover, counters the fallen tendency to pride and vainglory with its opposite, the humility of self-sacrifice. True heroism, then, involves a victory over, chiefly, the pride and intemperance of man's fallen nature. The discussion of tragedy and heroism at a point just prior to Adam's fall and regeneration should now begin to seem more appropriate: the Fall provides all future men with the pattern for, as well as the tendency to, false heroism; whereas true heroism, involves a regeneration of the spirit, the attainment of "A Paradise within thee, happier far" (XII.587) by a spiritual victory over the old Adam;[6] and it is this heroism which Adam will begin to experience by the end of the epic and which will find its exemplar in Christ and His triumph over the old Adam in the wilderness and on the cross. With the Fall tragedy enters human history, and the heroic and tragic become for the Christian hero inseparably interlocked: the false hero repeats the sins of the Fall and perpetuates the tragic misery and woe that entered the world through the Fall;

[5] On patience as the virtue opposite wrath, see Rosemond Tuve, *Allegorical Imagery* (Princeton, N.J.: Princeton Univ. Press, 1966), pp. 94-96.

[6] On the heroism of regeneration in *De Doctrina*, see George M. Muldrow, *Milton and the Drama of the Soul: A Study of the Theme of the Restoration of Men in Milton's Later Poetry* (The Hague: Mouton, 1970), pp. 9-53.

the true hero overcomes the sins of the Fall and triumphs over the tragic condition through the restoration of the inner garden. Paradoxically, however, the true hero's triumph over the generic or Adamic tragic condition makes him all the more vulnerable to the world. His establishing a garden in the wilderness becomes—as with his exemplar, Christ, who left the wilderness for the cross—a preparation for the martyrdom of Christian tragedy. With the Fall, all true heroism stipulates tragic loss, agony, and sacrifice; the hero must also be victim.

Adam and Eve provide the fallen pattern for the heroic and the tragic for all men after them. After Adam has joined Eve in the eating of the apple, the immediate consequence is lust, or intemperance of the concupiscible appetite; and after they have slept, the next consequence of their sin is wrath, or intemperance of the irascible appetite. (Once again Milton has schematized his materials, this time according to the bipartite nature of the appetitive soul. The end result of this is to clarify the causal thrust of the Fall; for the immediate consequences of the Fall are an index of, indeed the fulfillment of, Adam's and Eve's motivation for eating.) Eve, who was offered the parodic heroism of godlikeness by Satan, and Adam, who was offered the parodic heroism of the romance hero in a "glorious trial of exceeding Love" (IX.961) by Eve, quarrel:

> Thus they in mutual accusation spent
> The fruitless hours, but neither self-condemning,
> And of their vain contest appear'd no end.
>
> (1187-1189)

War, with its angry intemperance and willful vanity, has entered human history in this first "vain contest" between men for mastery. Adam and Eve, mastered by the intemperance and pride of the fallen mind, become the human prototypes of the false heroic—of Homer's Achilles and Neptune, of Virgil's Juno and Turnus.

The remaining events of *Paradise Lost* provide the heroic pattern for man's coping with his tragic condition. The movement from the loss of paradise in Book IX to the incipient regaining of paradise in Book XII, is a paradigm of the struggle of all true heroes throughout history to overcome the old Adam and to be recreated in the image of the new Adam. The inner landscape of Adam's own mind mirrors the outer landscape of the vision Michael puts before him in the last two books: the struggle in history is one between those who imitate the Fall of the old Adam and those few—Noah, Abraham, and Moses, for example—who prefigure the new Adam. In a crucial sense, however, history and the mind do not mirror each other, for in the outer world there is no sense of increase in goodness, nor is there any but a tentative and transient triumph over evil until the Apocalypse:

> . . . so shall the World go on,
> To good malignant, to bad men benign.
>
> (XII.538-539)

It is a world, as Hezekiah Holland says, of "grievous and continuall strifes" to which the Church and all men fall victim.[7] Only in each man's soul is any kind of really lasting victory over the old Adam and his sins possible—and even that victory, though it is his only possible defense against the world, ironically makes man more vulnerable to the world. This, of course, is the pattern set by Christ Himself on the cross, whose heroic triumph coincided with, indeed depended on, His death.

For Milton, then, the tragic and the heroic had to be interpreted not only in terms of the Fall and the loss of paradise but also in the ultimately Christian terms of the regaining of paradise. If I have read the prologue properly, it would seem that what Milton is suggesting is that tragedy is inescapable in the fallen world. It is part of our inheritance through Adam: we are born in sin and by that sin alienated from heaven, born to live in "a world of woe, / . . . and Misery"

---

[7] "Preface," *An Exposition . . . upon the Revelation of Saint John* (London, 1650).

190

and to die. In such a world heroism is possible only by attaining the inner paradise whereby the source of tragedy, Adam's sin, is overcome; but this heroism itself makes man even more a victim of the world, despised, persecuted, martyred. The paradox is that man can triumph over the tragic condition he inherits through the Fall only through tragedy—but tragedy in a different sense, one applicable not to all but only a few, the tragedy, like Christ's, of patient endurance and martyrdom. In the fallen world the heroic stipulates the tragic: one must lose oneself in order to gain oneself, one must die in order to be reborn; in order to triumph over the world one must become the world's victim. Adam provides the prototype of all tragic falls, but it is Christ, "coming in the Flesh / To a reproachful life and cursed death," Christ "nail'd to the Cross" (xII.405-413), who becomes Milton's exemplary tragic hero.

This same sense of tragedy, of triumph stipulating loss and agony, would seem to operate in *Paradise Regained* as well. When Mary says that her "favor'd lot" is an "Exaltation to Afflictions high," that she is "Afflicted . . . , it seems, and blest" (II.91-93), she imperfectly states and feels the tragic pattern of her son's triumph. In the word "blest," suggesting as it does at once divine favor and sainthood along with a state of being wounded, the wound and the triumph become one. It is therefore appropriate that in the lines immediately preceding these Mary alludes to her son's wounds at the Crucifixion: "through my very Soul / A sword shall pierce" (90-91). "Humiliation and strong Sufferance" (I.160) become the means of heroic victory; the wound becomes curative, redemptive. And indeed in the final events of the work Mary's intuition of Christian tragedy and heroism as being somehow inseparable is borne out: Christ's triumph on the pinnacle alludes to His martyrdom on the cross, and the heroic victory banquet prefigures the sacrament that will commemorate that martyrdom.

Samson Agonistes participates in the same tragic sense of life found in the closing books of *Paradise Lost* and in *Para-*

191

dise Regained, but it is, more than those works, "about" tragedy. Just as Milton's redefinition of the heroic became part of the action of his epic, so the redefinition of tragedy becomes part of the action of his tragedy. As I have suggested, Adam provides the prototype of all tragic falls, Christ the prototype of all tragic triumphs. The action of *Samson*, I contend, involves a progression from Adamic to Christian tragedy, and this progression parallels the hero's own progression from an *imitatio Adamis* in his fall to an *imitatio Christi* in his triumph and death. The portrayal of Samson as the work opens reveals him in his fallen, Adamic state, blind, groping his way in despair; it reveals him as a victim of the chief passion classical tragedy could make no claim to purge, doubt and despair. He resembles, as many readers have felt, Adam of Book X of *Paradise Lost*, his eyes and reason dimmed by his fall, in his complaint despairing of his own fate and distrusting the ways of God.[8] Like Adam, then, Samson is a chosen man who falls from lofty station to despair. Both heroes, moreover, experience a regeneration involving an externalization of their flaws, a confrontation with the Adamic mirror, a homeopathic purgation of like by like. Adam and Samson are both *agonistai* caught up in a psychomachia between the old Adam and the new. The triumph over doubt and despair, if it is to be more than a tentative, secular victory, stipulates Christian faith and hope. Accordingly, the movement of both Adam and Samson out of despair coincides with their recreation in the image of Christ and their imitation of His triumph over the Fall. Adam struggles against the pride and intemperance of his fall to take, in the end, Christ as his exemplar.

[8] Among the more useful comparisons of Samson and Adam, see E. L. Marilla, "*Samson Agonistes*: An Interpretation," *Studia Neophilologica*, 29 (1957), 70-73 esp.; E. S. Gohn, "The Christian Ethic of *Paradise Lost* and *Samson Agonistes*," *Studia Neophilologica*, 34 (1962), 261-264; Duncan Robertson, "Metaphor in *Samson Agonistes*," *University of Toronto Quarterly*, 38 (1969), 328-335; Jon S. Lawry, *The Shadow of Heaven* (Ithaca, N.Y.: Cornell Univ. Press, 1968), pp. 351-355; and, above all, Hawkins, pp. 211-230.

Samson imitates Christ's victory in the wilderness over the old Adam by resisting in the form of Manoa, Dalila, and Harapha the Flesh, the World, and the Devil, and proceeds to imitate Christ's victory over Adam and the devil on the cross. Samson's progress, then, to use Pauline terminology, involves a crucifixion of the old man, Adam, within him; Samson *agonistes* wrestles with the Adam of his own nature. The whole movement of the drama is towards a breaking of the Adamic community Samson, and also Israel, have with the Philistine enemy, and a reasserting of the integrity of their religious and spiritual identity. The central action of *Samson Agonistes*, on the part of the hero and his people, is a spiritual triumph over the old Adam; and precisely because this is the central action of the work, Milton will use the allegorical triad of the Flesh, the World, and the Devil to comprise the "middle" of the work. Needless to say, the kind of central action Milton's use of the infernal triad suggests is scarcely what we are accustomed to think tragic action to be. Indeed, Milton's tragedy begins where most would end, with the hero fallen. Obviously if Milton had felt the fall of a great man from high to low fortune the whole substance of tragedy, he would have focused on Samson's fall. But of course he could not have done that; for that would have confined his definition of tragedy to Adam's fall in the garden, ignoring Christ's triple victory in the wilderness and on the cross. Adamic tragedy, had Milton been able to accept it as the sum of tragedy, would not necessarily have run counter to classical theory. Christian tragedy, however, does. Milton, I believe, was amply aware of this, but he remained convinced that only Christian tragedy could provide the true fulfillment of the promises and claims of classical tragedy. It becomes significant, therefore, that although in his Preface Milton is at great pains to justify his work as modelled on the "best rule" of Aristotle and the great Greek tragedians in terms of the function and form of tragedy, he is perfectly silent on the point where he clearly differs from the "best rule"—the nature of the tragic hero. The omission is striking, for it is a central question in Renaissance discussions of tragedy. It is, in fact, no less central a question for Milton and his tragedy; but it is a question to which Milton, in putting forth his own opinions on the matter, would let the work itself speak.

If the progress of the hero reflects Milton's Christian redefinition of tragedy, so does the progress of the Chorus. Israel is, or must become, Israel *agonistes*; the struggle of the nation, as much as the struggle of the hero, is against not merely their physical enslavement to the Philistines but against all that that enslavement signifies, a spiritual bondage to Adam and the Fall. As the hero moves from an imitation of the tragedy of the old Adam to an imitation of the heroic tragedy of the new, simultaneously the Chorus, like the hero experiencing a catharsis within the confines of the tragedy itself, move from an Adamic or pagan conception of tragedy in terms of (as Satan says, offering the lesser wisdom of Adam's sons) "fate, and chance, and change in human life" (IV.265) to a Christian (or more accurately, pre-Christian) conception of tragedy. In the beginning the Chorus perceive Samson's tragedy in Adamic and pagan terms as a fall from high estate, a result of either pagan fortune or Jewish punitive justice; but by the end of the drama they perceive Samson's tragedy in terms of not only the justice they had doubted but also the mercy of which they were unaware. The Chorus' and Manoa's changing conception of the hero's tragedy correlates with, mirrors, their growing understanding of God, as they begin with a vacillating perception of Him as capricious pagan fortune and fate or as the Hebraic God of the *lex talionis* and progress to an understanding of Him as a god whose ways are merciful as well as just. What we witness in the development of the Chorus is not simply a growing understanding of God and His ways but also, what is the inevitable result of that, a growing understanding of the nature of tragedy. The transformation of the hero and the transformation of Israel witnessing the tragedy become Milton's means of dramatizing the transformation that has occurred to tragedy itself.

194

I

All is best, though we oft doubt,
What th' unsearchable dispose
Of highest wisdom brings about,
And ever best found in the close.

(1745-1748)

All of *Samson Agonistes* points to these words, and the whole
problem of the nature of tragedy in the work is embodied in
them; for *Samson*, every bit as much as *Paradise Lost* and
Paradise Regained, takes as its purpose one seemingly incompatible with tragedy, the justification of the ways of God
to man.[9] The promise of God at the annunciation of Samson's birth was that "the child shall be a Nazarite unto God
from the womb: and he shall begin to deliver Israel out of
the hand of the Philistines" (Judges 13:5); and yet as the
work opens, Samson, the promised deliverer, is in chains and
Israel herself in Philistine bonds. The spiritual progress and
triumph of Samson and the eventual deliverance of Israel
from the Philistine yoke thus bear a significance vastly greater

[9] This point is made, though somewhat perversely, by G. A. Wilkes,
"The Interpretation of *Samson Agonistes*," *Huntington Library Quarterly*, 26 (1963), 363-379, who, arguing against the modern critical
tendency to interpret *Samson* as a study in regeneration, claims that
the work is Milton's "last attempt to 'assert Eternal Providence'" (p.
367). Wilkes is right to insist on this perspective and theme, but he
somehow fails to see, as does John S. Hill, "Vocation and Spiritual
Renovation in *Samson Agonistes*," in *Milton Studies, II*, pp. 149-174,
that Samson's regeneration—whether expressed in terms of a movement from despair to patience (William O. Harris, "Despair and
Patience as the Truest Fortitude in *Samson Agonistes*," *ELH*, 30
[1963], 107-120), or a movement from despair to wisdom and fortitude (A. B. Chambers, "Wisdom and Fortitude in *Samson Agonistes*,"
PMLA, 78 [1963], 315-320), or a movement from despair and doubt
to faith, trust, and hope (John M. Steadman, *Milton's Epic Characters* [Chapel Hill, N.C.: Univ. of North Carolina Press, 1968], pp.
47-57), or a movement from passion to reason (E. S. Gohn, pp. 243-
268)—is part of "a larger whole: Samson's fulfilment of his divinely
predicted vocation" (p. 150). Samson's regeneration and the justification of the divine word are clearly inseparable matters.

195

than the intrinsic meaning of the events themselves, for what is at stake in *Samson* is nothing less than the justness of "the ways of God" (293) and the truth of the divine word and prophecy. That is to say, the central question in *Samson Agonistes* is whether or not man exists in a rational and morally purposeful universe.

As I suggested in the previous chapter, in the 1671 volume *Paradise Regained* and *Samson Agonistes* were designed as companion-pieces structured around the Flesh-World-Devil scheme; and this scheme provided the Christian context, that is the triumph over the old Adam and the Fall, for Milton's redefinition of heroism in the first work, of tragedy in the second. Accordingly, the opening of *Samson* reverberates with allusions to *Paradise Regained* and the portrayal of the Fall in *Paradise Lost*. *Samson* opens with the hero, very much like Christ in His first meditation in *Paradise Regained* and to some extent also like Adam in his complaint in Book X, meditating on his past—the portents that surrounded his birth, the prophecy of an elect mission—and the relationship between the past prophecy of exaltation and the present ordeal and humiliation. The similarities between Christ's and Samson's meditations extend even to verbal similarities. Both describe their thoughts in terms of swarming:

> O what a multitude of thoughts at once
> Awak'n'd in me swarm while I consider
> What from within I feel myself, and hear
> What from without comes often to my ears,
> Ill sorting with my present state compar'd.
>
> (I.196-200)

> Ease to the body some, none to the mind
> From restless thoughts, that like a deadly swarm
> Of Hornets arm'd, no sooner found alone,
> But rush upon me thronging, and present
> Times past, what once I was, and what am now.
>
> (17-22)

And both proceed from this to a reflection on their childhood, breeding, and the promises and portents surrounding them as liberators of Israel. Neither Christ, meditating in the "dark shades" (i.194) of the wilderness, nor Samson, mediating in "Irrecoverably dark" (81) blindness in a "land of darkness yet in light" (98), is aware of God's intent in leading him into darkness. Christ, of course, finally accepts the darkness patiently as part of God's mysterious and paradoxical ways, whereas Samson can at the moment consider his lowly darkness only as the punishment of a justice he cannot fully accept and a word he cannot understand, contradicting, as it seems to, its own prophecies. The divine word for Samson is not a paradox but a contradiction. Like Adam in despair after his fall, and to some extent like Christ in *Paradise Regained*, Samson attempts desperately to find some meaningful relationship between past prophecy and present reality; and he alternates between an overt questioning of God's ways and gifts, a doubting that reduces God to a false and capricious oracle, and, what can provide the only meaningful relationship he can at this point perceive, an acknowledging of his own guilt. The questions are obviously symptoms of despair, but so, in part, are the acknowledgments of guilt; for Samson's difficulty at this point is not simply that he is unaware of God's mercy (though, like Adam on Mount Speculation, he must become aware of it), but also that, through the same prideful self-reliance that led to his fall, he fails to place faith in God's power to verify His word and instead despairs of his own power to fulfill the word.[10] The statements of repentance following the overt questioning of God are thus themselves manifestations of distrust. For example,

[10] The two best accounts of despair and doubt in *Samson* are Don Cameron Allen, *The Harmonious Vision* (Baltimore, Md.: The Johns Hopkins Press, 1954), pp. 71-94, and Steadman, *Milton's Epic Characters*, pp. 44-57. See also the informative article of Raymond B. Waddington, "Melancholy Against Melancholy: *Samson Agonistes* as Renaissance Tragedy," in *Calm of Mind*, pp. 259-287.

after questioning God's intent behind the prophecy at his
birth ("O wherefore was my birth from Heaven fore-
told. . . ?" [30]) and the special preparation for his mission ("Why was my breeding order'd and prescrib'd / As of
a person separate to God. . . ?" [30-31]), and after lament-
ing that God's promise that he would deliver Israel has in
fact resulted in the very opposite of that, Samson checks himself: "Yet stay, let me not rashly call in doubt / Divine Pre-
diction" (43-44), and he proceeds to acknowledge that the
fault may not have been in the word but in himself:

> what if all foretold
> Had been fulfill'd but through mine own default,
> Whom have I to complain of but myself?
> . . . .
> O impotence of mind, in body strong!
>
> (44-52)

Samson's recovery here is also in part relapse. This acknowledgment of guilt is, like many similar acknowledgments in
the meditation, in part taken back in the act of giving; for the
acknowledgment takes the form of a question, and the passage concludes with an anger that, while no doubt partly self-
directed, is also, as the succeeding lines show, directed at
God. "But what is strength without a double share / Of wisdom?" (53-54), he asks; and Samson's confession of guilt
subtly modulates into an accusation that God's gifts made
him "liable to fall" (55)—which was, of course, Adam's
complaint, too, in Eden when he argued that "This Woman
whom thou mad'st to be my help, / And gav'st me as thy
perfet gift" (x.137-138) was the cause of his fall, and when
in his meditation later in Book X he impugned the sufficiency
of God's gifts for "Thy terms too hard" (751). Once again
Samson is forced to check himself, but once again the restraint modulates back into repeated accusation; for having
restrained himself from quarreling "with the will / Of highest dispensation" (60-61) in the sufficiency of his wisdom,

he proceeds simply to restate his earlier blasphemy in inverse terms, the insufficiency of the gift of strength:

> Suffices that to mee strength is my bane
> And proves the source of all my miseries.
>
> (63-64)

Samson then proceeds, in a lament for his chief misery, the loss of sight, to doubt God's wisdom in creation. For Samson, God seems perversely inconsistent in making light his "prime decree" (85) while confining "the sight / To such a tender ball as th' eye" (93-94). The meditation ends with a further lament over his afflictions, which suggests that Samson, for all his inner wrestling, has not progressed very far. The repentance necessary for his spiritual recovery is corrupted by the very sins he repents of. The pattern of regeneration as we witness it from the beginning is thus a tense and complicated interaction of old things with new, a subtle corrupting of new awarenesses with old vices.

The central question underlying Samson's dialogue with the Chorus, which concludes the first movement of the poem, is the same question underlying Samson's meditation, the justness of God's ways. That is to say that the Chorus, for all their religious platitudes, mirror Samson's Adamic distrust. In their first speech, the Chorus, echoing Samson earlier, focus on the contrast between past exploits and present misery and attempt to find some purpose and meaning in this contrast. Nonetheless, like Samson's their awareness is limited, and all that they can discover is a commonplace, with Samson as an "example" in the tradition of *de casibus* tragedy:

> O mirror of our fickle state,
> Since man of earth unparallel'd!
> The rarer thy example stands,
> By how much from the top of wondrous glory,
> Strongest of mortal men,

To lowest pitch of abject fortune thou art fall'n.
For him I reckon not in high estate
Whom long descent of birth
Or the sphere of fortune raises;
But thee whose strength, while virtue was her mate,
Might have subdu'd the Earth,
Universally crown'd with highest praises.

(164-175)

This is a common enough justification of tragedy in the
Renaissance, but it is hardly adequate as a justification of
God's ways with Samson, nor, for that matter, is it adequate
either as a description of or a justification of *Samson Agonistes* itself.[11] This speech obviously contrasts with the concluding speech of this movement of the drama in which the
Chorus express a faith, hardly demonstrated by them, that
"Just are the ways of God" (294). In their first speech,
however, the divine disposer is certainly not a god whose
ways are justifiable to man but rather a goddess Fortuna,
capricious and by no means just. The entire speech, in fact,
mirrors the limitations of the hero's own Adamic vision:
Samson, because of his distrust of the divine word and his
ignorance of mercy, can look at only the past and the sins
of the past and therefore, like Red Crosse Knight before him,
despairs of the future and the promise. Similarly, the Chorus
see Samson only as he is and, nostalgically, as he was. The
despair of the hero is also his nation's. The Adamic blindness
of the spiritually enslaved Samson is the blindness also of the
nation he was to liberate. By the end of the first movement
of *Samson*, the work's initial, that is Adamic, polarity has
thus been set up. This polarity provides the backdrop to the
ensuing three movements of the drama and their portrayal
through the Flesh, the World, and the Devil of the conflict
in Samson, but also in Israel, between the old Adam and the
new.

[11] Cf. Steadman, "The Tragic Glass," pp. 101-115.

II

In the first movement of the drama, Samson has been exploring with himself and the Chorus the identity of the old Samson. In the middle—that is, the second, third, and fourth movements—that identity is providentially mirrored by Manoa, Dalila, and Harapha. Once again Milton schematizes his materials; for in keeping with the homeopathic nature of the cure, the three representatives of Samson's progress in sin appear in *reverse* chronological order, from the most recent to the most remote, as part of the hero's journey backwards into the history of his soul. Providence provides Samson, as it had Adam on Mount Speculation, with a mirror wherein he can recognize and repudiate the Adamic corruption into which he has fallen. The chronology of this progress in sin is quite specific:

> Fearless of danger, like a petty God
> I walk'd about admir'd of all and dreaded
> On hostile ground, none daring my affront.
> Then swoll'n with pride into the snare I fell
> Of fair fallacious looks, venereal trains,
> Soft'n'd with pleasure and voluptuous life.
>
> (529-534)

After which, of course, he falls into the despair in which we find him at the beginning of the work. The chronology of sin, then, is from pride to intemperance to despair, represented by Harapha, Dalila, and Manoa, respectively. This is not to say that these three characters are equivalents to Samson's vices. There is about them an almost nightmarish distortion, though providentially it is a distortion which makes the truth of his identity clearer to Samson: Manoa's despair and distrust of God, which is at once something less and more than Samson's, takes the form of ingratiating concern and sincerely solicitous paternal love, and to resist it Samson must resist his own father; Dalila's lust and glory take the

201

form of a perfumed parody of masculinity and femininity, and to resist it Samson must see in all its ugliness the object for which he sacrificed everything and to which he has to some extent become; and Harapha's vainglory takes the quite un-glorious shape of masculine parading which fails to conceal its real cowardice and impotence. Like the visions at the end of *Paradise Lost*, these mirrors of the hero's identity must distort in order to reveal.

If Manoa, Dalila, and Harapha present Samson with a mir-ror to his Adamic corruption, simultaneously they also con-front him with the three temptations to which Adam had succumbed and which he in Gaza, like Christ in the wilder-ness, must resist and conquer. In the *Second Defense*, Milton remarks, in what is one of the few examples in his prose of the infernal triad, that

> Unless you expel avarice, ambition, and luxury from your minds, yes, and extravagance from your families as well, you will find at home and within that tyrant who, you believed, was to be sought abroad and in the field—now even more stubborn.[12]

This familiar Miltonic (and biblical) notion that the freedom of the soul, attained through resistance of "all temptation," is the essential prerequisite to triumph in the outer world; this notion, which played such a substantial role in the mean-ing and structure of *Paradise Regained*, plays an equal role in *Samson Agonistes*.[13] In *Paradise Regained* Christ, before

[12] *Complete Prose Works of John Milton*, ed. Don M. Wolfe (New Haven, Conn.: Yale Univ. Press), IV (pt. 1), 680.

[13] This thesis was proposed over twenty years ago by F. Michael Krouse, *Milton's Samson and the Christian Tradition* (Princeton, N.J.: Princeton Univ. Press for the Univ. of Cincinnati, 1949), pp. 119-132, but not until recently has it begun to receive from Milton-ists the serious consideration due it. Barbara Lewalski, *Milton's Brief Epic* (Providence, R.I.: Brown Univ. Press, 1966), p. 172, remarks diplomatically that she "remain[s] unconvinced by Michael Krouse's typological interpretation . . . largely unsupported by explicit allu-sions or statements in the poem inviting such a reading"; and in her

He can defeat the devil and begin mankind's salvation, must be "fully tried / Through *all temptation*" (i.4-5); and so Samson, before he can liberate Israel, must attain the "virtue which breaks through all opposition, / And *all temptation* can remove" (1050-1051). The structure of temptation in *Samson*, like its counterpart in *Paradise Regained*, which it virtually parallels, has its origins in the double-triadic scheme of Spenser and Fletcher: once again we discover a linear

---

"Samson Agonistes and the 'Tragedy' of the Apocalypse," p. 1055, she still remains unconvinced. H. R. MacCallum, "Milton and the Figurative Interpretation of the Bible," *University of Toronto Quarterly*, 31 (1962), 397-415, also finds Krouse "unconvincing" (p. 411). Neither he nor Lewalski, however, goes so far as to accuse Krouse, as does Arnold Stein, *Heroic Knowledge* (Minneapolis, Minn.: Univ. of Minnesota Press, 1957), p. 228, of "not having mastered the poem he is dealing with." The problem in part is that Krouse overstated his case; for as Ernest Sirluck, *Modern Philology*, 48 (1950), 72, in his review of the book sagely observed, while Samson is like Christ he does not allegorically equal Christ. Largely, however, the problem is lack of evidence. My intention is to supply that evidence by comparing characters and episodes in *Samson* with comparable episodes and characters in *Paradise Regained* and *Paradise Lost*, also Book I of the *Faerie Queene* and "Christ's Victory on Earth." I should add that recent criticism—e.g., Robertson, Hawkins, Lawry, Shawcross, Sadler; also, Kenneth Muir, *John Milton* (London: Longmans, Green, 1955), p. 182, and Roy Daniells, *Milton, Mannerism and Baroque* (Toronto: Univ. of Toronto Press, 1963), pp. 211-213—has increasingly tended to follow Krouse.

I do not like to place myself in the unenviable role of a resurrector of old theories, but the influence suggested by George Wesley Whiting, *Milton's Literary Milieu* (1939; rpt. New York: Russell and Russell, 1964), pp. 251-264, of Francis Quarles's *History of Samson* on Milton's work is by no means as unlikely as most readers have thought. Although many of the works translated or described in Watson Kirkconnell's *That Invincible Samson* (Toronto: Univ. of Toronto Press, 1964) treat Samson as a type of Christ, only one employs the Flesh, the World, and the Devil, and that is Quarles's work. One of the most popular works of its time, the *History of Samson*, although unlike *Samson Agonistes* concerning itself with the whole of Samson's life, treats Samson typologically. In Quarles, Samson's life at once looks back to Adam's and prefigures Christ's. For example, Samson's temptation by the woman of Timnah is seen as a counterpart to Eve's

Flesh-World-Devil sequence, with the World-temptation sub-
suming a subsidiary version of the triad. As the representative
of the Flesh, Manoa tempts Samson to intemperance as well
as despair; as the representative of the World, Dalila embodies avarice as well as the lust and glory in terms of which
she tempts the hero; as the representative of the Devil,
Harapha, embodying the violent but ultimately empty and
impotent pride and might of the devil, attempts to persuade
Samson that he is a lesser version of himself (Harapha), that
Samson's growing sense of a new identity is in fact a repeti-

---

seduction of Adam (Section 11), and Samson in the temple is compared to Christ on the cross (Section 23). The Flesh, the World, and
the Devil are associated with Dalila in Meditation 20, in which, after
Dalila has acquiesced to her countrymen's proposals, Quarles reflects
on the soul's desire "since the losse / Of the faire freedom" through the
Fall of man for Wealth, Glory, and Pleasure/Lust. In Meditation 21
Dalila's temptation of Samson is specifically related to the temptation
in Eden by way of (1) paraphrase of Genesis 3, (2) the association
of Dalila with the serpent (both Adam and Samson call their faithless wives serpents), and (3) the enumeration of the three sins: "Art
thou growne *Covetous*?" "Art thou *Ambitious*?" "Wouldst thou enjoy the *pleasures* of the flesh?" Although Quarles's Dalila has no
specifically Circean attributes, she is, like Milton's (and the Renaissance's) Circe, associated with the Sirens through her verbal wiles
and skills; and she is seen, very much as in Milton, as an amorous
conqueror. Verbal parallels between Quarles and Milton are fairly
numerous, and most of them are catalogued in Whiting. By far the
most striking of these is the parallel between the reflection of Samson's fall in Meditation 22 and the reactions of the Chorus and
Manoa upon first seeing the fallen Samson:

> O, sudden change!
> Is this that holy *Nazarite*, for whom
> Heaven shew'd a Miracle, on the barren wombe?
> Is this that holy *Thing*, againe whose birth,
> Angells must quit their thrones, and visit Earth?
> Is this that blessed *Infant*, that began
> To grow in favour so, with God and man?
> What, is this hee, who (strengthned by heaven's hand)
> Was borne a *Champion*, to redeem the Land?

(All citations from Quarles are to *The Complete Works in Prose and
Verse*, ed. Alexander B. Grosart [1880-81; rpt. New York: AMS
Press, 1967].)

tion of his earlier pride and presumption. The three visita-
tions, then, present the three temptations of the Flesh, the
World, and the Devil to which Adam and Christ were
tempted, while at the same time they provide the means
whereby Samson, moving from an imitation of Adam's fall
to Christ's triumph, can undergo an interior journey which
carries him farther and farther backwards from his present
despair (Manoa) to his lust for Dalila to, finally, in all of its
terrible impotence, the pride of the giant Harapha.

In *Paradise Regained*, as in the Despaire episodes of the
Faerie Queene and "Christ's Victory on Earth," the temptation of the Flesh involved a complex of related vices: distrust
of oneself and one's mission; disbelief of the word; distrust
of the goodness and justice of God; a sense of heaven's desertion, and, with that, an unwarranted reliance on illegitimate
means for self-preservation. These, as we have seen, are the
major tendencies Samson has been wrestling with in the first
movement of the drama. They are also the weaknesses which
Manoa embodies and to which he tempts his son. As in *Paradise Regained*, the appearance of the tempter is a symbolic
index of the nature of the temptation. For the temptation of
the Flesh on the first day, Satan assumed the disguise of "an
aged man" (1.314), as had Fletcher's Satan, "an aged
Syre," for the Flesh-temptation in "Christ's Victory." Similarly, it is the old age of Manoa which the Chorus stress as
he approaches:

> But see here comes thy reverend Sire
> With careful step, Locks white as down,
> Old *Manoa* . . .
>
> (326-328)

In his own description of himself Manoa also stresses his age:

> . . . hither hath inform'd
> Your younger feet, while mine cast back with age
> Came lagging after . . .
>
> (335-337)

205

As in *Paradise Regained*, the temptation of the Flesh is introduced by an old man offering himself as the hero's guide out of the unknown to the known in an act of hypocritical or genuine but misplaced charity. Ironically, the doting father plays the devil to his son. Lacking trust in his son and in the power of God to deliver Samson from "this uncouth place" (333), Manoa, for all the doubtlessly sincere and touching love he feels for his son, ironically works, like Satan to Christ in the stones-temptation, to foster doubt in Samson. He attempts to persuade Samson to accept the easy way back to the known and the native, just as Satan offers Christ the easy way out of the unknown wilderness back to known country; whereas both heroes must pass through the dark ordeal of temptation before they can return to the hearth, the one to return "Home to his Mother's house" (IV.639) to begin his work, the other, his work accomplished, to be brought in triumph "Home to his Father's house" (1733).

As for Satan, so for Manoa the contrast between past prophecy and present circumstances introduces the temptation of the Flesh to distrust. Satan's opening words to Christ, one recalls, employ the contrast of the divine sign of high mission with the present lowly state of Christ to suggest a distrust of the prophecy and, correspondingly, disbelief in the identity of Christ as the Son of God. So, for Manoa, in a speech which repeats many of Samson's feelings in his meditation, the contrast brings the hero's identity into question: "O miserable change! is this the man, / That invincible Samson . . . ?" (340-341), and he proceeds, again mirroring Samson (and also Satan in the stones-temptation of *Paradise Regained*), to question the meaning and purpose of the divine sign:

> For this did th'Angel twice descend? for this
> Ordain'd thy nurture holy, as of a Plant?
>
> (361-362)

Manoa's distrust of God is so deep that not only does he, like his son, question God's gifts but also, manifesting a distrust even greater than Samson's, he goes so far as to wonder if God does not tempt man to want His goodness in order for Him to inflict pain on man:

> Nay, what thing good
> Pray'd for, but often proves our woe, our bane?
> . . . .
> O wherefore did God grant me my request,
> And as a blessing with such pomp adorn'd?
> Why are his gifts desirable; to tempt
> Our earnest Prayers, then, giv'n with solemn hand
> As Graces, draw a Scorpion's tail behind?
>
> (350-360)

This is a deity as unjust, uncharitable, and morally capricious as the one Satan portrays to Eve in Eden and to Christ in the stones-temptation as selfishly keeping knowledge to Himself. For Manoa, there is little if any point to Samson's humiliation—even as a working out of God's justice, which seems to him out of proportion to the fault:

> Alas! methinks whom God hath chosen once
> To worthiest deeds, if he through frailty err,
> He should not so o'erwhelm, and as a thrall
> Subject him to so foul indignities
> Be it but for honor's sake of former deeds.
>
> (369-372)

God is not only unjust; he is also, as Satan implies in his account of God's treatment of him, ungrateful. What Manoa describes is certainly no god of mercy, not even the just god of the Jews, but a capricious pagan Fortuna, superior in no way to the god of Israel's enemies. If it is true that Milton's tragedy begins where most would end, it is equally true that at the beginning of the tragedy Manoa and Samson assert what is in the end the vision of most tragedy. Indeed Manoa articulates, and may even be said to represent, a vision central to non-Christian tragedy—the injustice of a universe that can permit a vicious disproportion between "frailty" and the "foul indignities" that ensue.

Not only, then, does Manoa's speech mirror Samson's meditation in its despair and distrust, but also it is expressed like Samson's in terms of the contrast between past promise and glory and present degradation, and phrased like Samson's in a series of questions. However, unlike his son, Manoa cannot check his doubting but must be checked by Samson himself:

> Appoint not heavenly disposition, Father,
> Nothing of all these evils hath befall'n me
> But justly. . . .
>
> (372-374)

Samson's confrontation with Manoa, like the confrontations after it, permits the hero to see and hear himself. Temptation provides a means whereby the inner struggle takes the form also of an outer struggle; it provides, from one perspective, the means whereby the soul can move outside itself, direct its energies outwards, in order that it may perceive itself more clearly and return to itself cleansed and purified. What Samson perceives upon the approach of Manoa as a renewal of "th'assault" (331), part of God's Hebraistic, *lex-telionis* way of achieving vengeance and exacting the due punishment, is really a manifestation of divine providence and grace, a means of redemption. The conception of the ordeal Samson voices to his father is, like the Chorus' conception of it, Mosaic and Old Testament: God, as part of his "Just . . . ways" (293), is merely establishing equivalents in punishment for past offenses in order to set the balances straight and restore a past but now violated parity. In actuality, temptation, like the tragedy itself, proceeds beyond Old Testament parity to a foreshadowing of New Testament mercy, beyond a retribution for past error to a new point of triumph. Samson's firmer trust in divine justice takes him beyond his father, who, as his age and the description of his feet "cast back with age / . . . lagging after" (336-337) suggests, is, like

Spenser's Despaire, rooted in the errors (and triumphs) of the past. Ironically, Manoa, as he questions God's justice, is an instrument not only of that justice but also of what goes far beyond his understanding, namely God's mercy. Samson's expression of firmer trust in God's justice is in fact—and this is the wonderful irony of the passage—part of the workings of a merciful providence, part of a tentative movement towards the future things grace will permit, a movement, like Samson's own tentative "dark steps [moving] a little further on" (2), into the future and a new illumination.

Samson's assertion of the justice of "heavenly disposition" leads him to a confession of guilt and an account of his error which bears many resemblances to Adam's fall: as Samson through uxoriousness "profaned / The mystery of God giv'n . . . under pledge / Of vow, and . . . betray'd it to a woman" (377-379), so Adam; as Dalila "The secret wrested from me in her height / Of Nuptial Love profest" (384-385), so Eve to Adam; as "the *Danite* strong" (*PL*, ix.1059), by allowing his reason to be overcome by feminine wiles, is reduced to unmanly yoke and "foul effeminacy" (410), so Adam; as Samson fell by himself deceived ("This well I knew, nor was at all surpris'd, / But warn'd by oft experience" [381-382]), so Adam. To this confession of an Adamic betrayal of God, Manoa, characteristically perceiving God in the most provincial Jewish terms, merely criticizes Samson's marriage choices, yoking the two together as though they were one. Manoa will not go so far as to deny altogether that there was "Divine impulsion" (422), but pragmatist of the spirit that he is, he notes the consequences and sees they are not good, implying of "Divine impulsion" the same sinister capriciousness he had earlier implied of divine favor; and he repeats his earlier distrust of God's punitive justice:

> . . . thou bear'st
> Enough, and more the burden of that fault;
> Bitterly hast thou paid, and still art paying
> That rigid score.
>
> (430-433)

Manoa, at the same time that he expresses fear that Samson will blaspheme God by serving Dagon, is himself a blasphemer. The Adamic flaw of her enemies is in Israel herself.

Samson's reply expresses trust in God's ability to "arise and his great name assert" (467), but he continues in his distrust of the prophecy concerning himself. "This only hope relieves me," he says, "that the strife / With mee hath end" (460-461). It is an expression of despair and continued doubt on one level, the one Samson consciously voices, and is false; but on another level, of which neither Samson nor his father is aware, it is true.[14] Even in the language of despair the operation of grace, working towards Samson's release and triumph, is implicit. The contradictory attitude towards God which Samson expresses is expressed in even stronger terms by Manoa, who repeats Samson's trust that God has the strength to vindicate his own glory and who repeats also Samson's distrust of God as far as Samson's own fate is concerned. The conception both men have of God is literally an anthropomorphic version of the old Samson: both men have faith in the might of God (it is revealing that Samson sees Dagon entering "lists with God" [462], and Manoa sees God "in competition" [476]); and both men see only superior might used as God's means of asserting "the glory of his name" (475). This is not the God of the end of the tragedy, whose name is vindicated not only by His might but also by His power to restore the hearts of His people, as Dagon cannot. This is "a petty God" indeed, to be "admir'd of all and dreaded / . . . none daring [His] affront" (529-531); it is a god who, except for the brute strength he uses to affirm his glory, seems hardly superior to Dagon. God seems merely the old Samson writ large. Such a misconception of God argues once again that Israel and her sons, as much as her

---

[14] This is but one of many of what Anne Davidson Ferry, *Milton and the Miltonic Dryden* (Cambridge, Mass.: Harvard Univ. Press, 1968), p. 151, calls the "unspoken meanings" of the play. See also Anthony Low, "Action and Suffering: *Samson Agonistes* and the Irony of Alternatives," *PMLA*, 84 (1969), 514-519.

enemies, worship a false god, different more in name and nationality than in substance from Dagon. Such a misconception, too, leads Manoa to suggest a repetition of Samson's old error of distrusting God and relying excessively on secular power:

> But for thee what shall be done?
> Thou must not in the meanwhile here forgot
> Lie in this miserable loathsome plight
> Neglected.
>
> (478-481)

This, of course, is what Satan argued in the stones-temptation: the hero must rely on his own powers and Satan's aid; he must despair of God's help, for He has obviously deserted him. And so, like Satan to Christ in the wilderness, the aged "Sire" and false guide offers to find an easy way to rescue the hero and lead him out of his ordeal. In *Paradise Regained*, part of Satan's strategy in the temptation of the Flesh is to convince Christ that God, while He wields superior power, is not morally superior to Satan. This assumption, which, as we have seen, has been implicit all along in Manoa's and Samson's discussion of God, underlies Manoa's proposal to ransom Samson. For while Manoa has found his own god unrelenting in His "rigid score," he has trust that the followers of Dagon "well . . . may by this [time] / Have satisfied thir utmost of revenge" (483-484). The followers of Dagon are more just than the God of the Hebrews. When Manoa in his next speech will pose the possibility of God's mercy as a reason why Samson should agree to his scheme, all the while arguing for deliverance by human hands, we should recognize at once the hypocrisy of Israel and her people, an hypocrisy rooted in a doubt they have neither the courage nor the self-knowledge to admit.

The crime for which Samson is being punished is, as he says, one which even the Gentiles punish with infernal pains; and yet Manoa, once again revealing the corruption of Israel, would have Samson evade that punishment:

211

Repent the sin, but if the punishment
Thou canst avoid, self-preservation bids;
Or th' execution leave to high disposal,
And let another hand, not thine, exact
Thy penal forfeit from thyself; perhaps
God will relent, and quit thee all his debt;
Who evermore approves and more accepts
(Best pleas'd with humble and filial submission)
Him who imploring mercy sues for life,
Than who self-rigorous chooses death as due;
Which argues over-just, and self-displeas'd
For self-offence, more than for God offended.
Reject not then what offer'd means, who knows
But God hath set before us, to return thee
Home to thy country and his sacred house,
Where thou mayst bring thy off'rings, to avert
His further ire, with prayers and vows renew'd.

(504-520)

It is easy to be gentle with Manoa, difficult not to be sympathetic and forgiving. Nonetheless, his proposal contradictorily reveals a profound disbelief in mercy while using the very terms of mercy as a means of evading a justice he does not accept. It is disbelief camouflaged as belief, blasphemy justifying itself as trust; it is an hypocrisy born of a largely unconscious doubt. The whole proposal has, in fact, significant similarities to three other temptations of the Flesh, Belial's proposal in *Paradise Lost* and Satan's stones-temptation and the banquet-temptation—though Manoa, it should go without saying, "equals" neither Satan nor Belial. Belial, like Manoa fearful of further pain and possible death, urges the fallen angels to accept Hell as home, and he extends the hope that

Our Supreme Foe in time may much remit
His anger, and perhaps thus far remov'd
Not mind us not offending, satisfi'd
With what is punisht. . . .

(II.210-213)

Belial and Manoa, both hoping "to avert / His [God's] further ire," present a temptation of the Flesh in the form of the necessity of acting according to what "self-preservation bids." It is a strategic hope in a mercy as unmerited as the belief in it is facile, and the consequence is "ignoble ease, and peaceful sloth" (II.227).[15] Similarly, Satan, requesting bread from stones, argues that "So shalt thou save thyself" (I.344); and in the banquet-temptation, he claims that taste "life preserves, destroys life's enemy" (II.372).

Until Manoa's offer of ransom, the temptation of the Flesh has taken the Protestant form of distrust of God and despair of His aid. Only in Samson's desire of rest from toil, in which sloth and despair are mingled, have we had any indication of the more traditional association of the Flesh with intemperance. With Manoa's offer, however, the temptation to slothful intemperance, "to sit idle on the household hearth" (566), takes more explicit form. From this point on until Manoa's departure, intemperance becomes the focal point of discussion. Samson's reply to Manoa's offer makes the proper transitions: he begins with a statement, like Adam's, of death-longing and proceeds to justify this desire by pointing to the seemingly irreconcilable contrast between his past promise and his fallen state. The Chorus then reflect on Samson's Nazaritic temperance in his restraint from "Desire of wine and all delicious drinks" (541); Samson echoes this in the parallel speech following it; and the Chorus reply extolling the virtue of abstinence. The interest in temperance at this point may seem a bit sudden, and Milton's structure wobbly; but neither is true. The discussion is clearly an outgrowth of the question Samson has been asking again and again: why the promise, why the special training, if he was to end so ungloriously? From another perspective, however, the discussion functions to bring Manoa's offer into focus as a renewed version of the temptation to "pleasure and voluptu-

---

[15] Stein, p. 155, also compares Manoa's offer to Belial's.

ous life," which Dalila offered. Samson's reply makes this clear:

> But what avail'd this temperance, not complete
> Against another object more enticing?
> What boots it at one gate to make defence,
> And at another to let in the foe,
> Effeminately vanquish't? by which means,
> Now blind, disheart'n'd, sham'd, dishonor'd, quell'd,
> To what can I be useful, wherein serve
> My Nation, and the work from Heav'n impos'd,
> But to sit idle on the household hearth,
> A Burdenous drone. . . .
>
> (558-567)

It seems at first that Samson is speaking of Dalila, but as the speech progresses it becomes obvious that he is also speaking of his father. To accept Manoa's offer is to make himself as much a "Bondslave" (411) to the senses as he was with Dalila; he would be merely exchanging the slothful effeminacy of "the lascivious lap / Of a deceitful Concubine" (536-537) for the slothful effeminacy of his father's hearth. Ironically, for all his good intentions, the father is playing Dalila to his son, Omphale to Hercules, Armida to Rinaldo, unwittingly tempting him to the sloth and despair of the Flesh and, even in his feeble hope for a return to past glory, a repetition of the Adamic sins and an acceptance of the limitations of the old Samson. "Better at home lie bedrid, not only idle, / Inglorious, unemploy'd, with age outworn" (579-580), advises Manoa; and in a slothful reliance on God to cure everything, he offers the hope of a miracle of renewed sight, that is, a return to the past but without regeneration, without change, without effort. Throughout this temptation, Manoa has continually offered Samson the slothful alternative, the easy way out, as opposed to the "many a hard assay even to the death" (*PR*, I.264), which is required of him as a tragic hero. Ironically, while trying to persuade his son not to despair, he is tempting him to a facilely presumptuous hope, which is the vice complementing despair as an opposite of trust.[16] That Samson resists this appeal is obviously to his credit, though clearly he resists it for less than perfect reasons. As the second movement of the drama ends, although Samson has refused the temptation to distrust the justice of God's ways and the temptation to slothful intemperance, he has not fully overcome his despair, nor have the Chorus. Indeed for Samson despair will not be fully overcome until the end of the Harapha episode or, possibly, until he accepts the Officer's invitation; and for the Israelites it will not be overcome until the end of the poem. In his last speech in this movement of the drama, Samson repeats the lament he has voiced again and again, that he who was God's "destined from the womb, / Promis'd by Heavenly message twice descending" (634-635) is now "cast . . . off as never known" (641), his evils "Hopeless . . . all remediless" (648). Nor have the "swoonings of despair, / And sense of Heav'n's desertion" (631-632) been overcome by the Chorus, who, after extolling "Patience as the truest fortitude" (654), proceed immediately to question God's justice as "contrarious" (669). "To *Israel*," Samson has indeed, as he confessed, brought "diffidence of God, and doubt / In feeble hearts" (454-456). Samson and Israel function as Adamic mirrors to each other, the weakness of the one being the weakness of the other; and both mirror the faithlessness of the enemy. Not until this mirror is broken will either Israel or her hero be free. And yet even in the expression of doubt, by Samson and the Chorus both, is suggested the operation of grace and the prophecy of new things: the "speedy death" Samson asks for is, more than he realizes, "The close of all [his] miseries, and the balm" (650-651); and the Chorus's petition for God to turn Samson's labors "to peaceful end" (709), while echoing Samson's despairing longing for death, carries, unknown to them, a meaning that by the end of the drama will be theirs as well as Samson's.

[16] See *De D.*, ii.iii; CE, xvii, 53-57.

215

III

The Dalila episode is, like the temptations of the World in *Paradise Regained*, the *Faerie Queene*, and "Christ's Victory on Earth," the most broadly based temptation in the work: the Flesh-temptation anticipates it, the Devil-temptation refers back to it. For like Satan in *Paradise Regained* in the World-temptation, Spenser's Lucifera, and Fletcher's Panglorie, Dalila, as the representative of the World, embodies not only the avarice of the World which the biblical account has as her motivation but also the intemperance of the Flesh and the vainglory of the Devil. The temptation of the World is, then, a composite temptation. Moreover, Dalila is, once again like her Miltonic and Spenserian predecessors, a Circe-figure.[17]

In *Paradise Regained*, the Circean Satan assumes for the temptation of the World a disguise of worldly courtliness, fashionable dress, and fair speech, like the disguise that Lucifera and Panglorie had assumed before him. Similarly, Dalila's courtly appearance suggests worldly success and fraudulent refinement:

> But who is this, what thing of Sea or Land?
> Female of sex it seems,
> That so bedeckt, ornate, and gay,
> Come this way sailing
> Like a stately Ship
> Of *Tarsus*, bound for th' Isles
> Of *Javan* or *Gadire*
> With all her bravery on, and tackle trim,

[17] John Steadman, "Dalila, the Ulysses Myth, and the Renaissance Allegorical Tradition," *Modern Language Review*, 57 (1962), 560-565, examines the major features Dalila shares with Circe— "her meretricious and libidinous nature, her skill in the arts and snares of the harlot, her flattery and deceit, her appeal to the *vita voluptuosa*, her eloquence" (p. 564). It should be added that Samson's repeated emphasis on his bestiality and effeminacy is also part of the Circean fabric of the poem. See Richard Sáez, "The Redemptive Circe," diss., Yale, 1967.

Sails fill'd, and streamers waving,
Courted by all the winds that hold them play,
An Amber scent of odorous perfume
Her harbinger, a damsel train behind;
Some rich *Philistian* Matron she may seem,
And now at nearer view, no other certain
Than *Dalila* thy wife.

(710-724)

The Chorus' description of Dalila suggests the entire complex of worldly sins she embodies—avarice, lust, and vainglory. Dalila's whole appearance, spectacular and vain in
its ornate flamboyance, reflects her vainglory. This vainglory
has two related forms: the first might well be called
"feminine" vainglory, that to which Comus tempts the Lady
and Satan Eve, of being the focus of all eyes, the belle of
the ball; the other, "masculine" vainglory, or excessive ambition, the pursuit of heroic honor and action. The ships of
Tarshish to which Dalila is compared are, as Merritt Hughes
notes, symbols of pride in the Old Testament.[18] The heroic
simile suggests both the masculine and feminine aspects of
Dalila's pride. The comparison of Dalila to a "stately" ship,
attracting all eyes through "her bravery" (her feminine finery
but also, possibly, her masculine bravery) and her "tackle

---

[18] *John Milton: Complete Poems and Selected Prose*, p. 568n. G. M.
Young, *Times Literary Supplement*, 9 January 1937, 28, suggests that
the source for this simile is Harrington's comparison of the Common-
wealth to a ship " 'with all its tackling, full sail, displaying its streamers, and flourishing with top and top-gallant' " in *A Word Concerning
a House of Peers*; and Peter Ure, "A Simile in *Samson Agonistes*,"
Notes and Queries, 195 (1950), 298, suggests parallels in Jonson's
The Divell is an Asse and *The Staple of Newes*. But surely the ana-
logue is, as Geoffrey and Margaret Bullough, *Milton's Dramatic
Poems* (London: The Athlone Press, 1958), p. 211, first noted, and
as Barbara Lewalski has also argued, "The Ship-Tempest Imagery in
Samson Agonistes," *Notes and Queries*, n.s. 6 (1959), 372-373,
Fletcher's description of Presumption in "Christ's Victory on Earth."
Lewalski has some brief but astute comments on the ship imagery of
the poem, as does John Carey, "Sea, Snake, Flower, and Flame in
Samson Agonistes," *Modern Language Review*, 62 (1967), 396-397.

trim," suggests the vanity of her feminine exhibitionism. At
the same time, however, the image of the ship in *Samson* is
generally a metaphor for the heroic life and voyage. The
two male heroic or pseudo-heroic figures, Samson and
Harapha, are both portrayed as ships: Samson sees himself
as "a foolish Pilot" who has "shipwreck't / My vessel trusted
to me from above, / Gloriously rigg'd" (198-200); the
Chorus speak of Dalila as Samson's copilot in his sea voyage
("What Pilot so expert but needs must wreck / Embark'd
with such a Steer-mate at the Helm?" [1044-1045]); and the
giant Harapha enters as a ship (1068-1072). This heroic
simile, like many in Milton, thus says more than it seems
to say; for we are called upon to view Dalila not only as a
meretricious parody of femininity but also as a corruption
of the masculine and the heroic. There is something unnatural
and perverse about Dalila as there was, too, about Eve; for
Eve, succumbing to her feminine desire for flattery and attraction, becomes, as John Steadman has shown, an "heroic
eidelon" in her desire to dominate Adam and replace him
with herself.[19] The suggestion of unnatural sexuality is at
least part of the meaning behind Samson's calling Dalila a
hyena, for the hyena was thought to be able to alter its gender
from one moment to another.[20] It is also part of the opening
two lines of the Chorus' description of her: "But who is this,
what thing of Sea or Land? / Female of sex it seems . . . "
(710-711). This is splendidly appropriate confusion; for not
only are the Chorus uncertain of the approaching object's
sex—it seems feminine but it is still "it," neuter—but they are
also uncertain whether it is a human being at all. For a

[19] *Milton and the Renaissance Hero* (Oxford: The Clarendon Press,
1967), p. 126.
[20] See Robert A. Van Kluyve, "Out, Out Hyaena!" *American
Notes and Queries*, 1 (1963), 99-101; also, Lee Sheridan Cox, "Natural Science and Figurative Design in *Samson Agonistes*," *ELH*, 35
(1968), 66, and Kester Svendsen, *Milton and Science* (Cambridge,
Mass.: Harvard Univ. Press, 1956), pp. 150, 164-165, 172, 277.

moment, in a marvelous bewilderment, the splendid spectacle becomes for the Chorus merely an unidentified species. The Chorus strain to discover what the object really is, for it "seems" feminine and "may seem" a "rich *Philistian* Matron," but it is obviously difficult to tell; and not until the last line of their speech can the Chorus answer the question that began it. The strained effort of the Chorus to perceive and identify the image before them dramatizes the whole difficulty of discovering who Dalila really is and what she really feels. The sexual confusion is, therefore, only part of a general confusion. The object before us, traditionally a classic *femme fatale*, the quintessence of seductive femininity, is portrayed as none of that but as parodically feminine and parodically masculine, indeed even neuter. And in this she mirrors her victim. Samson, "swoll'n with pride," fell into the snares of Dalila and the "voluptuous life," with the result that he has become at once neuter ("Like a tame Wether" [538]) and effeminate ("foul effeminacy" [410]). Ironically, as Samson has become through Haraphan pride foully effeminate, Dalila, the transforming Circe who is herself transformed by her own vices, becomes foully masculine, finding in her husband's fall her heroic ascendancy.

In addition to pride, Dalila is also characterized by fleshly lust and avarice. "Courted by all the winds" as an amorous object, Dalila's appeal to the senses is blatant: "bedeckt, ornate, and gay," flamboyantly dressed, she appeals to the sight; announced by "An Amber scent of odorous perfume," she appeals to smell. But in her appeal to the senses there is a suggestion of excess—too much clothing, too much perfume —which suggests at once "a deceitful Concubine" and a *nouvelle riche*. "Some rich *Philistian* Matron she may seem," says the Chorus; and although more of a whore than a matron, she is obviously rich and well-rewarded, dressed as she is and attended with "a damsel train behind." Throughout her confrontration with Samson, Dalila will until the end disclaim avarice as her motivation; but if we remember the introductory portrait of her, richly clothed and well-attended, we need be deceived no more than Samson about the woman who sold her husband for thirteen-hundred pieces of silver from each of the Philistine lords.

In this opening portrait of Dalila, Milton has provided us with a superlatively condensed image of what Dalila represents. She is, like Lucifera and Panglorie before her, the eternal woman that is the World, false-seeming and inconstant, indeed the goddess Fortuna, as she who has laid Samson low would also, it seems, raise him up again; and she embodies all the sins of the World—pride, lust, and greed. The opening portrait leads us, then, to expect that the notion of "all sin" and its triadic formulization will play a role in the ensuing confrontation. This expectation is, I believe, confirmed.

The underlying assumption of Manoa's temptation of Samson was that Samson should forgive himself, at least deal with himself less harshly; the underlying assumption of Dalila's temptation is that Samson should forgive her. In reality, of course, the end is the same in both: for Samson to pardon Dalila is for him to pardon himself, thereby accepting the sins of his past. Accordingly, Dalila's strategy in her appeal to pardon is, to a considerable degree, one of arguing community in vices which she will camouflage as virtues. Samson continually perceives these fraudulent virtues for what they are, versions of his own vices; so that he says to Dalila, as he must, "Such pardon therefore as I give my folly, / Take to thy wicked deed" (825-826), and when in her final request, in which the request to touch has ostensibly replaced the request to pardon, Samson, perceiving the strategy of her substitution, says "At a distance I forgive thee" (594)—which, of course, in the terminology of touch is no forgiveness at all—and he condemns her. As he must: for to accept Dalila's justification of herself is to justify the Adamic errors of the old Samson and to concede, every bit as much as if he had acceded to his father's proposal, that his offense was not that severe and that the ordeal is therefore unjust.[21]

If the Dalila-episode is part of a schematic conceptual design, it is also itself schematically designed to reveal Dalila's association with the entire triad of the Flesh, the World, and the Devil. Dalila speaks seven times. The first speech is prefatory, wherein Dalila, claiming fear of Samson, attempts to make of herself an object of pity, and claiming love for Samson ("conjugal affection" [738]), attempts to make of herself an object of admiration and desire—all, ostensibly, to obtain Samson's "pardon" (738) and "to recompense / My rash but more unfortunate misdeed" (746-747). The next three speeches emerge from the first and form a unit associating Dalila with the infernal triad and all the sins of the world. The first two are appeals for pardon through argument; the third—"In argument with men a woman ever / Goes by the worse, whatever be her cause" (903-904)— functions merely to conclude this stage and set it apart. In the fifth and sixth speeches Dalila shifts her tactics from an appeal for pardon through argument to an appeal for pardon through, first, an offer of recompense and, second, an offer and request to touch. And in her final speech she retracts all that has gone before as self-congratulation replaces repentance and the appeal for pardon.

Dalila's second speech consists of two arguments for pardon. The first is

> . . . a weakness
> In me, but incident to all our sex,
> Curiosity, inquisitive, importune
> Of secrets, then with like infirmity
> To publish them, both common female faults.
>
> (737-777)

---

[21] Cf. Charles Mitchell, "Dalila's Return: The Importance of Pardon," *College English*, 26 (1965), 619.

(How biting that "our sex" is!) In the second argument,
Dalila shifts the grounds of defense from the weakness of
her sex to the strength of her love: Samson's public life of
glorious but "perilous enterprises" (804) threatened to undermine their private life of love. Both of these excuses are
rationalizations for vices, and both, as Samson's reply makes
amply clear, are part of the triad Dalila represents. The first
defense is a cover-up for the sin of the World, avarice:

> Weakness is thy excuse,
> And I believe it, weakness to resist
> *Philistian* gold . . . .
>
> (829-831)

The connection Samson draws between avarice and Dalila's
stated motive of her sex's weakness, curiosity, makes sense
enough when it is remembered that the desire for forbidden
knowledge was the desire also of Eve, which the theologians
described as *avaritia scientiae*. The second defense is a cover-
up for the sin of the Flesh:

> But Love contrain'd thee; call it furious rage
> To satisfy thy lust . . .
>
> (836-837)

The vice Samson describes is more than lust, it is intemperance; for whereas lust is an excess of the concupiscible appetite, "furious rage" implies an excess also of the irascible
appetite.

In her third speech Dalila proceeds to a completely different tack and now camouflages the vainglory of the Devil
as honor: it was not love, but honor and duty triumphing over
love, that motivated her. Now labelling her love as "weakness" (843), Dalila has shifted the grounds of her appeal
from the weakness of her sex and flesh to the strength of her
character. In keeping with the double gender of the Chorus's
portrait, Dalila now appeals to her husband not so much as
wife and lover but as a hero to her people. The "assaults,"
"snares," and "sieges" she endured, she claims, "Might have

aw'd the best resolv'd of men, / The constantest to have
yielded without blame" (845-848); and continuing the
martial imagery of masculine combat, she proceeds to justify
herself in terms of duty to her nation and gods. "It was not,"
she argues, "gold, as to my charge thou lay'st, / That wrought
with me" (849-850)—a motivation she must deny, for it is
one incompatible with her basic strategy of making her vices
imitations of her husband's, and it is one which contradicts
the claims of service to Samson in love and to her country in
duty; rather it was the arguments of Philistine princes, who

> . . . press'd how just it was,
> How honorable, how glorious to entrap
> A common enemy, who had destroy'd
> Such numbers of our Nation: and the Priest
> Was not behind, but ever at my ear,
> Preaching how meritorious with the gods
> It would be to ensnare an irreligious
> Dishonorer of *Dagon.*
>
> (854-861)

"Public good" triumphed over "Private respects" (867-868).
This may seem a selfless sacrifice—unless we visualize Dalila
dressed up in her rewards. As in her previous arguments to
a common sexual weakness and a common lust, Dalila is
once again justifying her actions as the mirror of Samson's;
couching her meaning in the imagery of masculine combat,
Dalila implies that as in weakness so in masculine glory and
strength, "Thou show'd'st me first the way" (781).

Samson rejects as hypocritical Dalila's selfless claim to have
acted for the glory of god and country; but as a point of
argument, he accepts the possibility of sincerity in order to
expose Dalila's contradictions and the essential vainglory
underlying her pretenses. Arguing that Dalila's countrymen
by urging her to break "the law of nature, law of nations,"
the subjection of the wife to the husband, are therefore not a
country "but an impious crew" (890-891); arguing that gods
who cannot defend themselves except "by ungodly deeds"

(898) are therefore not gods at all, Samson is in effect applying the assertions Christ made about glory in *Paradise Regained*. True glory, Christ asserts, comes from God's "showing forth his goodness" (III.124), an imparting of what makes
Him God. The corollary is obvious: unjust gods are not godly
and not glorious, and therefore cannot impart glory. Moreover, according to Christ, the glory gotten among "a herd
confus'd" (III.49), who cannot weigh right from wrong,
justice from injustice, is "but the blaze of fame" (III.47),
transient and meaningless. True glory, Samson also suggests,
is not to be found among "an impious crew." Theirs, of course,
is the vainglory of the Devil; but that, as Samson's rebuttal has implied all along, is precisely what Dalila has sought,
and Dalila's final speech, claiming for herself fame among her
people, proves him right. It is true, of course, that as of this
moment Dalila can imply that as liberator of her people she
has succeeded where her husband has failed. Nonetheless, on
the tomb Dalila hopes for would be placed "annual flowers"
(987); Samson's will be planted "round with shade / Of
Laurel ever green, and branching Palm" (1734-1735), both
symbols of triumph over death, and eternity; and in the contrast is symbolized the different rewards of their different
glory.

Once Samson has rejected the three arguments for pardon wherein Dalila has camouflaged the three sins of the
World—the avarice of the World, the intemperance of the
Flesh, and the vainglory of the Devil, respectively—Dalila
shifts her tack and makes an offer of "recompense" (910)
to earn her pardon. If one is as chivalrous as Professor Allen,
this offer may well seem "a selfless proposal to a broken and
blinded man,"[22] well-meaning, like Manoa's, and mistaken.
Indeed the offer is embarrassingly similar to Manoa's: Dalila
will intercede with the lords to permit Samson to be "At home
in leisure and domestic ease" (917), and like Manoa she

[22] *The Harmonious Vision*, p. 90. The classic argument on Dalila's
behalf is William Empson's, "A Defense of Delilah," *Sewanee Review*, 68 (1960), 240-255.

urges Samson not "To afflict thyself in vain" (914). But this offer is hardly as selfless as Manoa's (nor was his, for that matter, altogether selfless); for while the worldly Dalila will share the pleasures of the flesh with her husband, her gold and glory she reserves for herself. Moreover, Dalila adds to the offer of sloth what one would expect of her as Circe, the prospect of sensual delight—an appeal she repeats in the next offer, to touch Samson. Samson's rejection of Dalila's final offer and request provokes Dalila into an angry revelation of herself. Her Lucifera-Panglorie ancestry comes to the fore as she exults in the fame she will have among her own people. "Nor shall I count it heinous to enjoy / The public marks of honor and reward / Conferr'd upon me" (991-992), she says in marked understatement; and the one sin she has persistently denied throughout, avarice, "reward," in this last gesture of contempt finally emerges.

Who is Dalila, and why does she come to Samson? She represents, as I have suggested, the World and is associated with "all sin"; and accordingly after Dalila leaves rejected, the Chorus proceed, in one of those attacks on women that have for some justified the label "anti-feminist" being applied to Milton,[23] to celebrate the virtue which can remove "all temptation" (1051). It would, of course, be insensitive to deny that the portrayal of Dalila includes more than her allegorical *significatio*. But while the allegorical association of Dalila with the World does not necessarily deny her the psychological complexity customarily granted her, Milton's relating his Circe to such feminine World-figures as Spenser's Lucifera and Fletcher's Panglorie makes absolutely clear that, whatever complexity of feeling Dalila may have, whatever

[23] One would have thought that the remarks of Parker, *Milton's Debt to Greek Tragedy*, pp. 129-135, and Watson Kirkconnell, *That Invincible Samson*, pp. vi-vii, would have disposed of this curious belief, as would the arguments, were they applied, put forth by John Halkett, *Milton and the Idea of Matrimony* (New Haven, Conn.: Yale Univ. Press, 1970). Milton is no more anti-feminist than Spenser, Fletcher, or Quarles, who provide the main literary precedents for his character.

sincerity may mingle with her fraud, Samson has no more choice than Christ in the kingdoms-temptation: Dalila's offers must be rejected with as much "disdain" (*PR*, IV.170) as Christ rejects Satan's. There is a real temptation, and many readers have succumbed to it, to be sympathetic to Dalila to the point of accepting her at face value. However, the extent, if any, to which Dalila is sincere is probably an ultimately unanswerable question. Dalila's protestation of love, for example, or her claim of contrition, can, if one listens with a certain ear, ring true (but that, after all, is the nature of successful fraud); and if one listens with another ear, it may seem hollow. Drama by its very nature allows a certain latitude in interpreting the motivation of characters; but by associating Dalila with the World Milton requires that we control our reading, perhaps also our own fallen tendency to forgive our vices. Possibly there is some measure of love in Dalila for Samson and her country. We cannot be completely sure. Be that as it may, the association of Dalila with the World insists that we must ultimately view Dalila as harshly as does Samson, eschew sentimentality, and realize that the same selfishness that led her to sell her husband for gold corrupts love into lust, duty into vainglory. To do otherwise is to reduce the stature of the hero and muddle the moral sense which makes Samson's regeneration and triumph truly heroic. It is also to run directly counter to the biblical account Milton was working from, where Dalila is a woman who for entirely selfish reasons, greed, sells out Samson (indeed, as many readers have noted, it would seem that Milton's making Dalila Samson's wife is intended to emphasize her culpability). The "real" Dalila, then, must to some extent remain an enigma to us. There is a genuine complexity in the episode, but this complexity may arise less from Dalila herself than, as the Chorus dramatized in their confusion upon her approach, from our relationship to her, as we, like them, try to perceive exactly who she is and what she is. Whatever flashes of sincerity we may see, or think we see, we must in the end find Dalila as unreliable, mutable, and un-constant as the World she represents. Not to do so is to succumb to the fair appearances of the siren and Circe that is the World, with whom, as Samson has well learned, there can be no compromise.

IV

Although Dalila's World-temptation is the central and most inclusive temptation Samson faces, Harapha's is the culminating and, in terms of Samson's spiritual recovery, the most important temptation; for insofar as Samson's regeneration involves a journey backwards into the history of the self, Samson confronts in Harapha the initial cause of his downfall, the vainglorious presumption of thinking himself "a petty God," "swoll'n with pride." This is, of course, the sin of the Devil; and as in the temptation of the Devil in *Paradise Regained*, also in Spenser's Orgoglio and dragon episodes, Harapha's Devil-temptation is one of violence and intimidation, as the fraudulent appeal to pleasure is replaced by the threat of adversity. Correspondingly, just as the pinnacle-temptation was introduced by a storm, Harapha is portrayed as an approaching storm:[24]

> *Chorus.* But had we best retire, I see a storm?
> *Samson.* Fair days have oft contracted wind and rain.
> *Chorus.* But this another kind of tempest brings.
> *Samson.* Be less abstruse, my riddling days are past.
> *Chorus.* Look now for no enchanting voice, nor fear
> The bait of honied words; a rougher tongue
> Draws hitherward, I know him by his stride,
> The Giant *Harapha* of *Gath*, his look
> Haughty as is his pile high-built and proud.
> Comes he in peace? What wind hath blown him hither
> I less conjecture than when first I saw
> The sumptuous *Dalila* floating this way . . .
>   (1061-1072)

[24] I am happy to acknowledge my indebtedness to my friend and former student, Harriet Petersen, for this observation.

The "pile high-built and proud" recalls the "stately ship" Dalila resembled. Moreover, just as Manoa's offer of the hearth anticipated Dalila's offer, so Dalila's pride anticipates Harapha's, and the violent words she uses at the end anticipate the "rougher tongue" and violent threats of Harapha.

The relationship, first suggested by Michael Krouse,[25] of Harapha to the Devil-pinnacle temptation in *Paradise Regained* has commonly been attacked on the grounds that Harapha is not violent in action whereas Satan is.[26] Nonetheless, Harapha does attempt to intimidate Samson through the threat of violence as Satan did to Christ; and the Chorus, reflecting on the episode, specifically associate Harapha with "The brute and boist'rous force of violent men" (1273). Furthermore, the fact that Harapha's threat is windy and hollow and that he himself is weak and cowardly is all part of Milton's intention in his portrayal of Harapha of revealing the essential weakness of the old Samson's being "fearless of danger, like a petty God / . . . admir'd of all and dreaded." This *fiducia carnalis*, a prideful reliance on one's own strength instead of "trust . . . in the living God" (1140),[27] is ultimately weak—as the giants in *Paradise Lost* demonstrate and as Christ asserts in the glory- and Parthia-temptations in *Paradise Regained*. Harapha is weak because the heroism he represents is weak, because the god upon which he claims to rely is weak, and because his trust in that god is weak. According to Milton's notion of the ultimate weakness of a heroism solely of physical might, he was required to modify

[25] *Milton's Samson and the Christian Tradition*, pp. 129-130. Marcia Landy, "Character Portrayal in *Samson Agonistes*," *Texas Studies in Language and Literature*, 7 (1965), 249, relates Harapha to the kingdoms-temptation.

[26] See, for example, Merritt Hughes's "Introduction" to *Samson* in *Complete Poems and Selected Prose*, p. 541.

[27] In *De D.*, II.iii (CE, XVII, 57), *fiducia carnalis* is, along with distrust, presumption, and idolatry, the opposite of trust in God.

the temptation by violence and fear in *Paradise Regained*. It
must be realized, too, that while the devil does use violence
in *Paradise Regained*, that violence is easily subdued by
Christ; and the impotence of the devil's power before the
living faith is as much demonstrated in *Paradise Regained*
as in *Samson*. That differences exist between the two episodes
need not be denied, but more important is the similarity,
which we have seen in the portrayal of Moloch, in the
glory- and Parthia-temptations, as well as in the pinnacle-
temptation, of associating the devil's sin of glory with
presumptuous might. Appropriately, therefore, Harapha's
name means "the giant," and in his self-proclamation it is his
gianthood that he stresses:

> Men call me *Harapha*, of stock renown'd
> As *Og* or *Anak* and the *Enims* old
> That *Kiriathaim* held . . . .
>
> (1079-1081)

And as he leaves, Samson says:

> I dread him not, nor all his Giant-brood,
> Though Fame divulge him Father of five Sons
> All of Gigantic size, *Goliah* chief.
>
> (1247-1249)

These giants, like those in *Paradise Lost*, represent prideful
strength and, in their association with the Titans, presumption.[28] Indeed, the connection between a giant and the devil's
violent prideful presumption had already been made by
Spenser in his portrayal of Orgoglio, whose gianthood is
repeatedly stressed; and no doubt Spenser's Devil-episode
must have played some part in Milton's casting a giant for
his Devil-temptation—a giant who is blown by the wind if
not blown up with wind and who is also ultimately impotent,

---

[28] On the association of the biblical and pagan giants with pride
and presumption, see Steadman, *Milton's Epic Characters*, pp. 177-
193, and Chambers, p. 319.

without the wind of his pride merely, as Spenser says of
Orgoglio, "an emptie bladder" (vii.24).[29]

Like its counterpart in *Paradise Regained*, the third temptation in *Samson* involves, more than any of those preceding
it, a demonstration of the identity the hero has been discovering and becoming. From his first words to Harapha—
"The way to know were not to see but taste" (1091)—we
are aware that Samson reveals renewed confidence in himself and his identity. The whole temptation consists of
Harapha's attempt, like Satan's in the storm-pinnacle
sequence, to intimidate Samson through threat of force and
the argument of "a rougher tongue" to distrust his own powers
and strength, also his relationship with God: "Stand if thou
canst," says Satan mockingly, and Harapha persistently encourages Samson to doubt his powers; Satan encourages
Christ to presume upon God's favor by casting Himself down,
whereas Harapha tries to convince Samson that his new
sense of identity is in fact presumption upon God. Here, as
in the previous two temptations, also as in the temptations in

[29] This is not to deny the possibility that Milton was influenced, as
Daniel C. Boughner claims, "Milton's Harapha and Renaissance
Comedy," *ELH*, 11 (1944), 297-306, by the *miles gloriosus* of classical and Renaissance comedy, or by the Euripidean boaster as Parker,
Milton's Debt to Greek Tragedy, pp. 122-124, claims; for the general features of Milton's character are such that they can, in one com-
bination or another, be found in a number of traditions and works.
Nonetheless, for the crucial element in the portrayal of Harapha—
a giant who is a Devil-figure and whose strength is ultimately hollow—Milton would seem to be most indebted to Spenser's Orgoglio,
even more than he is to Spenser's comic braggart, Braggadocchio
(Boughner, p. 297, finds Harapha "strongly recalling" Braggadocchio). Besides, I very much doubt that Harapha is meant to be the
object of our laughter so much as the object of our (and Samson's)
revulsion and contempt. If there is comedy here, it is a divine comedy
and the laughter is that of the gods; and from this perspective all evil
is ultimately comic as are all human limitations—from Samson's
self-contradictions, to Manoa's and the Chorus' contradiction of their
unexamined platitudes, to Dalila's vacillations and self-posturing, to
the presumptuous folly of the Philistines.

Paradise Regained, the hero is tempted to accept the identity that his tempter reveals in the mirror and to become not himself but an imitation of his tempter.

Harapha has two principal strategies for undermining Samson's sense of identity: he attempts to persuade Samson either that he is unworthy of him, Harapha, or that he is unworthy of his god. Harapha first attempts to cast doubt upon Samson's past identity and worth by suggesting Samson's inferiority in strength, to which Samson replies by asserting his present strength. Harapha then proceeds to question Samson's present worth as an opponent, blind and unwashed. Samson counters by placing the blame for his condition on the cowardly tactics of Harapha's own people; and disparaging the accoutrements and pageantry of combat associated in *Paradise Lost* and *Paradise Regained* with the false heroic, Samson offers to meet Harapha with only an oaken staff. Harapha's next tactic for undermining Samson's sense of worth and his identity as God's champion is to suggest that, even if Samson's strength were what he said it was, the source of this strength was not divinity but magic, "black enchantments [of] some Magician's Art" (1133); which implies that Samson's identity was not and is not, as he asserts in his next speech, that of the champion of "the living God, who gave me / At my Nativity this strength" (1140-1141). Harapha then proceeds once again to cast doubt on Samson's identity: his "trust . . . in the living God" is not trust at all but its opposite, "an overweening presumption,"[30] the sin, as Fletcher puts it in describing his tower-temptation, of unworthy man thinking himself of "wondrous price" with God.[31] Just as Satan argues from the storm that God has cut Christ off, Harapha argues from Samson's adversity at the mill:

> Presume not on thy God, what'er he be,
> Thee he regards not, owns not, hath cut off

[30] See *De D.,* ii.iii; CE, xvii, 55.
[31] "Christ's Victory on Earth," st. 33.

Quite from his people, and delivered up
Into thy Enemies' hand, permitted them
To put out both thine eyes . . .

(1156-1159)

Samson can assert his identity as God's champion by offering
"combat to decide whose god is God" (1176) and not sin
through presumption because he is already experiencing the
new impulse and realization that he is God's instrument. This
is not, as Harapha would have Samson believe (and as some
readers have been tempted to believe), a repetition of the
old Samson's error of excessive reliance on his role as God's
elect and favorite; rather it is a demonstration of the opposite of presumption, the "trust in God . . . whereby we wholly
repose on him."[32] What Harapha is tempting Samson to is
the belief that his new virtue is a vice, the trust of the new
Samson really the Haraphan presumption of the old. It is
also, he implies, vainglory:

> Fair honor that thou dost thy God, in trusting
> He will accept thee to defend his cause,
> A Murderer, A Revolter, and a Robber.

(1178-1180)

And the argument he advances in proof of this ironically carries the implications and much of the substance of Samson's
rebuttal of Dalila's claim to be her nation's and god's champion: Samson has broken the laws of nature and nations by
murdering, revolting against, and robbing the Philistines, to
whom his own nation was subject; as a result, either he does
his god no honor or his god is not an honorable god. From
either perspective, the implication Harapha would have Samson draw is the same as that which Samson would have had
Dalila draw: he is guilty of vainglory. Harapha's imputation,
however, does not dampen but in fact encourages Samson's
growing sense of identity. He replies that those who conquer
by force legitimately are overthrown by force and that he,

[32] *De D.*, II.iii; CE, XVII, 53.

the instrument of force, acted according to "command from Heav'n" (1212); and once again Samson issues a challenge.

The thrust of Harapha's temptation is the same as the thrust of Satan's temptation of Christ on the pinnacle. For Satan, "Son of God to me is yet in doubt," which is truth and strategy at once, as it is for Harapha, who again and again challenges from many angles Samson's past identity as God's champion and his present growing renewal of that sense of identity; and like Satan, Harapha attempts through intimidation and the threat of violence to undermine that sense of identity. That this is the thrust of the temptation, and therefore also the import of the entire triple ordeal, is made clear by the Chorus' discourse on the two forms of heroic identity, the more active heroism of those who "all thir Ammunition / And feats of War defeats / With plain Heroic magnitude of mind / And celestial vigor arm'd" (1277-1280) and the more passive heroism of "patience" (1287) and martyrdom. "Either of these," they say, "is in thy lot" (1292)—either the active heroism of the old Samson or a new heroism of fortitude. In fact, as Anthony Low has effectively argued,[33] Samson fuses both: victor by the force of "heroic magnitude" in his final act, he is also saintly in patient martyrdom. Samson's regeneration does not involve a categorical repudiation of his past. The active heroism of the old Samson, lesser than the other but certainly not invalid, is by no means rejected, only the sinful parody of it, so that the heroism of the old Samson is in effect incorporated into a new and larger heroism. Temptation has led to a dying to the sinful self of the old man, both personal and Adamic; but it has also permitted a resurrection of virtue, a revival of the old into something new. Samson in his encounter with the Flesh, the World, and the Devil has journeyed backwards

---

[33] "Action and Suffering," pp. 517-519; see also, *inter alia*, Woodhouse, "Tragic Effect," p. 213, Robertson, p. 329, and Joseph H. Summers, "The Movements of the Drama," in *The Lyric and Dramatic Milton: Selected Papers from the English Institute*, ed. Joseph H. Summers (New York: Columbia Univ. Press, 1965), p. 169.

into the past to confront and examine himself, but his point of return is greater than his point of departure. The temptations, which seemed at first merely the ordeal of justice, become in the end a means of grace and mercy. What was lost and wasted is recovered and with it more is gained, as divine grace working with the cooperative will of the hero transforms him, raising him "to a far more excellent state of grace and glory than that from which he had fallen."[34]

V

In adopting the Spenserian double-triadic structure for the middle of *Samson Agonistes* as he had for the companion poem in the 1671 volume, *Paradise Regained*, Milton called attention to the three-temptations motif and thereby also to his Christian redefinition of tragedy; and that motif, with its typological dialectic between Adam and Christ, provides the essential, polar terms of this redefinition. In *Paradise Lost*, Milton had prefaced Adam's fall and subsequent regeneration in the new Adam with the discussion in Book IX of the heroic and tragic modes. This preface, as we have seen, was not without purpose: the progress of Adam from the Fall to his regenerative *imitatio Christi* on the mount involved not only a redefinition of the man but also a redefinition of the tragic and the heroic as his fall had defined them. Adam and Christ, then, provided Milton with the human exemplars or prototypes of the two modes, the false heroic and the true, Adamic tragedy and Christian tragedy. Nonetheless, although the temptations in the garden and in the wilderness become the focus for Milton's redefinition of tragedy, it is in the image of Christ nailed to the cross that the mode finds its fulfillment. For neither Christ nor Samson does the resistance of the Flesh, the World, and the Devil signify a total triumph over Adam: the triumph becomes total only with the debelling of the antagonist. Just as Christ, after his two days of resistance, must proceed to a triumph on the pinnacle which

---

[34] *De D.*, I.xiv; CE, xv, 251.

foreshadows His martyrdom, so Samson, having imitated Christ's resistance in the wilderness, must now also imitate Christ's tragic martyrdom.

The triumph which fulfills Samson's mission stipulates, like Christ's crucifixion, the hero's death. Christ on the cross and Samson in the temple are brought into conjunction not only in the nature but also in the time of their sacrifice: Christ, atoning for Adam's fall at noon, is crucified at noon; Samson's martyrdom at noon at once looks back to Adam's fall and ahead to Christ's triumph over Adam on the cross.[35] If Samson's destruction of Philistia prefigures Christ's victory over Adam on the cross, it also signifies the culmination of Samson's own inner struggle against Adam. Accordingly, the Philistines are portrayed in terms linking them both to Adam and to the old Samson. Through their representatives, Dalila and Harapha, the Philistines mirror the intemperance and pride of both Adam's fall and Samson's; and they continue to mirror both figures in the idolatry and intemperance of their feast at the end of the drama. As Eve, soon to take the tree as her idol, feasts at noon on the fruit and becomes "hight'n'd as with Wine, jocund and boon" (IX.793), so at their noonday feast the Philistines are "jocund and sublime, / Drunk with Idolatry, drunk with Wine" (1669-1670). As Adam and Eve "As with new Wine intoxicated . . . / . . . swim in mirth" (IX.1008-1009), so do the Philistines, when "noon grew high and Sacrifice / Had fill'd thir hearts with mirth, high cheer, and wine" (1612-1613). As a mirror to Samson's Adamic idolatry and intemperance, Philistia is appropriately described in terms of his blindness at noon. Like

[35] On the role of noon-midnight in the Fall, see Albert R. Cirillo, "Noon-Midnight and the Temporal Structure of *Paradise Lost*," in *Critical Essays on Milton from "ELH"* (Baltimore, Md.: The Johns Hopkins Press, 1969), pp. 215-225. In "Time, Light, and the Phoenix: The Design of *Samson Agonistes*," in *Calm of Mind*, pp. 218-229 *passim*, Cirillo uses the noon-midnight motif to relate Samson to Adam and Christ; and Sadler, pp. 195-210, uses the motif to relate *Samson*'s ending to both the Crucifixion and the Apocalypse.

the diminishing eyesight of Adam and Eve after the Fall, Samson's blindness represents a blinding of the inner sight by sin. It is therefore significant, in terms of the Adamic and Christlike polarities between which Milton's tragic hero operates, that Samson's great lament, "O dark, dark, dark, amid the blaze of noon" (80), at once looks ahead to his imitation of the Crucifixion and back to the Fall: at the Crucifixion, the sun is eclipsed at noon; and during the temptation in Eden, Satan (midnight) leads Eve to the tree at noon, and Eve is compared to a "Night-wanderer" (IX.640). And the Philistines are "with blindness internal struck" (1686) at noon. Consequently, when Samson, "With inward eyes illuminated" (1689), destroys Philistia in her noon blindness, he completes, almost allegorically, the outer act consummating his own inner struggle against the old Adam. The mirror confusing the identities of hero and antagonist, confusing also the absolute moral disjunction between God and Dagon, is now finally broken, but the very act that finally breaks the mirror linking Samson with Adam and Philistia also brings him in tragic union with his victims amidst the rubble of Philistia. Tragically, the assertion of Samson's new, Christlike identity requires that he, as well as his enemies, be the victim of it.

The last day of Samson's life has epitomized prophetically the public life of Christ, begun in the wilderness and completed on the cross. Samson's triumph on this day, however, looks forward to a final and more lasting triumph: just as Christ in *Paradise Regained* receives as His reward fruits from the *arbor vitae*, a symbol of the triumph over death awaiting all men who in their pilgrimage imitate His victory over the Flesh, the World, and the Devil; so Samson receives his reward after a similar pilgrimage, a monument planted round "with shade / Of Laurel ever green, and branching Palm" (1734-1735). Samson's monument images forth the *arbor vitae* of which the saved will partake at the end of history; it represents the promise of eternal triumph which grace permits beyond justice—the triumph that provides the final

answer to Samson's, and the work's, central question about
the moral nature of the universe.

The promise of the Apocalypse is shadowed forth in Samson's monument; it is shadowed forth also in his final act.[36]
Nonetheless, these are only shadows, intimations, implications; and the central allusive thrust behind Samson's martyrdom is not to the Apocalypse but the Crucifixion. For Milton
to have stressed the Apocalypse more strongly would no
doubt have diminished the tragic impact of the work; it would
also have run counter to his own conception of the tragic
hero as victim. Samson's tragedy occurs within, and is interpreted in terms of, the fallen world. The obvious cannot be
too forcefully emphasized: tragedy occurs within history as
part of a world now altered by the Fall. This life, not the end
of it, provides the tragic perspective; it is not the Son but
Christ who is Milton's exemplary tragic hero. If *Samson* is
tragic, it is not through the hero's prefiguring the Son rolling
untouched in His chariot over the forces of evil; rather it is
through his imitating Christ nailed on the cross triumphing
in agony. For in this world triumph comes at great price and,
as Milton's "authority" says, "through many tribulations":
the Church "was established . . . in the blood of Christ, It
began and increased in the blood of the martyrs: And in
their blood it shall continue unto the end."[37] The history and
tragedy of the saints is a constant expenditure of the self in
sacrifice. The end to this expenditure comes not through a
utopian progression of history but through the termination
of history; for if the bloodshedding and sacrifice of the saints
is continuous, their triumphs are not. That, in fact, is the
vision underlying all of Milton's last works. Adam leaves
Eden, his regeneration in Christ begun, in one sense victori-

[36] Lewalski, "Samson Agonistes and the 'Tragedy' of the Apocalypse," p. 1054, relates Samson's martyrdom only to the Apocalypse,
arguing that there is "no clear evidence that Milton intended to in-
voke the antitype of Christ's sacrificial death in the drama"; whereas
Sadler, pp. 195-210, finds both events alluded to.

[37] Pareus, p. 111.

ous; but to be recreated in Christ means to be victim, albeit a learning victim, of forces now no longer under his control. The foul change that Adam, like Satan and Samson, initially perceived as his tragic agony is in the end only a preliminary to more agony for himself and his descendants. Even in Christ's triumphs in *Paradise Regained* there is no final victory: the temptations over which He triumphs are those to which His church will succumb again and again throughout history; and His victory in the wilderness is but proof of His worthiness to die for man, the full promise of that sacrifice to be fulfilled finally only at the end of history. *Samson* provides no more finality: the conflicts within the nation he dies for, their disloyalties and treacheries, are to be repeated again and again; this is not the first time Israel will hand over her savior to the enemy, nor is this the last of her captivities. A common sense of the tragedy of the human condition suffuses all three of Milton's mature works—a sense that in the fallen world man is capable of limited triumphs only and these through "humiliation and sufferance," the continuous shedding of blood.

Samson Agonistes is a heroic tragedy of transformations. It is also a transformation of tragedy. The justice and mercy of Milton's God transform both the genre and the hero. Transformed as well are the witnesses of the tragedy, Israel and ourselves; and as the tragedy ends, it is we who have become its focus. Let us turn again to the final words of the poem:

> All is best, though we oft doubt,
> What th' unsearchable dispose
> Of highest wisdom brings about,
> And ever best found in the close.
> Oft he seems to hide his face,
> But unexpectedly returns
> And to his faithful Champion hath in place
> Bore witness gloriously; whence *Gaza* mourn
> And all that band them to resist

His uncontrollable intent;
His servants he with new acquist
Of true experience from this great event
With peace and consolation hath dismist,
And calm of mind, all passion spent.

(1745-1758)

With these words the Chorus bring together the transformation that has occurred to the participants in the tragedy and
the transformation that has occurred to the genre itself. Accordingly, the opening four lines of the speech are based on
the concluding choruses, all essentially the same, of Euripides' *Alcestis, Medea, Helen, Andromache,* and the *Bacchae*:

> The gods have many shapes.
> The gods bring many things
> to their accomplishment.
> And what was most expected
> has not been accomplished.
> But god has found his way
> for what no man expected.[38]

A sense of the obscurity, unexpectedness, and ineluctability
of God's ways Euripides' chorus shares with *Samson*'s; but
there is a difference, of course, and a crucial one. The emphasis in the Euripidean concluding chorus is on how surprising
and strange the unravelling of events is. Some of this is in
Samson's Chorus, too; but more important is what is absent
from Euripides, the sense of the justness behind the unravelling of events. Bacchus, or rather Zeus operating through
Bacchus—to cite the most obvious example—is the antithesis
of Milton's God. His ways are capricious, mercilessly venge-
ful, as he reduces Pentheus to low estate and wrecks havoc
on Thebes. The punishment seems all out of proportion to
the offense, and the suffering this punishment involves leads

[38] *The Bacchae*, lines 1387-1393, in *The Complete Greek Tragedies*,
ed. David Grene and Richmond Lattimore (Chicago: The Univ. of
Chicago Press, 1958), IV, 608.

to no substantial spiritual renewal, certainly not renewal of the extent or kind Milton portrays. Zeus has an "unsearchable dispose," but not "Of highest wisdom." The dispose of Euripides' Zeus is not, therefore, one that could invite the "calm of mind" which classical tragedy claimed and which Milton's Chorus actually experience.

The limitations of Euripides' unjustifiable gods should be familiar, for they are precisely the same limitations implied at the beginning of *Samson*—by Samson himself, by the Chorus, by Manoa—about Israel's God. The limited understanding of all the participants of God and His ways is mirrored in their limited understanding of tragedy. The conception of tragedy put forth at the beginning of the work is a conventional one with its roots in part in classical tragedy, in part in medieval *de casibus* tragedy: Samson's tragedy is perceived again and again as a change of circumstances, a fall of the hero from "high estate" to "lowest pitch of abject fortune" (169-170), which is where most tragedies would end. It is a tragedy of the fickleness of fortune, at best a tragedy of punitive justice, at worst a tragedy of capricious and ineluctable fate. Correspondingly, Israel's God is alternately perceived as rigorously just or as capricious. Perceived as an exemplum of the ways of fortune, Samson's fall has therefore inevitably brought "To *Israel*, diffidence of God, and doubt / In feeble hearts." But by the end of the drama, Samson has become an exemplum of a different sort, an exemplum of the operation of grace, extended not only to him but also, through him, to Israel.

For Israel as well as her hero, the consequence of grace is physical and spiritual liberation. By the time of his sacrifice and his physical liberation from the torments of the flesh, it is clear that Samson, whom the messenger describes as "patient but undaunted" (1623) and the Semichorus describe as being "With inward eyes illuminated," has attained a liberation of the spirit, the paradise within which Christ is perfectly to reveal and which for Milton, as I have suggested, is the Christian fulfilment of the promises of classical tragedy. To

Israel comes a similar transformation. They are freed from
the yoke of the Philistines, but that in itself is of no more
importance than it would have been for Samson had he returned unbound to his father's house; for as Samson, like
Christ in *Paradise Regained*, asserts, Israel, by preferring
"Bondage with ease than strenuous liberty," is by her own
"vices brought to servitude" (269-271). The physical bondage of Israel to Philistia is, like Samson's, a spiritual bondage.
Samson perceives his Adamic nature not only in the Philistines Dalila and Harapha but also in his own father, a Jew;
and as Samson establishes in his first exchange with the
Chorus, those who would bind their savior with cords and
hand him over to their enemy are themselves already enslaved
to the enemy. The physical enslavement that follows is as just
and inevitable as it is anticlimactic. The Philistines worship
a false god, but the Israelites do not really worship, because
they do not really understand, the true. There is something
of Harapha in Israel as well as Samson, Dagon in their God.
Israel is Philistia; and if she is to end the equivalence that
enslaves her, she must herself become *agonistes*. The movement of the drama, then, on the part of Israel as well as the
hero, involves a progression away from an identity conflated
with that of their enemy to a morally and religiously distinct
identity. They, too, must be purged of their Adamic community with the enemy. That is what the whole work has
been moving towards, and that is what we witness in the
closing movement of *Samson Agonistes*.

The significance of Samson's sacrifice and tragedy is, therefore, not so much the liberation of a nation as the liberation
of a nation's spirit. If Samson learns from the Chorus, it is
equally true that Israel (Manoa and the Chorus) learns from
him. At the end of Samson's resistance of the Flesh, the
World, and the Devil, the Chorus remark:

> Oh how comely it is and how reviving
> To the Spirits of just men long opprest!
> When God into the hands of thir deliverer

Puts invincible might
To quell the mighty of the Earth, th' oppressor . . .
(1268-1272)

The Chorus then propose two alternatives for Samson, an active heroism whereby the oppressed are liberated, and a heroism of patience whereby "each [is] his own Deliverer" (1289). The implication of the speech is that either Samson will liberate them, Israel, or by endurance liberate himself and himself alone. As we have seen, these two modes of liberation are for Samson inseparable. They are as inseparable for Israel as they are for Samson. The meaningfulness of Israel's physical liberation through Samson the active hero is contingent upon Israel's attaining the same inner "fortitude" and "patience" (1287-1288) of Samson the passive hero. It is precisely because the significance of Samson's tragedy lies so largely in the response of Israel's spirit to it that, quite in addition to the requirements of classical dramaturgy, it is Israel, and not Samson himself, that occupies center stage at the end of the tragedy. Accordingly, by the end of the work Israel has progressed, like the hero, from initial doubts to trust, gaining from Samson's sacrifice the same "internal peace" (1334)—or "peace and consolation" (1757) or "calm of mind" (1758)—of Samson liberated by patience. Samson's destruction of Philistia involves not only the liberation of Israel from physical bondage; it is also the final means to, and is symbolic of, the purging of Philistia from Israel. Israel is recreated in Samson's image. The final chorus, therefore, not merely states, it demonstrates, the meaningfulness of Samson's tragedy, also the meaningfulness of God's superiority to Dagon, in terms of their own inner victory over Adam in the mind's garden. The final chorus is more than the conventional commentary on the events of the drama; it is itself the final event.[39]

[39] Recent criticism—e.g., John Huntley, "A Revaluation of the Chorus' Role in Milton's *Samson Agonistes*," *Modern Philology*, 64 (1966), 132-145; Marcia Landy, "Character Portrayal in *Samson*

The profit of tragedy, writes Milton in the Preface, is through its power of "raising pity and fear, or terror, to purge the mind of those and such like passions, that is to temper

---

Agonistes," *Texas Studies in Literature and Language*, 7 (1965), 251-252—has increasingly stressed the Chorus's growth throughout the drama. This is as it should, and must, be; but, unfortunately, there has simultaneously occurred what seems to me an overemphasis on the limitations of the Chorus's, Manoa's, and even Samson's awareness at the end of the drama. For Franklin R. Baruch, "Time, Body, and Spirit at the Close of *Samson Agonistes*," *ELH*, 36 (1969), 319-339, Manoa and the Chorus represent "the limited effect that this kind of development [i.e., the growth of spiritual insight and power] in one man may have on others without their participation"; they exemplify "men who stop at the level of admiration, who remain passively dependent on a foolish idea of vicarious regeneration" (p. 320); "Milton turns classical tragic purgation into Puritan anathema" by making the traditional *consolatio* of tragedy a morally unjustifiable self-contentment which ignores responsibility of commitment to action. John T. Shawcross, "Irony as Tragic Effect," argues similarly but more temperately, that Manoa and the Chorus reach a false hope in which they expect God to keep working miracles for them and ignore their responsibility to be the agents through which He works. Irene Samuel, "*Samson Agonistes* as Tragedy," extends her sense of the limits of Manoa and the Chorus, whom she finds gloating over the bloody massacre of the Philistines, to Samson himself. In her attempt to detract from the stature of Samson's final act, she argues that Samson is motivated by a revengeful desire to visit physical destruction on the enemy, which means that Samson's apparent triumph over Philistia and himself is in reality a result of the self-concern and egomania from which he has not totally been able to extricate himself; Samson's slaying of the Philistines in fact runs counter to Milton's own attitude towards revenge, as Miss Samuel understands it (in Milton "*revenge* and *vengeance* are regularly linked with the tyrannical and diabolical rather than the divine" [p. 236]), and even to God's word ("Samson's announced vocation was to deliver Israel, not to slay Philistines" [p. 252]).

These three essays all demand our respect. The realization of Manoa's and the Chorus's limitations is, within limits, salutary; but those limits should be more clearly demarcated than they are. One may agree that the Chorus and especially Manoa fall short of Samson's awareness (if one will grant that awareness), but that, after all, is to be expected: Samson is the hero; the Chorus is composed, as no

and reduce them to just measure with a kind of delight,
stirr'd up by reading or seeing those passions well imitated."[40]
The homeopathic purgation of Miltonic catharsis is dramatized in Samson's own experiences in the triple ordeal; it is

doubt are the readers who are also to profit from Milton's tragedy,
of lesser mortals. At the same time, however, one must also realize
that unless Manoa and Israel have profited from Samson's tragedy
by some sort of inner transformation and liberation Milton has con-
tradicted himself not only on the function of tragedy but also on the
nature of Christian liberty, for mere physical liberation hardly suffices
as the verification of the divine promise.

Miss Samuel's adventurous and often highly commendable reading of the work merits special response, more than I can give it here.
In the first place, as the situation is set up, if Samson is to liberate
his people and fulfill the divine prophecy, the only means offered for
that involves the destruction of Philistia: the "announced vocation"
and the slaying of the Philistines have become inseparable, revenge
or no revenge. In the second place, Samson's mental state ("patient
but undaunted" [1624]) is clearly described in contrast to the Philistines' drunken debauchery; one wonders why Samson would be described as "patient" and "With inward eyes illuminated" [1690] if he
is still disturbed by egomaniacal passions. But my main objection to
Miss Samuel's reading, and all of those that detract excessively from
the growth and triumph of Samson and Israel, is that their detraction
is based on an unwarranted tendency to expect of pre-Christian, Old
Testament characters a full-fledged Christian or New Testament out-
look. Whatever Christian framework the play itself has, Milton's
characters themselves are located in their Old Testament, Hebraic
context. By the standard of a wholly Christian, or a wholly Miltonic,
vision they of course fall short—it could be no other way; at best
they can prefigure, in words, gestures, and experiences whose meaning they obviously cannot fully grasp, the Christian truth that will
ultimately be fully revealed. What vision they do attain is as close to
the heights (and limits) of Old Testament religious experience as one
can reasonably expect. The work concludes, after all, with the lesser
mortals of the Chorus voicing sentiments in the spirit of the great
Psalmist's *Dominus illuminatio* or *Ad te, Domine*. Limits there no
doubt are to their vision; they are not David. But surely the spirit
and vision upon which Milton's tragedy places, at the end, its emphasis is not on the limits of what the Israelites have become but on
their breaking beyond the limits of what they were.

[40] The most stimulating account of Milton's conception of catharsis
is Hawkins' "Samson's Catharsis." Hawkins finds Samson experienc-

also dramatized by the Chorus, who throughout the play have mirrored the weaknesses and passions of the tragic hero and in the end mirror him also in his inner victory. The suffering that seemed at first either pointless or unjust has proved to be an instrument of beneficence for Samson, for Israel—but also for us as well. Samson's revival is carried

---

ing catharsis in its two possible meanings, purgation and *lustratio* (= sacrifice and absolution); and purgation becomes for Milton as for Donne and Bunyan the symbol of repentance. The homeopathic nature of catharsis requires that Samson purge himself of pity (Dalila), fear (Harapha), and—an additional weakness, justified by the phrase "and such like passions"—grief (Manoa). From this perspective it would seem that Milton was dramatizing the action of catharsis much more specifically and schematically than one would have expected. My own conception of dramatized catharsis does not necessarily run counter to Hawkins', but I would be inclined to revise his argument slightly by suggesting that the "like passion" which must be purged in terms of Manoa (and the Chorus) is the principal passion which Samson and Israel share and which is the source of their grief, namely doubt and despair. T.S.K. Scott-Craig, "Concerning Milton's Samson," *Renaissance News*, 5 (1952), 45-53, also gives Milton's catharsis a theological meaning by relating *lustratio* to the Greek word *lusis*, from which the Latin word comes and which means "loosing." Scott-Craig concludes that "Milton regarded tragedy, and the tragedy of Samson in particular, as a lustration, a symbolic form of ransoming, of deliverance, of redemption—from fear" (p. 48). If my own discussion of *Samson* is true, it would seem that Scott-Craig's argument is not as exotic as some have thought—though one would not want to follow him all the way to his ultimate conclusion that "the celebration of the agony of Samson is a surrogate for the unbloody sacrifice of the Mass" (p. 47). Martin Mueller, *"Pathos* and *Katharsis* in *Samson Agonistes,"* in *Critical Essays on Milton from "ELH,"* pp. 234-252, contains an elegant treatment of Samson's catharsis. See also Waddington, "Melancholy Against Melancholy," p. 269, who argues for a dramatized catharsis on the grounds "that all three encounters involve thematic and character parody; that Samson successively is presented with images of himself; that the process of repudiating these images, the melancholy of Manoa, the sour of Dalila, the salt of Harapha, is the therapeutic action by which Samson reduces to just measure 'such like passions' in his own mind."

On the historical context of Milton's theory of catharsis, see Paul R. Sellin, "Sources of Milton's Catharsis: A Reconsideration," *Journal*

over into the souls around him, his heroic martyrdom a "memory" inflaming future "breasts / To matchless valor, and adventures high" (1739-1740); these are our souls. And his acts are to be "enroll'd / In copious Legend, or sweet Lyric Song" (1736-1737); this is *Samson Agonistes*. We, fellow witnesses of the tragedy with the Chorus, are ourselves drawn into the tragedy as participants; the consolation and the challenge are ours.

In the opening scene of *Samson Agonistes*, Samson lay in the bonds of despair. This scene, it now becomes clear, was Milton's challenge to the claims of classical tragedy. Embodied in the image of the languishing Samson is the principal "passion" which Samson, Manoa, and Israel share, despair and doubt. It is this passion Milton's tragedy deals with from its beginning to its end, and only with the purgation of this passion is the "calm of mind" of Christian catharsis fully realized. Through his portrayal of the despairing Samson, Milton added to the Aristotelian fear and pity, which pagan tragedy could to some limited extent purge, another, "like passion," which, because of its unjustifiable gods and because of its inherent Adamic limitations, it could not purge—doubt, despair, disbelief. The justification of God's ways to man becomes the basis for the justification of tragedy itself. Thus for Milton, however contrary it may be to our own feelings on the matter, Christianity, far from being antagonistic to tragedy, provided the only framework wherein the claims of pagan tragedy could be fulfilled. The therapeutic purgation of the emotions claimed by pagan tragedy goes beyond that in Christian tragedy to the redemptive purification of the garden of the mind. Milton's "new tragedy" becomes for the hero, for the Chorus, and ultimately for us as well a means

of English and Germanic Philology, 60 (1961), 712-730; Martin Mueller, "Sixteenth-Century Italian Criticism and Milton's Theory of Catharsis," *Studies in English Literature*, 6 (1966), 139-150; and John M. Steadman, " 'Passions Well Imitated': Rhetoric and Poetics in the Preface to *Samson Agonistes*," in *Calm of Mind*, pp. 175-207.

of overcoming the old Adam and imitating the new, of raising a paradise of the mind in the waste reaches of Gaza.

In the 1671 volume Milton completed a lifelong effort to
consecrate the profane. Working with the double-triadic
structure he inherited from Spenser, Milton has redefined
both the heroic and the tragic modes in terms of the dialectic
between Adam and Christ, the Fall and man's restoration,
inherent in the typology of the Flesh-World-Devil scheme.
He has supplied both modes with the fundamental Christian
premise his classical predecessors could not possibly provide,
the triumph over the Fall and the restoration of the inner
garden. It is this uniquely Christian triumph over the Fall
and Adam that makes the Christian hero of *Paradise Regained* a greater than Ulysses and Aeneas, that makes the
Christian tragic hero of *Samson Agonistes* a greater than
blind Oedipus at Colonus. The echoes between these two last
works—in argument, in the appearance of the tempters, in
language, and of course in structure—reveal them ultimately
as the companion-pieces Milton intended them to be. This
final volume emerges as the culmination of a lifetime of Milton's redefinition of the great modes of poetry; and within it
he has offered, as the English Homer, the English Virgil, the
English Sophocles, the Christian poet's fulfilment of the two
supreme classical modes of poetry, the heroic and the tragic.
In so doing, he concluded the challenge, made decades before, to those classical writers whose ranks he had dedicated
himself to join. From this perspective, the 1671 volume is the
fitting completion and summation of Milton's poetic career.

As it is from another: Dryden's famous account of Milton's
claiming Spenser as his "original" may be apocryphal, but
it is one of those accounts that deserve to be true. If in 1644,
in the *Areopagitica*, Milton could speak of "our sage and
serious poet Spenser" as "a better teacher than Scotus or
Aquinas," he would not have withdrawn that praise in 1671.
The influence of Spenser on Milton in the early pastorals,
and on *Comus*, has long been acknowledged—indeed from

247

the beginning when Humphrey Mosley said of the 1645 volume that he was "bringing into the light as true a birth as the Muses have brought forth since our famous Spenser wrote, whose poems in these English ones are as rarely imitated, as sweetly excelled." It has been a central contention of this study that Milton's imitating and excelling of Spenser did not die out in the course of his poetic development; for as we have seen, in the 1671 volume Milton adopted from Spenser a complex-triadic *schema* and embraced conceptions and portrayals, similar to his, of the Flesh-temptation (Despaire; the stones-temptation; Manoa), the triadic and Circean World-temptation (Lucifera-Panglorie; the kingdoms-temptation; Dalila), and the Devil-temptation (Orgoglio and Red Crosse's combat with the dragon; the pinnacle-temptation; Harapha)—to cite the most obvious relationships we have explored.

In Milton's attempt to provide his native literature with works that might rival the achievement of the ancients in the major genres, it is obvious that he saw part of his task as an English writer one of infusing the vernacular literature with a classicism that had not been the dominant spirit of his three great predecessors in the English pantheon—Chaucer, Shakespeare, and Spenser. In this sense, Milton's pursuit of a purer classicism relates him to the Restoration and to the next age of English literature. But if Milton's efforts were to point his country's literature away from its largely medieval and romantic orientation to a more authentically classical orientation, it is nonetheless true that Milton himself was profoundly indebted to the orientation whose sway, partly through his own influence, would be somewhat curbed in the next few generations of English poets. In terms of the two great traditions, the romantic and the classical, Arnold saw in English literature, Milton stands as a titanic Janus who could be claimed by the Neoclassicists and the Romantics alike; for as the older critics realized more clearly than many of the more modern, if Milton is a forerunner of the Neoclassicists, he is also the last of the Elizabethans. His poetry looks backward to a literary tradition rooted in medieval allegorical romance and in romantic narrative in general. This aspect of his poetry has been uncovered partially—and of course only partially—by the allegorical lineage I have traced in the preceding chapters and by that process, muted, subtle, and occasional, of schematizing materials in an older manner—a manner that, if it is not often strictly allegorical in the style of a Lydgate or Hawes, seems at least to emerge from medieval allegory and, more immediately and more importantly, from the diverse forms medieval allegory took in Spenser and his followers. Whatever the still improperly defined relationships are, differences as well as similarities, between Milton and the Elizabethans, one central point remains and deserves a final emphasis: that in *Paradise Lost* and in the 1671 volume, Milton continued to view that tradition which we may call romantic, Elizabethan, or Spenserian—a tradition at once moral, allegorical, heroic, and in some ways medieval—as the central tradition of English literature and the one central, to some degree, for him as well. Any great writer is his own literary moment, and he stands in his own unique place and time. To the extent, however, that the later Milton can be placed in a literary moment, related to the traditions he molds and transcends, chiefly his is the tradition of the *Faerie Queene*, of *Poly-Olbion*, of *The Purple Island*, of *Christ's Victory*; and of this tradition he was, as Arnold wisely remarked, "the continuation and close." It would be outrageous to make of Milton a neo-Spenserian; it is also obvious that—if we are to see him in the context of English poetry at all, certainly if we are to see him in the context of seventeenth-century English poetry—this is his principal context and heritage. It is true: we do not have an Elizabethan *Arthuriad*; we also do not have a medieval or Italian biblical drama on the Fall. But the poetic impulses and traditions behind these early conceptions and plans persist—even though one may feel them modified to the point that a difference in degree seems a difference in kind. It would be unnecessarily foolhardy, and naïve, to deny that of the two impulses we have been discussing, the classical and the vernacular, the classical did not come to prevail. Even so, if Milton set himself the task of joining the ranks of the great classical writers, he also set himself the task as a Christian poet of the English Reformation, writing in the vernacular, of joining the ranks of the greatest English writers; and to the end of his poetic career and the publication of the 1671 volume, it would seem that of these for him the chief English master was in fact his "original," Edmund Spenser.

APPENDIX

Biblical Passages:
The Fall and the Temptation in the Wilderness

Genesis 3:1-6: The Fall

1 Now the serpent was more subtil than any beast of the field which the Lord God had made. And he said unto the woman, Yea, hath God said, Ye shall not eat of every tree of the garden?

2 And the woman said unto the serpent, We may eat of the fruit of the trees of the garden:

3 But of the fruit of the tree which is in the midst of the garden, God hath said, Ye shall not eat of it, neither shall ye touch it, lest ye die.

4 And the serpent said unto the woman, Ye shall not surely die:

5 For God doth know that in the day ye eat thereof, then your eyes shall be opened, and ye shall be as gods, knowing good and evil.

6 And when the woman saw that the tree was good for food, and that it was pleasant to the eyes, and a tree to be desired to make one wise, she took of the fruit thereof, and did eat, and gave also unto her husband with her; and he did eat.

Matthew 4:1-11: The Temptation in the Wilderness

1 Then was Jesus led up of the spirit into the wilderness to be tempted of the devil.

2 And when he had fasted forty days and forty nights, he was afterward an hungred.

3 And when the tempter came to him, he said, If thou be the Son of God, command that these stones be made bread.

4 But he answered and said, It is written, Man shall not

live by bread alone, but by every word that proceedeth out of the mouth of God.

5 Then the devil taketh him up into the holy city, and setteth him on a pinnacle of the temple,

6 And saith unto him, If thou be the Son of God, cast thyself down: for it is written, He shall give his angels charge concerning thee: and in their hands they shall bear thee up, lest at any time thou dash thy foot against a stone.

7 Jesus said unto him, It is written again, Thou shalt not tempt the Lord thy God.

8 Again, the devil taketh him up into an exceeding high mountain, and sheweth him all the kingdoms of the world, and the glory of them;

9 And saith unto him, All these things will I give thee, if thou wilt fall down and worship me.

10 Then saith Jesus unto him, Get thee hence, Satan: for it is written, Thou shalt worship the Lord thy God, and him only shalt thou serve.

11 Then the devil leaveth him, and, behold, angels came and ministered unto him.

Luke 4:1-13: The Temptation in the Wilderness

1 And Jesus being full of the Holy Ghost returned from Jordan, and was led by the Spirit into the wilderness,

2 Being forty days tempted of the devil. And in those days he did eat nothing: and when they were ended, he afterward hungered.

3 And the devil said unto him, If thou be the Son of God, command this stone that it be made bread.

4 And Jesus answered him, saying, It is written, That man shall not live by bread alone, but by every word of God.

5 And the devil, taking him up into an high mountain, shewed unto him all the kingdoms of the world in a moment of time.

6 And the devil said unto him, All this power will I give thee, and the glory of them: for that is delivered unto me; and to whomsoever I will I give it.

7 If thou therefore wilt worship me, all shall be thine.

8   And Jesus answered and said unto him, Get thee behind me, Satan: for it is written, Thou shalt worship the Lord thy God, and him only shalt thou serve.

9   And he brought him to Jerusalem and set him on a pinnacle of the temple, and said unto him, If thou be the Son of God, cast thyself down from hence:

10   For it is written, He shall give his angels charge over thee, to keep thee:

11   And in their hands they shall bear thee up, lest at any time thou dash thy foot against a stone.

12   And Jesus answering said unto him, It is said, Thou shalt not tempt the Lord thy God.

13   And when the devil had ended all the temptation, he departed from him for a season.

Index

N.B. All works of Spenser and Milton, and the characters and events therein, are indexed under the author's name.

257

Index

261

Index

Waldock, A. J. A., 112, 113n-114n, 119, 121
Waters, D. Douglas, 25n-26n, 36n, 53n
Weber, Burton J., 127n
Werner, Abt. of St. Blase, xxviin
Weymouth, Richard Francis, xxxiiin
Whitaker, Virgil K., 20n, 25n, 53n
Whiting, George Wesley, 203n-204n
Whitney, J. E., 52n-53n
Wilkes, G. A., 195n
Williams, E. C., 17n
Williams, Kathleen, 78n
Wittreich, Joseph Anthony, Jr., 126n, 184n
Wolfe, Don M., 186n, 202n
Woodhouse, A. S. P., 90n, 132n, 150n, 169n, 170n, 172, 183n, 233n
World, temptation of, and Athens-temptation, 162-64; and Cave of Mammon, 31-32, 69-70; and Dalila, 204, 216-277; and the Fall (PL), 108-09; in Giles Fletcher, Christ's Victory, 178-79, 216; and gold-temptation (PR), 153-54; and House of Holiness, 63-66; and House of Pride, 40-51, 176, 216; and Mammon (PL), 102-03; and the World-temptation (PR, second day), 126-28, 148-65, 176
Wright, B. A., 121n

York Plays, xxviiin
Young, G. M., 217n

267

Library of Congress Cataloging in Publication Data

Cullen, Patrick, 1940-
  Infernal triad.

    1. Spenser, Edmund, 1552?-1599—Religion and
ethics. 2. Milton, John, 1608-1674—Religion and
ethics. 3. Spenser, Edmund, 1552-1599—Influence
—Milton. I. Title.
PR2364.C8   821'.009'31   73-16753
ISBN 0-691-06267-6